W9-ANJ-819

THE POLITICS OF LITERARY THEORY

PHILIP GOLDSTEIN

The Politics of Literary Theory

An Introduction to Marxist Criticism

THE FLORIDA STATE UNIVERSITY PRESS / TALLAHASSEE

The Florida State University Press is a member of University Presses of Florida, the scholarly publishing agency of the state university system of Florida. Books are selected for publication by the faculty editorial committees of Florida's nine public universities: Florida A&M University (Tallahassee), Florida Atlantic University (Boca Raton), Florida International University (Miami), Florida State University (Tallahassee), University of Central Florida (Orlando), University of Florida (Gainesville), University of North Florida (Jacksonville), University of South Florida (Tampa), University of West Florida (Pensacola).

Orders for books published by all member presses should be addressed to University Presses of Florida, 15 NW 15th Street, Gainesville, FL 32603.

Library of Congress Cataloging-in Publication Data

Goldstein, Philip.
The politics of literary theory: an introduction to marxist criticism / Philip Goldstein.
p.   cm.
Bibliography: p.
Includes index.
ISBN 0-8130-0949-9 (alk. paper)
ISBN 0-8130-0976-6 (alk. paper) (pbk.)
1. Marxist criticism. 2. Politics and literature. I. Title
PN98.C6G6 1990
801'.95–dc20   89-33187 CIP

©1990 by the Board of Regents of the State of Florida
⊗ Printed in the U.S.A. on acid-free paper.

CONTENTS

THREE: The Politics of Reading   100

FOUR: Poststructuralism—The Politics of Skepticism   162

ACKNOWLEDGMENTS

I WANT TO THANK THE MANY PEOPLE WITHOUT WHOSE HELP AND SUP-port I could not have written this book. Philip P. Wiener enabled me to learn what professional philosophy was all about. Gaylord LeRoy, who introduced me to Marxist literary criticism, stimulated my study of Thomas Hardy. George MacFadden encouraged me to study the "new" literary theory. The Marxist Literary Group provided numerous opportunities for me to meet literary theorists from this country and abroad and to share my ideas with them. Jane Tompkins gave me the chance to write a dissertation on literary theory and showed a very encouraging confidence in my work. Susan Stewart and Stephen Zelnick read early drafts and provided important insights. Temma Berg, Wendell V. Harris, Gerald Graff, Michael Sprinker, and Suresh Raval also provided helpful readings. I owe a special thanks to Mark Amsler, who enabled me to teach literary theory and who frequently contributed insightful readings and stimulating discussions. Lastly, I cannot sufficiently thank my wife, Leslie, for generously supporting my work even in difficult times.

A few portions of this manuscript have been published elsewhere. Part of chapter 2 was published as "Humanism and the Politics of Truth" in the Fall/Winter 1984/1985 issue of *Boundary 2*. Part of chapter 3 was published as "The Politics of Fredric Jameson's Totalizing Marxism: A Critique" in *Postmodernism/Jameson/Critique*, edited by Douglas Kellner (Washington, D.C.: Maisonneuve Press, 1989). This material is used here by permission of the publishers.

In Defense of Politics

IN THE 1970S RICHARD OHMANN URGED LITERARY CRITICS TO RE-
turn to the politics from which formal study had divorced them. In
the 1980s this divorce persists; the study of the humanities remains
a neutral area where, as E. D. Hirsch, Jr., says, valid interpretations
of literature represent the unbiased wisdom of common sense or the
universal truths of canonical texts, not the individual commitments
of the interpreter (*Aims*, 146–53). Conservatives such as William
Bennett, a former United States Secretary of Education, and Allan
Bloom, a professor at the University of Chicago, insist that the study
of the humanities requires an unyielding commitment to canonical
texts and to unbiased wisdom. These conservatives fear that liberals
who yield to Afro-American, feminist, or other "special" interests
undermine the high standards of American academic life and embroil
the country in socioeconomic ills. Those liberal critics who refuse to

make changes in the canon responsible for the country's socioeconomic problems still affirm the traditional belief that the study of the humanities is ultimately apolitical (Poirier, *The Renewal,* 8). Those radical critics disgusted with the McCarthyism, the racist and sexist discrimination, and the uncritical apologetics of the Reagan era understand the humanities in equally apolitical but more negative terms. For example, Russell Jacoby argues that in the 1920s and 1930s New York's bohemian intellectuals, who did not know where their next check would come from, established an independent public stance; by contrast, modern, conformist academics live securely, in true complacency, adopting arcane professional jargon and ignoring public issues (5–17). Even the New Left scholars who, in their militant youth, attacked and rejected the complacent university life, have in their middle age accepted its apolitical conformity (140–41).

I admit that these conservative accounts of the humanities face serious opposition. Certainly feminist, Afro-American, and third-world critics have shown that the established canon is neither neutral nor objective. It represents women, blacks, and Hispanics as fearful "others" who reveal the repressed longings of dominant white males. These critics have won such accomplished but overlooked writers as Edith Wharton, Susan Ashton-Warner, and Zora Neale Hurston a well-deserved place in the literary canon. In fact, these critics have gone on to assemble impressive anthologies of hitherto neglected and marginal writers, who now form whole new literary traditions. However, as Jane Tompkins points out, to upgrade forgotten writers and neglected traditions, these critics appeal to traditional, apolitical standards, including the complexity of a text's language, the subtlety of a writer's insight, or the uniqueness of her nonwhite, nonmale experience (*Designs,* 123). What is more, the critic who describes feminist, Afro-American, or third-world literature in these traditional terms reaffirms the conservative faith in neutral objectivity and ignores the political interests behind the established canon.

A more forceful challenge to the conservative view comes from literary theorists like Terry Eagleton, Edward Said, Frank Lentricchia, and Stanley Fish, who oppose the conservative faith in transcendent values and neutral truths. Influenced by Jacques Derrida, Michel Foucault, and other poststructuralists, these critics "scandalously" expose a "microphysics" of power embedded within traditional criticism and certifying its "disinterested" results. A mere facade, the traditional ideal of neutral form hides an entrenched apparatus of discourses and practices establishing the place of a theory, reproducing its attitudes, and legitimating its results. This apparatus frees itself from governmental interference but still constructs a perceiving, interpreting subject.

This poststructuralist approach makes possible a professional politics in which the interpretive strategies of a literary scholar gain their power from his or her communities' implicit political interests, utopian visions, and ideological beliefs, not from his or her unbiased objectivity. Nonetheless, many literary critics deny the political import of their criticism and reaffirm the conservative ideal of neutral truth. Why do they do so? Why does the conservative view remain so powerful? One of my distinguished colleagues, who holds a chaired professorship and a high administrative office, believes that the university cannot judge research on political grounds and still encourage scholarly pursuits of all sorts. My colleague does not share the Platonic belief that artists and critics who fail to adopt the political values of the ideal republic have no place in it, yet he unhesitatingly assumes that a political approach must censor and repress scholarly freedoms in a Platonic manner. Another, more artistic colleague, who cannot bear administrative duties, fears that politics would set vulgar practical interest above art. In her Kantian terms, formal literary language transcends the degrading utilitarian norms of a political approach. The critic who imposes his methods or his biases on a text obscures its unique voice.

In an article that praises the "old literary elite" of "neutral humanists," Barbara Christian voices similar concerns. She complains, as my colleagues do, that "writers are often seen as *persona non grata* by political states," and she defends apolitical criteria of literary value, according to which the free play of artistic language explains "why creative literature, even when written by politically reactionary people, can be so freeing" (59). On similar grounds the eminent Hazard Adams argues that long before Foucault's notions of discursive power became popular, Blake, who defended the autonomous imagination of the great artist, refuted them (441–43). Lewis Feuer, a veteran of numerous political battles, formulates such objections in broad sociological terms. "Intellectuals in politics" are, he says, the blind instruments of transient styles and biased outlooks: "Ideologists rather than philosophers, their 'ideas' are much more the by-products of intellectual fashion; their concern is less with the truth of things than with ideas as weapons" (202). Less harshly, Mark Krupnik welcomes the "worldword" movement of criticism but still fears that "when American literary intellectuals get involved with politics they often betray their vocation as intellectuals" (168). Like Krupnik, Jacoby dislikes the academic retreat from the "public" realm, yet he argues that professional academic scholarship is invariably withdrawn, apolitical, and private, for academia represses committed, public, critical work. He laments what Hook, Christian, and others favor—the university's preservation of a neutral humanism, yet he too excludes politics from the humanities.

By contrast, poststructuralists deny that the professional and the political, the private and the public, and the scholar's "vocation" and transient "fashion" inevitably exclude each other. Academic discourse imposes complicity and restraint upon its rebellious practitioners but still retains a critical, disruptive function. To assume, as Jacoby and Hook do, that academics are apolitical and uncritical, while public scholars are free, independent, social, and political, is to adopt too simplistic a notion of institutional discourse. Its constraints do not stem solely from insecurity or unemployment, excess comfort, or mindless chores, for such discourse also defines the terms of intelligible speech. As Foucault points out, institutional discourse imposes the terms in which insiders and outsiders conduct their debates. The outsider must speak the language of the insider if the insider is to understand what the outsider says. Resistance and critique do not occur in a neutral, public space but on a terrain already structured and contested by opposed discourses. Michael Walzer rightly contends that "the outsider can become a social critic only if he manages to get himself inside, enters imaginatively into local practices and arrangements" (39). Isolation and unemployment may make the scholar independent and rebellious, but they do not destroy his or her complicity with the dominant discourses.

Marxism and the Humanities

The Marxist versions of this poststructuralist approach also reject the traditional belief in a neutral humanities and expose the political commitments of the established methods. The poststructuralist Marxists have not escaped the institutional constraints of their disciplinary discourses nor have these Marxists produced an alternative public culture or a viable political party, let alone a working class revolution. They have established a radical cultural politics, not a political coalition. Nonetheless, scholars still fear that the "failures of communism" destroy the viability of all Marxist approaches. For example, William Cain complains that our taking a "Marxist position can be no more than a futile gesture. . . . Marxism . . . has no vital connection to the real political scene and hence is destined to remain a marginal enterprise" ("English," 101). In a more negative vein, the neoconservative Norman Podhoretz faults *The God That Failed,* which documented many distinguished writers' disillusionment with communism, for distinguishing Marxism and communism: "It was a book which said, in effect, that one could be an anti-Communist without ceasing to be a liberal . . . or a socialist or a Marxist" (26). In *The Master Thinkers,* André Glucksman, who also refuses to distinguish Marxism and communism, says that Marx reluctantly hands social institutions over to the bureaucrats organizing the Soviet gulags (226). Such works as *Marxism: An Autopsy,* by Henry Parkes; *The God That Failed,* by R. H. S. Crossman; *The Dialectic of Defeat,* by Russell Jacoby; and *Marx and the Disillusionment of Marxism,* by Walter L. Adamson, show equally pessimistic estimates of Marxism's possibilities.

However, even reduced to a totalitarian nightmare, Marxism has not died. In the United States it lives in newspapers, magazines, and television, where unending reports of imprisoned artists, divided families, missing soldiers, inadequate production, stolen technology, exploding nuclear reactors, and oppressed satellite countries expose the "inhumane" character of Marxist regimes. Moreover, communist societies, which reveal sharp tensions between their Stalinist and their "liberal" proponents, are awakening us from this satanic nightmare. Indeed, the pessimistic conservatives mistakenly assume that one definitive essence informs the communism of the world, the writings of Karl Marx, Friedrich Engels, V. I. Lenin, and Joseph Stalin, as well as the theories of Fredric Jameson, Terry Eagleton, and other contemporary critics. However, splintered and fragmented, Marxism is not basically determinist, totalitarian, or even liberating. Not only do communist countries disavow their Stalinist lineage but cultural Marxism, distinct from classical Marxism, also possesses not one basic self but numerous competing strands. The historical, existential, Frankfurt, structuralist, and poststructuralist schools composing cultural Marxism represent a complex assortment of competing methods, practices, and ideals—not a simple set of doctrines attached to the name Karl Marx.

If modern literary theory has broken into a confusing array of philosophies, techniques, and practices, cultural Marxism, which includes an established body of Marxist texts and the various schools and traditions of literary theory, must be doubly confusing—why else would Cornell University Press publish a book-length explanation (William Dowling's *Jameson, Althusser, Marx*) of Jameson's *The Political Unconscious?* The varied and opposed reactions of these texts, schools, and traditions have so fractured Marxism that no simple essence clearly unifies its many proponents.

Classical versus Cultural Marxism

While the classical Marxism that we inherit from Karl Marx and Friedrich Engels insightfully demonstrated that ideology plays an essential role in social life, this Marxism does not escape its historical contexts or establish the essence of Marxism. Marx discovered and explained the crucial importance of ideology, but his account of it does not resist the narrow positivism of nineteenth-century Europe. His early writing, which presents this groundbreaking account of ideology, takes on a determinist tone, especially if we leave the nineteenth-century Hegelian context of Marx's early work and enter the twentieth-century world of powerful institutional discourses.

In *The German Ideology* and *The Economic and Philosophic Manuscripts of 1844,* for example, Marx drew the philosophical lessons of his youthful academic life. During it, he adopted a "left" Hegelian outlook and, subsequently, accepted Feuerbach's anthropological critiques of Hegel. In this period he also wrote economic analyses for the *Neue Rheinische Zeitung.* Not only did these analyses precipitate his physical expulsion from Germany, they stimulated his intellectual growth beyond Hegel and Feuerbach. What Marx discovered was a theory of ideology according to which philosophy, theology, art, and other cultural discourses do not have a history apart from that of their socioeconomic systems. The theoretical activity of the ruling class or its representatives brings these discourses together to form a unity ("form of consciousness") which expresses and justifies the social system. As Marx wrote in *The German Ideology:*

> Morality, religion, metaphysics, all the rest of ideology and their corresponding forms of consciousness, thus no longer retain the semblance of independence. They have no history, no development; but men . . . alter, along with . . . their real existence, their thinking and the products of their thinking. (14)

In light of the *Manuscripts of 1844,* we can say that this passage is not reductive: it simply denies the Hegelian belief that the mind or spirit ("forms of consciousness") is self-determining or self-constituting. Given the Hegelian subtext, the passage means that the "forms of consciousness" do not determine themselves because the mind of the intellectual does not control or change historical circumstances; rather, these circumstances influence the development of consciousness and its forms. The slave society of the classical Greeks, the feudal society of medieval England, and the capitalist society of eighteenth-century England all give rise to different cultural forms because "men . . . alter, along with . . . their real existence, their thinking and the products of their thinking" (14).

In a particular society certain ideas prevail because they and not other ideas best defend the interests of the ruling class; as Marx says, "The ideas of the ruling class are in every epoch the ruling ideas" (*Ideology,* 64). Although the figure of the ruling class compresses the sources and the power of ideas into one godlike entity, the figure stresses the interested character of ideas, what Gramsci calls their hegemonic force. As Althusser argues, this account of ideology's roots and functions opens up a new terrain, the history of the "social formations" producing and reproducing a society's ideologies. Still, Engels, who wrote letters and commentaries insisting that philosophy and art create distinct histories within that of their initiating systems, admitted that his love of "content" led him to forget "form": "I have done that too and the mistake has struck me only later" (*Correspondence,* 458–60). This forgetfulness is not accidental. As scholars point out, Marx's account of ideology minimizes the political import of ideological practices. For example, Raymond Williams complains that the language with which Marx describes ideas—"reflexes," "fantasms," or "chimeras"—is too decidedly positivist and anti-intellectual (*Marxism*, 59). Jürgen Habermas fears that Marx remains too committed to the Fichtean "ego" of the industrial engineer to provide for that moment of self-reflection in which the theorist acknowledges and critiques the sociohistorical contexts influencing social thought (*Knowledge*, 46–48).

In Marx's defense, I am tempted to argue that these critiques neglect Marx's hatred of intellectual pretentiousness. That Hegelians derive social change from theory, not from institutions, appalled Marx, who readily adopted the scientific positivism growing very prestigious in his era. However, I believe that Marx, Engels, and the classical Marxists did not treat culture as seriously as twentieth-century Marxists do. In the unfinished *Grundrisse,* Marx and Engels planned to write extended cultural theory, but they produced only occasional commentary, not formal theory. For example, the continuing appeal of Greek drama puzzled Marx, who wondered why the dramas "still afford us aesthetic enjoyment and in certain respects prevail as the standard and model beyond attainment" (*Critique,* 311) even though Greek socioeconomic conditions disappeared long ago. To account for this anomaly, he drew a suggestive analogy between the Greeks and childhood: "Why should the social childhood of mankind, where it had obtained its most beautiful development, not exert an eternal charm?" (*Critique,* 312). Engels commented insightfully on radical novelists, praising their "demystificatory negativism." He also established what became a central point of Marxist realism—that artistic technique reveals more of social life than positive exposition does. In a well-known example, he commends the work of Balzac, who, despite his monarchist outlook, could produce a wealth of critical insight because he successfully depicted the internal conflicts of representative or "typical" characters and did not polemicize in favor of the monarchy. In a similar manner, Georgei Plekhanov discussed the relations of thought and style, Leon Trotsky analyzed the weaknesses of formalism, and V. I. Lenin assessed the social import of Tolstoi's fiction; yet these discussions too were occasional essays, not formal theory.

To explain this embarrassing paucity, some scholars suggest that Marx, Engels, and others were too preoccupied by socioeconomic matters to examine cultural questions at any length. The unacceptable implication of this suggestion is that all serious Marxists should be equally preoccupied with socioeconomics and not with culture. Other, more cynical scholars have suggested that in the twentieth century, the continuing defeat of western European and American working-class parties, as well as the emergent Stalinism of eastern European countries, led the frustrated revolutionary to vent his spleen in cultural studies (Anderson, *Considerations,* 42–43). This harsh suggestion also implies that cultural Marxism neglects the central issues. However, in the twentieth century culture has exerted much greater political influence than it could in the nineteenth. As Nicos Poulantzas points out, despite brutal warfare and economic depression, twentieth-century European and Anglo-American institutions preserve and enhance their power by disseminating positive, affirmative rituals, discourses, and practices, not by exerting bare economic force (5–30). What keeps these institutions so remarkably stable is the causal efficacy of their established discourse.

During the last two centuries, educational institutions, in particular, have markedly increased their influence on social life. Speaking of American universities, for instance, Burton Bledstein says that "not only has higher education brought coherence and uniformity to the training of individuals for careers, it has structured and formalized the instrumental techniques Americans employ in thinking about every level of existence" (*Culture,* 289–90). American and European institutions of higher education acquired this influence once they ruptured with the scholastic classicism that dominated them in past centuries. Previously confined to dissenting academies and to irregular apprenticeships, physics, chemistry, biology, law, medicine, and dentistry did not enter the university until the nineteenth century passed its midpoint. Around that time women, Afro-Americans, and third-world people who sought positions in the emerging public educational system began to penetrate the cultural studies traditionally reserved to the upper-class Western males seeking positions in the church or the government. Around that time also, the middle classes turned to education to foster the unifying values of a national culture. As scholars point out, at that time British schools made English an autonomous discipline in order to ensure that the national culture would assimilate the working classes and perpetuate the dominant ideologies (Doyle; Batsleer, 13–40; Eagleton, *Literary Theory,* 17–53). After the Civil War, American educational institutions adopted the study of English for similar reasons but did not succeed so well (Graff, *Professing*, 12). During the nineteenth century, French educational institutions made similar changes: the study of French language and literature became a sign of the bourgeoisie's natural "superiority" to the working classes, for working-class students learned only the national language and its prescribed forms, while the elite bourgeois students learned the effects of literary language (Balibar, 25–28). In the twentieth century, the emergence of professional literary associations independent of church authorities, academic administrators, and political officials has only enhanced culture's importance.

By contrast with Marx's era, culture has so sharply increased in importance that the Hegelian "forms of consciousness" do not simply fail to exert influence, they come to mirror socioeconomic history passively, losing any vestige of autonomous development. Such culture homogenizes art, ethics, and industry, reducing these influential discourses to useful but helpless puppetry. An artistic text can only echo a predetermined world if the socioeconomic base governs the ideological superstructure. Should economic structures rule artistic production, a text serves as the instrument of higher powers, not of political action. (See Wellek and Warren, 94–110; Brooks and Wimsatt, 468–70; Jameson, *Prison-House*, 213–14; Eagleton, *Marxism*, 34; as well as Caute, 153–57, and Swingewood, 21).

The tragic experience of eastern European Marxists illustrates this passivity, for they did not consistently resist the doctrines or expose the failings of Stalinist policies. The classical theory became official doctrine in eastern Europe, yet Marxists did not fully oppose the unrestricted authority claimed by political leaders. In Solzhenitsyn's *Cancer Ward,* for example, the displaced academic Shulubin regrets that Soviet intellectuals were unable to oppose Stalin even though they knew his policies were inhumane (429–44). Conformity replaced criticism, for Stalin and his followers acquired an unlimited power to decide which works mirror the true causes and which do not. It was those leaders who judged the accuracy of the artist's insight, and we know all too well the fate of "inaccurate" artists.

Solzhenitsyn goes on to trace this Stalinist power to classical Marxism, but the true sources of Stalinism are Soviet conditions, not Marxist theory. To an extent, Stalinism developed because in the 1920s provincial superstition and feudal tyranny so oppressed the Soviet people that they could provide few well-educated Marxists to fill the offices of the state. To an extent, the unbroken hostility of the Western world and the collapse of the worker/peasant alliance generated fears that the Stalinists exploited successfully. For example, to impose collective farming and liquidate the kulacs (rich peasants), the Stalinists built up the secret police, which they also used to eliminate their communist opponents. In short, as scholars have shown, classical Marxism does not give birth to Soviet Stalinism, whose origins are largely indigenous (Ellenstein; Lukács, *Marxism,* 61–71; Stephen Cohen, 38–70).

Nonetheless, classical Marxism does not encourage its proponents to adopt a critical view of their institutional authorities; rather, the classical Marxists remain relatively limited and passive, expecting history to foster progressive changes. While Marx's discovery of ideology has been very influential, the classical Marxism that we inherit from him too readily exposes artists and critics to an uncritical complicity with institutional authorities.

In *Culture and Society* (1948), Raymond Williams, a communist militant in his youth, disavowed Marxism because of this reductive passivity (209–84). In the 1960s, when he discovered the work of Georg Lukács and Lucien Goldmann, he returned to Marxism, but he rightly insisted that to overcome the classical passivity cultural Marxism must be a distinct realm independent of classical Marxism (*Problems,* 18–22).

My reader may object that traditional Marxists have always distinguished between vulgar determinist approaches and genuinely elevated dialectical approaches. A genuinely dialectical approach would preserve the distinctions between form and content, ideology and history, subject and object. However, this objection restates the traditional humanist faith in objective truth. Classical Marxism does not fail to maintain a dialectical analysis, to preserve formal standards, and to oppose vulgar determinism; rather, this Marxism fosters an empiricist passivity that the historical, speculative, structuralist, and poststructuralist schools of Marxism repudiate. Moreover, like classical Marxism, the historical and the speculative schools emphasize the illusory independence of the "objective" theorist and minimize the determining influence of authoritative institutional discourse; by contrast, (post)structuralist Marxism disavows that autonomy and objectivity and acknowledges the determining force exerted by twentieth-century institutional discourse.

Historical Varieties of Cultural Marxism

Consider, for example, the historical criticism of Georg Lukács, who justifies the historical narrative and the autonomous theory of classical Marxism, and that of Lionel Trilling, who repudiates the narrative but preserves the autonomy of cultural theory. The later Lukács defends classical Marxism and rejects modernist art; Trilling rejects "Stalinist" Marxism and defends modernist art. Yet both critics share the traditional faith in artistic objectivity and in cultural autonomy.

Lukács's Procommunist Realism

In *The Theory of the Novel* and other early works, the young Lukács poses the dilemma of modern culture in phenomenological, not in historical, terms. He argues that the fragmented, alienated culture of modern society ruptures with the organic, unself-conscious culture of ancient Greece. The Greek epic takes for granted a coherent totality in which the meaning of life is only a matter of the hero's position, not of his character or his labor. By contrast, the modern novel, which does not find a totality implicit in life, can only lament this loss by depicting fragmentation and incoherence in ironic ways. Like the lawful necessity of unjustifiable social conventions, the subjective feelings of the lyric affirm the reified condition of modern culture; by contrast, the novel undermines this condition, ironically contrasting the narrator, whose transcendental structures embody the values repudiated by the fallen world, with the hero, whose quest reveals that the world has repudiated the values affirmed by the narration. This ironic narrative outlook is subjective yet necessary, inadequate but meaningful (92).

Bernstein denies that this ironic opposition between the modern novel and the Greek epic shows that a nostalgic Lukács idealizes the Greek epic (64–65); however, Lukács does impose on the epic and, indeed, on all fiction the impossible burden of traditional humanist study—to establish the objective norms of social life. After Lenin died and Stalin triumphed, Lukács, who had been deeply involved in Hungarian and Soviet socioeconomic matters, withdrew from politics and returned to cultural studies (Löwy, 205–6). In his new work, the human subject no longer suffers what the younger Lukács considered a tragic fall into a fragmented society; rather, history acts in a positive way. Its distinct periods of development culminate in full communism, which unites and reconciles the fragmented subject with itself. The subject passes through distinct, historical stages until it reaches the communist era, where its alienation and fragmentation will come to an end. His new accounts of the novel reflect this orthodox historical perspective but preserve the impossible burden of the old accounts.

In the new accounts, the great novels show historical realism: the conventions of the novel include typical characters, which are those revealing the individual development possible in an aristocratic or a peasant society, not the standard features of the aristocracy or peasantry; an intention or totality articulating the structure of a transindividual subject, not a unique personality; and a plot showing an objectively valid (e.g., Marxist) insight into social conflict, rather than human nature. At the same time, Lukács attributes to this generic realism a normative purpose: to define the ideal against which a critic judges a particular text—does it have the greatness of scope and the objectivity of insight characterizing the great eighteenth- and nineteenth-century realists? When Lukács wrote *The Historical Novel, Studies in European Realism, Realism in Our Time,* and other historical works, his aim was not only to define the major literary modes, including realism, modernism, naturalism, and romanticism, but also to teach his Soviet readers good standards of judgment.

In light of this grand purpose, it is not surprising that Lukács's greatest achievements were in literary history, where his accounts of realism, naturalism, modernism, and other movements insightfully explained the general features of literary periods and their underlying socioeconomic determinants. Under his aegis, Marxist theory could tell why one period evolves from another, why the dominant literary traits shift so radically from period to period. Since the major artists show a personal, subjective sensibility in the romantic but not in the neoclassical era, Lukács suggests that this change corresponds to distinct socioeconomic developments, such as the aristocracy's declining power or the bourgeoisie's political compromises. In fact, the theory has become a commonplace among historians of the novel, who argue that England's burgeoning middle classes turned the novel into a successful literary form because, more than the epic or the drama, the novel satisfied their interest in individual character, realistic contexts, and moral improvement (Watt, 35–59).

The grand historical vision has its weaknesses as well as its strengths, for Lukács reduces a work's virtues and limitations to social conditions and neglects the impact of the artist's and the reader's productive activities. Thus the naturalism of Emile Zola or Stephen Crane does not yield objective insight because, faced with incipient working-class rebellion and a weak, defeated aristocracy, the bourgeoisie of the naturalist period gave up its progressive attitudes. Modernist art like Kafka's also lacks objectivity: in the modernist era an imperialist ruling class finds radical politics and colonial rebellion an absolute nightmare foreshadowing the end of class rule, and in horror this class repudiates the rationality and the objectivity informing the realist art of earlier periods. Such analyses condemn the fiction if the era does not provide the great political struggles enabling the artist (or the reader) to meet the norm of realist objectivity. Overlooking the artist's labor allows the critic to devalue the literature of uneventful eras.

This difficulty stems from Lukács's commitment to classical Marxism, which kept him from fully questioning Stalinist practices. For example, during the Stalin-Hitler pact, when the Soviet Communist party prohibited any attacks on Hitler, Lukács, Hitler's unrelenting critic, went to jail for attacking an ally. When the Soviet Union crushed the Hungarian rebellion of the 1950s, Lukács, the Hungarian minister of culture, went to prison again. All the same, before Nikita Khrushchev revealed the horrors of Stalin's rule, Lukács would not criticize the Stalinists in public; only in private interviews would he fault them, and even then he feared that his criticism would merely aid the imperialist enemy. After Khrushchev's exposé Lukács wrote caustic analyses of Stalin's "civil war" mentality and praised the new realism of Aleksandr Solzhenitsyn. He believed that history was undermining the Stalinist regime, yet he remained loyal to the Stalinist belief that Soviet socialism was a historical necessity and not a disastrous aberration (Löwy, 193–213). Although Lukács provided a powerful account of historical periods and their development, he mistakenly expected cultural study to transcend the conformity and complicity imposed by Stalinism and to grasp the objective truths of historical development.

Trilling's Anticommunist Realism

Lionel Trilling, who also produced a historical account of literature, preserves the traditional autonomy ("authenticity") of cultural study in a decidedly anti-Stalinist way. One of those distinguished "New York intellectuals" associated with the influential *Partisan Review,* Trilling became warmly procommunist in the 1930s, when his Jewish background combined with his progressive beliefs nearly cost him his position at Columbia University. By the 1940s, however, he adopted that harsh anticommunism which came to characterize Sidney Hook, Irving Howe, Norman Podhoretz, Midge Decter, and other New York intellectuals. Indeed, he devoted *The Liberal Imagination* to cleansing the middle-class intelligentsia of its Stalinist proclivities. He argues that except for the "humanist" Marx, liberal intellectuals busily attacking Western democracies inevitably minimize and ignore the evils of communism. Like Lukács, he equates Stalinism and communism, but his variant of this equation is negative and even tragic.

Nonetheless, his account of culture is both historical and political, both realist and oppositional. While he and Lukács expect great art to produce complex insight into sociopolitical life, Trilling formulates this insight as a matter of the subject's individual authenticity and not of realism's historical development. Scholars say that Trilling does not follow a distinct method (Krupnik, 162), but he does insist that, while literature is inescapably historical, great art possesses a "moral realism" resisting the artist's culture and transcending history. In the influential "The Sense of the Past," for instance, Trilling writes that "literature, we may say, must in some sense always be an historical study" (*Liberal,* 181). The anarchists in *The Princess Cassimassima,* Iago, Becky Sharp, and other dissembling villains from classic English literature—these characters reflect social life because literary ideas grasp sociohistorical reality accurately.

At the same time, Trilling expected the artist to overcome the limits of his era's ideologies. Trilling is aware that artistic ideas may degenerate into ideology, which he defines in Freudian terms as "the habit or the ritual of showing respect for certain formulas . . . of whose meaning and consequences in actuality we have no clear understanding" (*Liberal,* 272). However, great artists rise above ideology's blinding influence and produce a critical insight into and repudiation of ideology's reassuring formulas. As he says, art can achieve an "intense and adverse imagination of the culture in which it has its being" (*Self,* i). For example, he interprets *Huckleberry Finn* as, in part, an account of Huck's moral development. When Huck resolves to help Jim, Huck heroically "discards the moral code which he has always taken for granted" (*Liberal,* 113). While this interpretation neglects Huck's persistent fear that, by helping Jim, Huck dooms himself to hell and to damnation, the interpretation does imply that fiction can overcome ideologies as deeply rooted as the Old South's racist fundamentalism.

Moreover, Trilling believes that modernist art also rises above the influence of ideology. While Lukács argues that modernism shows only the disintegration of the subject, whose solipsistic withdrawal from social life and from historical reality erases history and its potentialities, Trilling extends art's oppositional, adversarial character to modernism too. In it he finds a congenial opponent of liberal intellectuals and democratic writers whose Stalinist proclivities lead to simplistic abstractions and stylistic ineptitude. The aristocratic values and religious commitments of modernists, especially their "imagination of disaster," have produced works of much greater value than those of liberal artists: as Trilling says, "The sense of largeness, of cogency, of the transcendence which largeness and cogency can give, the sense of being reached in our secret and primitive minds—this we virtually never get from the writers of the liberal democratic tradition of the present time" (*Liberal,* 286). Of course, Trilling has some reservations, including the Lukácsian fear that the modernist's "conscious preoccupation with form" may be harmful (*Liberal,* 260); still, as late as 1970 he insisted that the "authenticity" of modernist art "is implicitly a polemical concept" (*Sincerity,* 94).

This insistence on modernism's adversarial stance parallels the views of Theodor Adorno, who also esteems the subversive force of modernist art, condemns the totalitarian practices of the USSR, and dismisses the committed views of liberal and radical writers. Moreover, Trilling's sensitivity to individual artistic practices enables him to produce a fuller, more balanced account of realism and of modernism than Lukács produces. Indeed, Mark Krupnik rightly praises Trilling's pursuit of an Arnoldian grace and balance in which the virtues of the aesthetic modernist and the liberal realist compensate for their failings (162). Nonetheless, Trilling goes too far: not only does this pursuit of grace and balance transcend the institutional commitments of the writer and the critic, it represents the Western subject as though Stalinism and not racial prejudice, social injustice, and class conflict kept it from unifying itself. As Trilling suggests, the disintegration of the modern self may undermine liberal realism and romantic sincerity, but the moral force of modernist authenticity does not erase all social or historical limits except Stalinism. Lukács, who went to the opposite extreme, insists that nothing but the critical realism of a liberal or a socialist sort can guarantee the social progress enabling the subject to regain its autonomy. Lukács believed what Trilling rightly denied—that only critical realism steadily opposes established social institutions and as a result loyally ensures their advance. Yet Lukács and Trilling both insist that great art shows the autonomy of the artist, who overcomes the ideological limitations and achieves a forceful insight into social life.

The Frankfurt School of Social Theory

The Frankfurt social theorists, who also defend the traditional autonomy of the subject, repudiate the traditional narrative of classical Marxism and the realist method of the historical critics. Like Trilling, the Frankfurt theorists fear that classical Marxism, especially its division of base and superstructure, leads to Stalinist totalitarianism. Like Lukács, they doubt that the human subject can achieve unity and autonomy under capitalism, which reveals an endless capacity to fragment the subject. In those dark, barbaric times, when fascism and Stalinism triumphed in Europe, the Frankfurt school rightly sought to keep alive the rapidly dying forms of critical thought, but the school did so in an unacceptable way, by reaffirming a speculative, Hegelian version of traditional humanist objectivity.

The Frankfurt school repudiates the objective historical realism of the older Lukács, but not his youthful Hegelian critique of capitalism's "reified" forms. This critique forcefully exposes the sociohistorical contexts "underlying" empirical disciplines but restates and even extends the theoretical potency of the subject. Lukács argues, as Husserl does, that experience reveals real essences (underlying conditions) which make experience possible. In the influential essay "Reification and Class Consciousness," he shows that empirical disciplines like economics ignore the "ontological" conditions which explain the disciplines' conditions of possibility. However, to explain these conditions, Lukács does not seek to bracket the empirical standpoint, to intuit an essence, and to attain absolutely certain knowledge; rather, as Goldmann points out, he assumes that humankind is situated in history, which alone reveals being or totality (*Lukács,* 7). Insofar as humanity and history produce each other, a discipline comes to understand its underlying realities by transcending the standpoint of the autonomous self and examining the history of social life.

The history that Lukács chooses to tell is Marx's history of capitalism, especially the violent origins and the debilitating effects of commodity production. According to Marx, capitalist production imbues commodities with the mystical powers that tribal societies reserve for their totemic gods. Instead of using commodities, people worship them. People have diverse ends and purposes, but commodity production destroys the ability of individuals to define themselves; their products—cars, machines, theories—impose definition, self, and purpose upon them. Such "fetishized" commodities displace and conceal the social relations organizing society and acquire the rationality and the value lost to humanity (Marx, *Capital,* 69–84; Fromm, *Man;* Jameson, *Form,* 232–57).

Revising and extending this critique of commodity production, Lukács argues that capitalism imposes the commodity's illusory autonomy on all social institutions. He contends that an instrumental rationality, which calculates means and not ends, evaluates techniques and not values, and seeks autonomy and not community, governs the economic institutions of bourgeois society. Moreover, as Bernstein points out, Lukács argues that, once economic institutions gain their independence, capitalism imposes this rationality on all realms, including the intellectual (82). As a result, the sciences, the humanities, and the other disciplines functioning within this context examine the internal relations of their discipline and ignore its social relations. The "exchange value" of their works matters more than their "use value." Like commodities, these "reified" disciplines consider themselves autonomous and ignore their underlying social conditions.

To subvert this reified condition, Lukács adopts the totalizing method, not the absolute totality, of Hegel. In the *Phenomenology of Mind,* Hegel says that outside of consciousness or "appearance" the Kantian essence or thing-in-itself reduces to an empty abstraction, a substanceless ideal. Moreover, by systematizing accounts of experience, consciousness grasps its whole context and renders the "thing-in-itself" superfluous. Consciousness, whose phenomena do not conceal this hidden reality, develops by distinct stages. At the same time, Hegel expects this system of consciousness to transcend the interpreter's experience and to attain the status of "absolute knowledge," a "position where essence becomes identified with existence" (144–45). As Habermas points out, this pursuit of absolute knowledge contradicts Hegel's account of consciousness' experience. Systematizing experience into historical stages radically undermines the autonomous ego, but absolute knowledge transcends the stages of historical experience and affirms positive, static truth (*Knowledge*, 20–21).

Lukács repudiates Hegel's faith in absolute knowledge but preserves and extends the systematizing critique of experience. Possessing the critical potency which phenomenologists attribute to classical norms or to literary figures, this systematizing method enables the critic to challenge the illusory autonomy and false independence which the capitalist mode of production instills in science, art, philosophy, and other disciplines. The critic who adopts the perspective of the totality questions the limits imposed by the dominant instrumental rationality. He asks about values and not just forms, examines his social relations and not just his discipline, and synthesizes disparate disciplines and not only isolated facts.

The great achievement of this Hegelian critique is that it poses such fundamental questions about academic disciplines; the great failing is that the method moves the critic to seek "independent" grounds outside academic institutions. In the early, phenomenological work, Lukács expects the lost totalities of the past to provide such independent grounds, but in the reification essay, Lukács argues that history does not provide a perspective critical enough to demolish the reified state of modern society. The autonomous ethical subject of the modern era can oppose but cannot destroy society's reified forms. The critic must also adopt the terrain of the working class, the only class whose practical activity can overcome the divisions and conflicts of social life. In 1921, when the Soviet revolution was still flowering and even Western revolutions looked possible, an optimistic Lukács announced that the working classes were "the identical subject-object of the social and historical processes of evolution" (*History,* 149).

While some early members of the Frankfurt school shared Lukács's enthusiastic view of the working classes, the school's original members, especially Herbert Marcuse, Theodor Adorno, and Max Horkheimer, grew very pessimistic. In the 1920s, when Lukács argued that the working class could overcome the traditional oppositions of the subject and the object, the successful revolutions in the USSR and elsewhere seemed to confirm his argument; by the 1940s and 1950s, when conservative trade unions and Stalinist political parties assimilated the working classes into reified bourgeois society, the Frankfurt school could no longer believe in its revolutionary potential. Lukács's identical subject/object gives way to Marcuse's one-dimensional man, whose newly gained position within communist and capitalist institutions ironically destroys his critical thought and vitiates his radical action. While Marcuse preserves Lukács's dismay at the ability of empiricist, instrumental reason to divorce fact and value and to divide theory and practice, he laments the fact that the modern world does not provide meaningful historical agents. Marcuse writes that "social theory is concerned with the historical alternatives which haunt the established society as subversive tendencies and forces," yet "advanced industrial society," which appears "to reconcile the forces opposing the system and to defeat or refute all protest," deprives social theory "of its very basis" (xii). Moreover, he fears that in modern industrial societies "domination—in the guise of affluence and liberty—extends to all spheres of private and public existence, integrates all authentic opposition, absorbs all alternatives" (18). Capitalism "integrates" into itself all its traditional opponents, including the working class, African-Americans, and radicals.

Not only is the working class no longer a viable alternative, an inescapable subjectivity alienates the theorist. Totalizing thought still reveals the social relations concealed by fetishized discourses, but objective truth does not undermine the reified structures of capitalist institutions. If historical agents no longer promise to negate the instrumental divorce of action and value, history loses its subversive force. The saddened Marcuse complains that "even the most empirical analysis of historical alternatives appears to be unrealistic speculation, and commitment to them a matter of personal (or group) preference" (xiii). For similar reasons, Horkheimer labels the Marxist notion that history follows necessary stages a "metaphysical error" (106).

He adds that "critical theory . . . confronts history with that possibility which is always visible within it" (107). The theorist reveals repressed possibilities, not objective laws; utopian visions, not historical truth. As a result, it is artists, rebels, academics, and other marginal groups, rather than opposed classes and their political parties, who create alternative worlds and utopian visions undermining the rigid structures and loosening the restricted possibilities of our "fetishized" society. On these subjective grounds, Adorno, like Trilling, defends the adversarial stance of modernism: more effectively than the committed work of Bertolt Brecht, the modernist work of Samuel Beckett and Franz Kafka repudiates the rigid structures of capitalist discourse: "Kafka's prose and Beckett's plays . . . have an effect by comparison with which officially committed works look like pantomine" ("Commitment," 315).

On the one hand, as Goldmann points out, Lukács, like Heidegger, ends up the defender of a dictatorship whose inevitable downfall he patiently awaited (*Lukács,* 16–17); on the other, the Frankfurt school turns into alienated theorists whose interpretations lose any objective import. Still, the original members of the Frankfurt school retained the Lukácsian notion that systematizing Hegelian phenomenology overcomes the reified structures of social life. Since the 1920s, when the Frankfurt school began, this forceful affirmation of theory's potency has preserved the integrity of Marxist studies. In the 1930s and 1940s, when the black night of Stalinism and fascism darkened the world, when conservative institutions co-opted the working class and other rebellious forces and silenced critical forms of discourse, the Frankfurt school's defense of theory assumed a truly revolutionary status. The tragic suicide of Walter Benjamin, the school's flight from the Nazis, Marcuse's great influence in the United States, Horkheimer's and Adorno's ascendancy in postwar Germany—these events testify to the revolutionary import assumed by theoretical critique.

Still, the extravagant theoretical autonomy sought by Hegelians so disgusted Marx that in *The German Ideology* he ridicules their arrogant pretensions: such theorists foolishly imagine, he says, that men drown because they cannot get the idea of gravity out of their heads (1–2). Marx would rather report the death of philosophy than acknowledge theory's ability to change material conditions. Similarly, Habermas complains that to overcome the reified state of commodity production Lukács endows systematizing Hegelian thought with a fantastically potent force and identifies that theoretical potency with the working class' ideal perspective. As Habermas says, "In doing so, he has to credit theory with more power than even metaphysics had claimed for itself" (*Action*, 364). Even though Hegelian theorists are among the most critical in the Western tradition, I think Marx and Habermas are right: the force of speculative thought is too limited. Rethinking Marxism's Hegelian roots may dissolve the impediments presented by the classical theory and uncover utopian norms and ideals repressed by capitalist society, but such Platonic constructs are ultimately ahistorical—they do not expose the entrenched institutions reproducing capitalist social structures. To insist, as Marcuse does, that modern society can absorb "all authentic opposition" is to construe all institutions as repressive and "one-dimensional" and to neglect their internal divisions or institutional politics. As Habermas and Althusser imply, the established organizations representing the traditional working class and other rebellious groups have not remained the silent victims of social domination; rather, they have become interested in theorizing and improving the institutional conditions which ensure their survival (Habermas, *Knowledge*, 196–97; Althusser, *Lenin*, 148–77). Even the Communist parties which accepted the repressive, dogmatic policies of the Stalinists reveal significant conflicts between liberal reformers and conservative dogmatists.

Poststructuralist Marxism

A more viable kind of cultural Marxism comes from Louis Althusser, a French philosopher who rejects both the historical and the Hegelian pursuit of an autonomous subject. Like Trilling and the Frankfurt school, he grants conservative objections to classical Marxism, yet his structuralist and even poststructuralist accounts of ideological discourse do not admit either the historical or the speculative reconstruction of an autonomous subject. For example, in his early work he praises the theoretical achievements of Stalin, but in *Pour Marx* he acknowledges that Stalinist practices deformed Marxist thought.

To overcome this deformation, Althusser proposes a number of new concepts, the most important of which is an explosive account of ideology. Contrary to traditional views, ideology does not impose a false consciousness obscuring the ruling class' true aims or the working class' true interests. It does not invert or distort the subject's reflection of his true social relations. It does not efface those relations within a metaphysics of the commodity. Rather, ideology is an unsystematic, decentered network of socially necessary images, myths, structures, and concepts: "Ideology is a system (possessing its logic and proper rigor) of representations (images, myths, ideas or concepts according to the case) endowed with an existence and an historical role at the heart of a given society" (238).

This view of ideology does not break completely with classical determinism (the economic infrastructure still influences ideological practices but only in the "last instance"). Like Roland Barthes, Tzvetan Todorov, and other French structuralists, Althusser means to establish a science of such "representations," but he assumes that Marxism-Leninism is such a science. In *Pour Marx,* for example, he argues that "theory," which he equates with this science, engages in what he terms "theoretical production," which includes three mythical generalities: the materials of theory, the products (particular theories), and the criteria and standards ("means of production") (186–90). Theory produces scientific concepts from its discursive materials, not from its ostensible objects, and, by adhering to its standards and not to practice, intentions, or sources, theory struggles against ideological influences. Ideology puts practice ahead of theory, but theory divorces the two. Indeed, practice does not test theory; rather, practice has its ends and aims (those of ideology), and theory has its standards and ends. Moreover, the science of the theorist enables him to escape the influence of ideology and grasp its true aims. Because of science's high standards, the theorist—but not ordinary persons—can discover the gaps, inconsistencies, and incoherence that expose the ends of ideology. Any theorist (including the communist) who fails to preserve his scientific standards is merely ideological.

This account of ideology and science aroused a storm of objections. (For a thorough discussion of them, see Anderson, *Arguments,* and Hirst, *Marxism.*) Critics construed this account as anti-humanist, elitist, and even Stalinist, for ideology exercises its influence unconsciously, turning its subjects into its agents or instruments and denying them the ability to take meaningful action (see E. P. Thompson, 205–17, 276–95). Although Althusser does not fully answer these criticisms or disavow his elitist scientism, he develops an institutional kind of critique whose aim is not to preserve the autonomy sought by the traditional theorist or to reveal the objective truths concealed by ideology but to disrupt the ideological construction of the conservative subject. He preserves the conceptual truths of science but develops an institutional account of ideological discourse.

This development aligns Althusser's approach with that of Michel Foucault, his student and, as he says, his "master." Despite their many differences, they both assume that discourse/ideology possesses its own peculiar independence—what Althusser calls its relative autonomy and Foucault, its will to power. In "Ideology and Ideological State Apparatus" (1969), for example, Althusser roots ideology in institutions whose rituals and discourses reproduce it. It accounts for the subject's "lived" experience by interpellating the individual as a subject, mirroring his world and setting him to work. The essential ideological act is not distortion or misrepresentation but that recognition or, to use the psychoanalytic term, "introjection" whereby a specific person sees himself as the member of an institution that duplicates his view of himself. Ideology converts an institution's discursive representation of social relations into the objects of an individual's experience. Every society, including a communist society, needs ideology because ideology explains and justifies the social position of the subject, what Althusser calls the subject's relation to the relations of production (162–77). No longer a seamless, boundless space, ideology articulates the institutional practices that give it life.

Since Erik Erikson, American psychoanalysts have acknowledged that mature individuals form an identity by adopting the roles and ideals which institutions offer them, yet, committed to an autonomous ego, these psychoanalysts ignore the power of institutional discourse to form the individual's unconscious, that repressed and forgotten realm whose terms and framework account for individual response to and interpretations of experience. Conversely, influenced by Jacques Lacan, many European psychoanalysts ignore the institutional forces forming identity but emphasize the power of discourse to construct a subject whose experience mirrors and whose language symbolizes its prestructured discourse. Althusser's account of ideology implies that the institutional account of the subject's identity does not preclude the analysis and critique of the ideological discourse constituting the subject's unconscious. Warren Montag rightly remarks that the "subject, any subject, comes into existence only within the configuration described by the conjunction of" ideological practices and unconscious discourses (73). For example, to explain the contradictory subjectivity of Western women, Catherine Belsey says that they occupy an unstable position between hegemonic liberal discourse and traditional chauvinist discourse ("Subject," 56–67).

Moreover, to show that this account of ideology has genuine political value, Althusser reworks the views of Antonio Gramsci, who spent his last years in a cold, wet prison pondering the reasons why Benito Mussolini and his Blackshirts had come to power in Italy and Stalin and his followers in the USSR. Gramsci concluded not only that the intellectuals of a modern Western society are more numerous and more functional than those of other societies but that Western intellectuals also exercise more political force. The traditional distinction between civil society and the state is no longer applicable. In the private associations (schools, churches, trade unions, newspapers, television, businesses) composing civil society, intellectuals do more than express a personal opinion; in addition, they persuade subordinate groups to accept what Gramsci termed the "hegemony" (ascendancy) of the dominant class. Similarly, the state does more than enact laws and require conformity with them; it may also force subordinate classes to accept the rule of the dominant class. (For a full discussion of Gramsci's view, see "The Antinomies of Antonio Gramsci," by Perry Anderson).

Similarly, in "Ideology and Ideological State Apparatuses," Althusser divides the power of the state from the state apparatus. State power is what a distinct class exercises, whereas state apparatuses, which include repressive structures (courts, legislatures, prisons, police, army) and ideological structures (political parties, schools, media, churches, families) are what intellectuals run. State power is a political matter bearing on who does or does not rule a country, while state apparatuses are a structural matter revealing ideology's ability to reproduce society's organizations. However, while Gramsci expects intellectuals to join a new, historic bloc capable of winning state power, Althusser feels that intellectuals who subvert the ideological reproduction of bourgeois social relations undertake sufficiently revolutionary action. As Hirst says, Althusser poses the quotidian problem of how intellectuals can disrupt the reproduction of the bourgeois subject (*Law*, 14–17), not the long-term question of how intellectuals construct a revolutionary party.

Althusser shows that in a conservative Western society, ideological critique represents political action because the continuity of the bourgeois subject depends essentially upon the ideological apparatuses maintained by intellectuals. Moreover, theory, which Althusser comes to distinguish from science, exposes the gaps, incoherence, and lacunae of all ideological discourses including Marxism because theory retains its formal independence of those discourses. In the structuralist writing, Althusser construes this independence as a general epistemological rupture between science and ideology. In the poststructuralist writings, he repudiates the general distinction of science/ideology—it represents the harmful influence of positivist rationalism—and accepts a historical view in which, striving for autonomy, distinct discourses develop particular conflicts of theory/ideology.

Foucault also assumes that discourse possesses a peculiar autonomy, but he criticizes discourse by emphasizing its historical breaks. Althusser emphasizes its peculiar kind of autonomy but exposes its limits and its gaps, not its historical discontinuities. Both Foucault and Althusser describe the constitutive force and the historical particularity of discourse, but they understand its critical import in these opposed terms.

Critics object that this poststructuralist Marxism reduces "virtually any aspect of contemporary society" to "a symptom of 'bourgeois' ideology" (McLellan, 82), fragments and fetishizes the subject, and inflates and absolutizes language (Anderson, *Tracks*, 55), or imposes a robotlike "functionalist" conformity with established discourse (Montag, 72; Hirst, *Law*, 43–46; Said, *The World*, 244–45). These objections ignore the social changes that have made culture so important a force in the twentieth century and reaffirm the traditional humanist belief that objective truth escapes the political efficacy of established discourses and ensures the theoretical autonomy of the subject. Without a revolutionary working class, an autonomous subject, or an objective science, poststructuralist Marxism inevitably reproduces established approaches, yet that complicity does not force this Marxism to accept their conservative import. Unlike the

Derridean Marxists, whose *"mise en abyme"* dissolves institutional discourse and repudiates established practices altogether, this Marxism preserves the interpretive force of established approaches but undermines their conservative faith in the status quo. While deconstruction subverts all authoritative discourses, dismissing them as metaphysical quests for absolute meaning, this institutional Marxism reveals their political import and still acknowledges their interpretive power. Both this Marxism and deconstruction expect the indeterminate figuration of language to govern reading; however, while deconstruction assumes that this figuration dissolves the constraints of established practices, this Marxism argues that reading reveals the discursive formations or interpretive communities whose conventions and practices constitute the reader as a political subject.

Conclusion

To show how forceful this Marxism is, I suggest in the succeeding chapters that the unique, distinguished work of prominent scholars elaborates the premises of established approaches even though these scholars take political stances of diverse kinds. In these chapters, I restate the assumptions and criticize the politics of New Critical, authorial, reader-oriented, phenomenological, structuralist, and poststructuralist approaches. First, it is well known that the New Criticism successfully opposed historical, sociological, psychological, moral, and philosophical approaches and established irrational, figural language as a professional norm; nonetheless, New Critical formalism reveals a positive, radical potential elicited by Marxists, feminists, and Afro-American critics but ignored by conventional scholarship. Second, authorial humanists oppose the apolitical formalism of the New Critics but favor an equally apolitical notion of objective truth. Marxists and feminists of diverse kinds establish the radical possibilities of authorial humanism but accept its apolitical limits as well. Third, reader-response, phenomenological, and structuralist theories of reading radically undermine the limits of New Critical and authorial approaches. These theories open literary study to the reader's or the critic's subjectivity, freeing it from textual or authorial constraints. At the same time, though, these theories reinstate these constraints; even the most radical versions of these theories preserve the apolitical neutrality of traditional criticism. Fourth, poststructuralism, which challenges traditional criticism more consistently than those theories of reading do, forcefully undermines the disciplinary boundaries of literary study. A richer movement than its opponents acknowledge, poststructuralism includes textual versions, which take the subversive force of literary language to undermine all interpretive practices, authorial versions, which assume that historical accounts of literary works do not destroy the theoretical autonomy of the individual critics, and reader-oriented versions, which repudiate the subversive force of literary language and the theoretical autonomy of individual critics and situate readers in distinct, interpretive communities. Last, to demonstrate the practical value of this poststructuralist Marxism, I outline a political account of the pessimism saturating the later fiction of Thomas Hardy. In this account, the pessimism stems from the failed liberalism, the new detective fiction, the sensational journalism, and the positivist science of the late nineteenth century. Formal, authorial, reader-response, structuralist, and deconstructive approaches also explain Hardy's pessimism but not in these sociopolitical terms.

I do not mean this institutional critique of established approaches to compromise the independence and individuality of the unique accomplished scholars who make the study of the humanities so rewarding. However, I would like to suggest that insofar as the humanities function as a social institution, the study of the humanities does not escape the political involvement imposed by this function. If this study is situated in established literary communities, the humanities necessarily reproduce the injustice and the irrationality of our neocapitalist social system. To an extent, to acknowledge the institutional politics of the humanities is simply to underline the dereliction and the guilt inevitable in bourgeois life; more importantly, such an acknowledgment may tell us what good and bad things our approaches have done to us, what terrible yet wonderful kinds of people they have made us. Said complains that, unlike American historians, American literary scholars have not produced any serious revisionist accounts of their cultural discourse (167). To fill that void, my account of the terrible but wonderful prodigies (en)gendered by literary discourses turns to the New Criticism.

ONE

New Criticism As/Contra Politics

A MARXIST POSTSTRUCTURALISM UNDERMINES BUT DOES NOT DIS-
place the established discourses producing the many selves of the literary critic. Foremost among these discourses is the New Criticism,
which came by the 1950s to dominate American literary studies so
effectively than even in the 1980s historical, philosophical, and political criticism seem not simply mistaken but altogether unliterary. The
New Criticism became so natural that, as scholars say, it seems more
like a personal tone or a literary style than a critical movement or
a political practice (Krieger, *Apologists,* 4; Foster, 28; Cain, *Crisis,*
104–22). To explain this impressive success, scholars have shown that
the New Criticism confirms broad social and historical tendencies, including the decline of religious faith, the consolidation of American
monopoly capital, the limits of traditional liberal humanism, and the
emergence of the Cold War (Baldick, 223–31; Bové, 42; Eagleton,

Theory, 22–30; Fekete, "Modernity," xviii–xxiii; Graff, *Literature,* 22–29, and *Statement,* xiv; Said, *The World,* 164–65; Weimann, 71–78). However, in addition to these social developments, changes in literary study also explain the success of the New Critics. Before the New Critics, the literary scholar dabbled in psychology, history, philology, or religion; after the New Critics, he specialized in the distinct periods, authors, or genres of a formal discipline. With the New Critics' assistance, the status of the scholar changed from amateur to professional, from dabbler to specialist (Ohmann, 80). In the modern American university, where scientific disciplines have acquired the most prestige, the New Critics forcefully justified the disciplinary claims of literature, making it an independent field with critical potential.

As scholars have argued, the New Critics adopted many contrary approaches and outlooks, but what especially enabled them to justify the disciplinary status of literary study was a tough-minded contextual empiricism, which does not tolerate abstract, impressionistic responses to texts or distant, causal analyses of them. New Critics dismissed the scientific literalism of the empiricists but not their (con)textual objectivity. The all-too-familiar result is that readers describing the intention of the author or the responses of the reader violate this context, whose objective figural forms—irony, paradox, symbol—transcend authors, readers, and discourse. Cleanth Brooks, John Crowe Ransom, René Wellek, and the other New Critics no longer dominate American literary institutions, but the orthodoxy that they established takes for granted their belief that criticism is empirical or formal and not historical or political. I do not mean to suggest that, as an orthodoxy, the New Criticism lapsed into mechanical, formulaic practices or lost its perceptivity; I mean to show that even the neutral empirical stance enabling the New Criticism to make literary study a discipline does not exclude political differences. In fact, the orthodoxy which the New Critics established permits conservative, liberal, feminist, Afro-American, and even Marxist stances.

Empiricism as a Literary Tradition

The New Criticism weaves together romantic, theological, phenomenological, as well as empiricist strands of thought; however, its institutional politics stem from its empiricist strand or, rather, antistrand, for the New Critics turn empiricism against itself—they take its emphasis on verbal contexts and individual responses to undermine its faith in literal, scientific language. It is well known that the New Critics vociferously excluded science from literary criticism but not that they defend a literary kind of empiricism against the philosophical kind.

The philosophical kind is mainly factual and conceptual. As J. H. Randall, Jr., points out in *The Career of Philosophy,* the British empiricism of the 1700s was a largely unsuccessful drive to extend the methods of the natural scientist to social, political, ethical, and even literary matters (566–76). For example, in *A Treatise of Human Nature* (1739–40), David Hume proposed "the application of experimental philosophy to moral subjects" (xx). Hume's *Treatise* fell "stillborn" from the press, but in the 1900s, when Bertrand Russell, A. J. Ayer and others advocated a purified empiricism called logical positivism, British and American philosophers found it congenial. This positivism accepts the traditional faith in experience but rejects the traditional analyses of the subject's mental habits. As A. J. Ayer says, the positivists believe that "every factual proposition must refer to sense experience," yet they disavow "the psychological doctrines which are commonly associated with empiricism" (71). Such doctrines are hopelessly "metaphysical" because they depend upon the synthesizing activity of the human mind, not the empirical verification of public assertions.

Analytic philosophy turned this positivist account of knowledge into a philosophical program in which legitimate reasoning does not seek the impressions behind our ideas or our habitual modes of combining ideas; it confines itself to plainly empirical assertions and strictly necessary inferences, or it plunges into metaphysical nonsense. Should reasoning take into account the intentions of the speaker or the reactions of his auditor, it inevitably commits the infamous genetic fallacy, which is the mistaken belief that the truths of logic and the verification of facts depend upon these "psychological" matters.

It is in these philosophical terms, namely, as a drive to establish the empirical character of literary study, that I mean to discuss New Critical practices. That is to say, philosophical positivism makes philosophy a genuine discipline by repudiating intentions, effects, and discourse as psychological, not philosophical, and by separating the procedures of formal logic from the synthesizing activity of the mind; New Criticism makes literature a genuine discipline in a similar way: the New Critics construct an objective, figural realm whose empirical features alone justify interpretation, and they dismiss the traditional interest in readers' responses, writers' intentions, and sociohistorical or psychological truth as emotivist, relativist, historicist, subjectivist, or, in any event, nonliterary. This procedure is not unusual; Althusser points out that to produce a formal or scientific account of a discipline its proponents usually dismiss the ideologies of its past and construct independent criteria of evaluation.

In those famous essays "The Intentional Fallacy" and "The Affective Fallacy," Wimsatt and Beardsley outline a programmatic version of this procedure—to make criticism emphasize the conformity of interpretive statements and textual facts and to dismiss the impact of readers, writers, and discourse. Wimsatt and Beardsley acknowledge that the designs of the writer produce or "cause" a work but insist that such causal or intentional designs do not enable a critic to establish a genuine standard of evaluation. They admit that a work affects the feelings of readers but argue that only an impressionistic critic discusses such effects. The objective critic, who refers them to the text, provides a sufficiently reliable account of "what the poem is likely to induce in other—sufficiently informed—readers" (34), for "a great deal of constancy for poetic objects of emotion . . . may be traced through the drift of human history" (38).

This commitment to unchanging poetic emotions stems more from Matthew Arnold and T. S. Eliot than from Bertrand Russell and A. J. Ayer, yet, insofar as Wimsatt and Beardsley assume that emotions form "a pattern of knowledge," the commitment does suggest that they mean to make English a scientific discipline. In *Literary Criticism: A Short History,* Brooks and Wimsatt reveal a similar intention, for they expose the philosophical "errors" of classical, neo-classical, romantic, Arnoldian, Marxist, and historical approaches. For instance, Brooks and Wimsatt say that the Aristotelian notion of catharsis belongs to a scientific realm—experimental psychology—not to literary realms. While Aristotle would have considered psychology part of the soul and, as such, part of criticism, Brooks and Wimsatt divide psychology and criticism along disciplinary lines: catharsis belongs to the sciences, not to criticism, because psychology is a factual science and literature is not. Moreover, in Aristotelian mimesis they find an embarrassing dilemma: as they say, either mimetic theory comes "very close to putting a didactic clause in . . . poetry—closer than Aristotle himself seems to wish," or the theory makes the "apparently tautological statement . . . that the only *artistic fault* is to paint the animal *inartistically*" (28). Just as empiricists rigidly divide "is" from "ought," so too do Brooks and Wimsatt translate mimetic theory into a moral imperative lacking factual support and a factual statement without any normative force. In Arnoldian and Marxist theory they find an equally unacceptable didacticism (447, 469–70) because they distinguish so sharply between modern empiricist concreteness and classical Arnoldian or Marxist norms. Last, in disproving the theory of Wordsworth, Coleridge, and others, Brooks and Wimsatt do not distinguish the romantic from the empiricist view of emotion; instead, they translate romantic theory into positivist terms (it relies on the "principle of association by emotive congruity") and discover, as we might expect, that the theory does not make sense: "Emotion as such cannot become the formal or organizing principle of a poem without the disappearance of the principle" (408–9).

Brooks and Wimsatt do acknowledge the historical differences between their approach and traditional approaches, but the positivist terms in which they describe these differences ultimately dismiss those approaches. Confusing psychology and art or imposing "external" objects—mankind's ideals, universal truths, profound emotions, "sweetness and light," the "total state"—the older approaches do not show a partial sense or limited understanding of literary value; they "necessarily" neglect literary values, pursue "inherently" misleading, mistaken, or destructive aims, or express "essentially" nonliterary interests.

The Liberal Empiricism of I. A. Richards

The empiricist program so effectively established by Brooks, Wimsatt, and Beardsley originated, to a large extent, with I. A. Richards, who elaborated a liberal version of it. When Richards arrived at Cambridge, Bertrand Russell, Ludwig Wittgenstein, and other logical positivists had already begun their attack on abstract Platonic,

Kantian, and Hegelian "metaphysics." In the influential *The Meaning of Meaning,* Richards and C. K. Ogden oppose logical positivism but develop a similar attack on "metaphysical" thought. While Russell divides meaning from reference, Richards and Ogden reject that distinction: recurrent configurations of signs cause reactions which establish the meaning of the signs and explain interpretations of them (53–55). They argue that a fuzzy entity called "thought" does not create meaning, which is the "contextual" effect of "sign-making," or the "objective" result of verbal acts. In literature this emphasis on "effects" or "acts" qualifies the context indefinitely, rendering it complex and ambiguous. Any interpretive reference to society, history, or theology must abstract from this contextual complexity and invoke unclear, "metaphysical" entities. Literary statements are "pseudo-statements" involving only their own context because poems use abstract assertions for emotive, not for conceptual, ends, to generate feelings, not to avow beliefs (48–72; see also Russo).

In *Practical Criticism,* Richards modifies but does not abandon this bold dismissal of propositional truth. He grants that political discourse is intentional and that scientific discourse is propositional, but he denies that literary discourse is either intentional or propositional: "The statements which appear in . . . poetry are there for the sake of their effects upon feelings, not for their own sake. Hence to challenge their truth or to question whether they deserve serious attention *as statements claiming truth,* is to mistake their function" (180).

While conservative New Critics dismiss this account of feeling as a nonliterary subject and imbue literature with a unique spiritual or irrational truth, the liberal Richards construes the study of feeling as a civilizing force functioning in the everyday ideological realm. This realm, which he describes as "the whole world . . . of abstract opinion and disputation about matters of feeling," lies between the sciences, "which can be discussed in terms of verifiable facts and precise hypotheses," and practical affairs, "which can be handled by rules of thumb and generally accepted conventions." He explains that "to this world belongs everything about which civilized man cares most. I need only instance ethics, metaphysics, morals, religion, aesthetics . . . to make this plain. As a subject matter for discussion, poetry is a central and typical denizen of this world" (5). Not only does art occupy the "in between" world where "matters of feeling," not "verifiable facts" or "concrete affairs," are central but the world of art includes "everything about which civilized man cares most."

Situating art in that "in between" world of "comparative ideology," Richards affirms that liberal British tradition in which art's purpose is to shore up and to justify (as well as to undermine and to repress) the myths, beliefs, and customs discredited by science. Richards, who builds on Mill's and Arnold's versions of this tradition (see Baldick, 18–68, 134–56; Eagleton, *Theory,* 23–43; McCallum, 9–67), justifies literature's status as a discipline by endowing literature with an ethical aim—to civilize the reader. To perform this function, literary critics assume that traditional beliefs, customs, and practices (the realm of ideology) remain credible even though science has discredited them. The reader does not suspend his disbelief in them; he learns to respond in a more complex way. Juxtaposing opposed traditions and incompatible beliefs, good poetry accords them a unified realm in which they may still induce belief. Poetry rearranges them, harmoniously discharging the reader's impulses to action. As Richards says, "If a mind is valuable, not because it possesses sound ideas, refined feelings, social skill and good intentions, but because these admirable things stand in their proper relations to one another, we should expect this order to be represented in its utterances, and the discernment of this order to be necessary for understanding" (312–13). While the supple reader discerns the "proper relations" of "these admirable things," the gross reader remains mired in what Richards calls stock responses, irrelevant associations, doctrinal adhesions, and technical preconceptions. The job of the critic is to overcome such obstacles to good responses. As a scientific discipline, literary study will encourage the complex responses of the good readers and will debunk the mental blocks of the poor readers. In Richards's terms, "the belief that . . . finer, subtler, more appropriate responses are more efficient than crude ones, is the best ground for a moderate optimism that the world-picture presents" (240).

Critics argue that this "civilizing" program adapts the reader to the very mechanistic institutions that the program means to challenge (Baldick, 226–31; Bové, 58–59; McCallum, 93). This objection is forceful but one-sided, for it does not acknowledge that Richards's scientific account of language undermines the reader's ideological commitments. While conservatives like Brooks establish a hierarchic contextualism glorifying mythic discourse and parodying rational procedures, Richards opens literary study to the "in between world" where ideological analysis counts. Moreover, even though he believes that the "systematic investigation" of our linguistic "instruments" enables us to "master" them and to civilize ourselves (314–19), this belief does not preclude radical textual interpretations of a feminist, Afro-American, or Marxist kind.

The Conservative Empiricism of Cleanth Brooks

In *The Well-Wrought Urn,* Cleanth Brooks is amused to find that the "paradoxical oppositions" of *Macbeth* befuddle critics. Passages like "a naked new-born babe/Striding the blast, or heaven's cherubim, hors'd/Upon the sightless couriers of the air" reveal sharp tensions between the helpless and the powerful or the ordinary and the extraordinary, yet critics haplessly seeking "noble simplicity" strive to dissolve them (48). While this wry affirmation of the text's contrary tones or tensions parallels Richards's faith in an irreducible poetic context, the conservative Brooks considers the text irrational and not civilizing. Brooks rejects Richards's "in between" world of ideological feeling but not the figural language of his contextual empiricism.

Brooks clearly prefers Eliot's belief that a work is a "fusion of thought and feeling" to Richards's belief that "the emotional state of the reader" differs sharply from "the means used to produce this . . . state" (*Literary Criticism,* 623); still, as Krieger and Bové point out, Brooks takes up Richards's contextual account of literary language (Krieger, *Apologists,* 26–28; Bové, 46); in Brooks's words, Richards's "specific contribution lay in his account of . . . 'two uses of language' [e.g., the emotive and the scientific]" (*Literary Criticism,* 613). Just as Richards argues in *The Meaning of Meaning* that scientific language is cognitive, while poetic language is emotive, so too does Brooks say that "the terms of science are abstract symbols" or "pure (or aspire to be pure) denotations," while a poetic term is not a "discrete particle of meaning, but as a potential of meaning, a nexus or cluster of meanings" (*Urn,* 210–11).

Moreover, he too denies that literary texts assert propositions whose truth critics can judge in a scientific way. Literature expresses the depths of the artist's experience, not the "in between world" of ideology, yet we cannot summarize and evaluate that experience successfully. Since the multiple affects of language undermine a summary assertion of a work's meaning, we lose confidence in the assertion's power to picture the facts. Paraphrased assertions violate the "total context" of the work. The "ironic," "paradoxical" complexity of the context indefinitely qualifies the propositions of a paraphrase (*Urn*, 204–9). Such a result dismays philosophical empiricists: as Richard Rorty says, they fear that talk of Sherlock Holmes and other fictional entities threatens our grasp of the real (*Consequences*, 129). By contrast, this "irresponsible" talk delights Brooks, who warns us that "if we persist in approaching the poem as primarily a rational statement, we ought not to be surprised if the statement seems to be presented to us always in the ironic mode" (*Urn*, 211).

Since such "irresponsible" language is not denotative, the assertions of a literary work lose their cognitive value, becoming what Richards calls "pseudo-statements," yet Brooks still argues that literature voices important truths. For example, Brooks attributes the power of *Macbeth* to two powerful metaphors, the garment and the babe. The imagery of the garment includes Macbeth's ill-fitting honors, "hypocritical disguises," "unachieved hope and ambition," "manly readiness," and "dark night's screen or blinds." And the imagery of the babe includes Macbeth's "future limits," "womanly pity," "unmanly childishness," "irrational power or control," "helpless defiance," and "avenging justice." These metaphors "encompass an astonishingly large area of the total situation" (*Urn*, 49) but do not violate the play's poetic context or involve abstract historical or biographical claims.

At the same time, Brooks insists that the metaphors of the "babe" and the "clothes" exert more than this contextual force; in addition, they fit the real situation "on the deepest levels" (*Urn*, 38) and symbolize "all those emotional and—to Lady Macbeth—irrational ties which make man more than a machine" (*Urn*, 46). The conflict between Lady Macbeth's rationalism and the witches' irrationalism shatters Macbeth and reveals true "human experience," not only the poetic context. As Brooks says, "There is a sense, of course, in which every man is caught between them" (*Urn*, 44). I grant that the play's chains of imagery give "the babe" and "clothes" contextual force, but that fact by no means ensures that these symbols penetrate the "deepest levels" of the "real situation." To demonstrate the unifying force of these symbols is not to show that they reveal true "human experience" or that "everyman" experiences their power.

The immediate experience of the artist does not justify the complexity of poetic language if such language is truly contextual. Concrete, truthful, the poet's intuitive feeling does not explain the purely contextual nature of his language, the irreducibly immanent meaning of his poem. Yet Brooks warns us that "it is not enough for the poet to analyze his experience as the scientist does, breaking it up into parts, distinguishing part from part, classifying the various parts. His task is finally to unify experience. He must return us to the unity of experience itself as man knows it in his own experience" (*Urn*, 212–13).

Returning us to the "unity of experience itself," dramatizing its oneness, triumphing over its "apparently contradictory and conflicting elements"—these are quintessentially New Critical acts; however, they oppose a purely formal literary language. Brooks insists that the unified experience of the poet enables him to overcome the poem's "conflicting elements," yet, as scholars point out, this insistence contradicts the ambiguous complexity making paraphrase a heresy (Krieger, 130–32; Graff, *Statement,* 96; Fekete, *Twilight,* 38). Either poetic language has its own immanent meaning and requires no external justification or "at its higher and more serious levels" experience justifies the unifying thrust of the poem; either the poem's context creates a unique, unparaphrasable language or experience gives that language its meaning and justification.

This inconsistency suggests that to preserve truth Brooks sets artistic experience above the empirical text, which in turn stands above philosophical analyses. In other words, Brooks establishes an irrational hierarchy at the top of which stands artistic experience, religious faith, or mythic insight; in the middle, literary or poetic discourse; and at the bottom, scientific, philosophical, and other nonfigural discourses. He dismisses the historical realm of ideology, but he approves Allen Tate's belief that "'an *angelic imagination* is not possible. Angels by definition have unmediated knowledge of essences.' Man . . . can take hold of essences only through analogy" (*Literary Criticism,* 605). While science remains literal, "analogy" or figural language strives for but never achieves the wisdom of angels and gods. On similar grounds, he commends the traditionalism of T. E. Hulme, who construes art "not as a vehicle for, or simple statement of, ethics or religion but as a human artifact taking shape in the same universe where ethics and religion are sustaining principles" (*Literary Criticism,* 661).

While Hulme elevates ethics and religion into principles "sustaining" the universe, he voices a severe, classical contempt of human reason. Brooks's hierarchy implies a comparable contempt of philosophy, for the "heresy of paraphrase" dismisses all philosophical analyses, not only empiricism. In fact, in *The Well-Wrought Urn,* Brooks explains the truth of a poem by opposing "unity of tone" to "rational or logical unity," "scientific or philosophical truth" to "dramatic truth," and coherence based on "propositions logically related to each other" to coherence derived from a "complex of attitudes dramatically related to each other" (244). To an extent these oppositions allude to T. S. Eliot's belief that the good poet digests or dramatizes his ideas or he gives them up entirely. More important, the oppositions assume that philosophical or scientific paraphrase is not metaphorical or figural but purely propositional. Scientific minds desire "rational" unity and "logically-related" propositions, while literary minds seek "dramatic" coherence and "unity of tone." Just as logical positivists like A. J. Ayer insist that "scientific" knowledge cannot be figural, so too does Brooks claim that poetry is "dramatic," not "rational." Verifiable truth is literal, not poetic.

Brooks mistakenly supposes that philosophy as a whole shares the positivist fear of "irresponsible" figural talk. He accepts the contextualism of Richards, not the literalism of Ayer, for he believes that all philosophical assertions, not just the positivism of Ayer, repudiate figural language. By contrast, John Crowe Ransom, W. K. Wimsatt, and others do not dismiss rationality in this reductive way. Neither does Richards, in whose view art's purpose is not to affirm transcendent values but to shore up and justify (as well as undermine and repress) the myths, beliefs and customs discredited by science. Moreover, while logical positivism does oppose figural thought, philosophy as a whole does not. Certainly the existential phenomenology of Friedrich Nietzsche, Martin Heidegger, and Jean-Paul Sartre does not. Even analytic philosophy no longer does so. Indeed, poststructuralists have shown that philosophical writing employs figures and devices and so does not escape the discursive conventions undermining the capacity of "literal" terms to represent discrete contexts.

Nonetheless, Brooks's hierarchic contextuality has been remarkably influential. Certainly Brooks's approach influenced deconstructive critics like Paul de Man, who complains that the "heresy" of paraphrase depends upon a "purely empirical notion of the integrity of literary form" (*Blindness,* 32), but who still preserves the New Critical opposition of figural language and propositional assertion. Moreover, Brooks's approach enabled literary criticism to become a distinct discipline with an equally distinct subject matter—the canon. By fusing artistic experience with mythic realms, Brooks suggests that literature possesses a unique kind of wisdom and merits specialized study. By caricaturing rationality, he effectively makes the canon (but not particular canonical works) what Eliot believed it should be—the object of impersonal devotion. In the early *Modern Poetry and the Tradition* (1939), he simply defends the tradition of metaphysical wit against other kinds of poetry. In that work he argues that, unlike Coleridge, Wordsworth, and Arnold, T. S. Eliot, William Butler Yeats, John Crowe Ransom, and other modern poets create a precise, inclusive, and tough-minded poetry. In his later work, however, he campaigns on behalf of a formal method that dismisses the subjectivity of the critic. *The Well-Wrought Urn* (1947) is his greatest work because it weans the study of metaphor and other figures away from the metaphysical tradition. As Brooks writes: "The 'new criticism,' so called, has tended to center around the rehabilitation of Donne, and the Donne tradition. . . . What the new awareness of the importance of metaphor . . . results in when applied to poets other than Donne and his followers is therefore a matter of first importance" (22–23).

While the "rehabilitation of Donne, and the Donne tradition" limited his earlier account of metaphor, "the new awareness of the importance of metaphor" opens his account to other canonical poets, especially Milton, Wordsworth, Keats, Tennyson, and Yeats. This "new awareness" enables Brooks to set aside his bias in favor of metaphysical poetry and to adopt the "unbiased" canon as an object of analysis. While Richards gives literary study a civilizing purpose, Brooks makes the canon a transcendent object: devotion to it allows the formal critic to suppress his biases and to analyze literary forms objectively.

Brooks's achievement is to open the whole canon to unbiased formal analysis: not only does he make literary study a genuine discipline with a "scientific" method and objective object but he also encourages the endless interpretation and reinterpretation which keeps critics in business. At the same time, he demeans the subjectivity of critics, whose conventions and discourses seem arbitrary, if not irrelevant. Their reactions to figural language are subjective; critics can describe their responses to other readers, but, given the heresy of paraphrase, critics can only prove that the work justifies those responses, not that literary conventions make such responses possible or that other readers should share them. In other words, critics require an authoritative canon if they are not to lapse into irredeemably arbitrary responses. Without the unifying force of its authority, critics' responses must remain altogether unjustified. As William Cain suggests, the New Critic ends up impressionistic and subjective despite his empiricist opposition to impressionistic criticism (*Crisis*, 102).

Paradoxically, then, Brooks bolsters critical response by instituting a method that devalues it and exalts the canon. The irrational, mythic discourse in terms of which he glorifies literary language and caricatures philosophy legitimates the disciplinary status of literary study but represses the subjective commitments of the critic. While Brooks and Richards both defend an empirical, contextual version of literary study, the civilizing program of Richards enables the critic to subvert the ideological realm of everyday life; the hierarchic approach of Brooks objectifies the works in the established canon and denies the value of rational, ideological critique.

The Liberal Phenomenology of René Wellek

In the influential *Theory of Literature* (1942), virtually the only theoretical work read by graduate students of the 1950s, René Wellek and Austin Warren introduce American scholars to European phenomenology, which endows literary figures and forms with greater theoretical force than the more "impressionistic" empiricism allows them but remains squarely within the empiricist framework. Like Brooks, Wellek and Warren mean to overcome positivist literalism but deny critical subjectivity. Unlike Brooks, Wellek and Warren seek this hard objectivity in phenomenological theory, not empiricist facticity. Literary value does not come from what Brooks calls the "imaginative coherence" or achieved unity of a work; rather, value comes from a "structure of norms" "made up of several strata, each implying its own subordinate group" (150–51). Into these groups Wellek and Warren organize literary devices, ranking them from the lowest—the "sound-stratum," which includes euphony, rhythm, and meter—to the "highest"—"metaphysical" or generic qualities like the sublime, the tragic, or the holy.

Originating with Roman Ingarden, this "structure of norms" is real but elusive. Particular readings articulate or "concretize" it but only in part. The whole structure inevitably escapes the critic's grasp. Like the Kantian thing-in-itself, it possesses observable phenomena but an invisible essence. The structure does not represent the sort of unchanging form favored by Ingarden or the mythic figures defended by Brooks: as Wellek and Warren say, "There is no need to hypostatize or 'reify' this system of norms, to make it a sort of archetypal idea presiding over a timeless realm of essences" (153). Wellek and Warren still divide language into the poetic and the scientific and construe the poetic as ironic and paradoxical and the scientific as literal and pragmatic. At the same time, since phenomenology confers transcendent reality on intellectual ideals, the structures do not embody the empirical behaviorism of Richards: "The narrow assumptions of behaviourism define as 'mystical' or 'metaphysical' anything which does not conform to a very limited conception of empirical reality" (153–54). The structure of the text is formal but neither empirical nor mythical.

Wolfgang Iser also objects to mythic, archetypal essences and to narrow empiricism, but he requires the reader to produce a coherent text. Wellek and Warren acknowledge the reader's activity but construe the text as a normative structure independent of the reader's experiences or the author's intentions. To reduce the structure of a text to the experiences of readers (or the intentions of authors) would be to commit what empiricists call the affective fallacy and phenomenologists, the error of psychologism. As Wellek and Warren argue:

A poem . . . is not an individual experience or a sum of experiences, but only a potential cause of experiences. Definition in terms of states of mind fails because it cannot account for the normative character of the genuine poem, for the simple fact that it might be experienced correctly or incorrectly. In every individual experience only a small part can be considered as adequate to the true poem. (150)

Although the reader's experiences are never "adequate to the true poem," it can cause the (correct) experiences. Similarly, Brooks says that a poem "causes" appropriate reactions but to define the "genuine poem" in terms of "states of mind" is to accept an "affective" or "emotive" theory. Wellek, Warren, and Brooks consider the text something more than the experiences of readers; however, Brooks describes the something more as verbal and empirical—"imaginative (as opposed to rational) coherence"— while Wellek and Warren describe it as objective and social—an "intersubjective" "system of norms" "assumed to exist in collective ideology" (156).

While phenomenologists expand this "system of norms" into a theoretical force capable of transforming the reader, Wellek and Warren adopt the liberal humanism of Richards even though they repudiate his empiricist "behaviorism." To justify the contextual complexity of poetry, Wellek appeals to the structure's aesthetic autonomy, not to the poet's experience. While Brooks emphasizes the irrational nature of this experience, Wellek and Warren argue that the structure of a text exists for its own sake, its very independence obviating the need to claim, in justification of complexity, a referential or experiential force (240–46). I doubt, though, that the aesthetic autonomy of a text's norms is consistent with its objectivity. How can a text which exists for its own sake represent either values common to all competent readers or ideals valid in an objective sense? In a strikingly empiricist passage, Wellek suggests a questionable answer:

There is a difference between the psychology of the investigator, his presumed bias, ideology, perspective, and the logical structure of his propositions. The genesis of a theory does not invalidate its truth. Men can correct their biases, criticize their presuppositions, rise above their temporal and local limitations, aim at objectivity, arrive at some knowledge and truth. (*Concepts,* 14)

This distinction between the "psychology of the investigator" and the "logical structure of his propositions" or between the "genesis of a theory" and its "truth" is not a matter of artistic experience but of positivist/humanist belief, yet this belief is inconsistent with a work's aesthetic autonomy. A work that exists for its own sake need not ensure that its readers can overcome their bias, ideology, or perspective and arrive at a transcendent truth. A work that is autonomous need not promise to make our values objective. Wellek does not appeal to human experience, as Brooks does, but his humanist commitment to "objective" norms and values does not square with his notion of aesthetic autonomy. As an end in itself, a text need not guarantee that criticism remain objective or that critics overcome their subjectivity.

Moreover, describing the text as an autonomous complex of norms emerging from, yet independent of, the reader's responses allows Wellek and Warren to include past readings in a limited way—such interpretations reveal a text's development but invariably affirm its identity. A text's historical reception matters even though it must show the seamless continuity of its emergent structure. The phenomenological organization of a text does take into account the past reception or "concretizations" of a work but only in the form of an underlying identity. As Wellek and Warren contend:

A work of art is 'timeless' only in the sense that, if preserved, it has some fundamental structure of identity since its creation, but it is 'historical' too. It has a development which can be described. This development is nothing but the series of concretizations of a given work in the course of history which we may, to a certain extent, reconstruct from the reports of critics and readers about their experiences and judgements and the effect of a given work of art on other works. (155–56)

Wellek acknowledges a distinction between a timeless and historical structure, but he means to abolish the distinction. What destroys it is the structure's development, which is "nothing but the series of concretizations given a work in the course of history." To fashion "a substantial identity of 'structure' which has remained the same throughout the ages," we "reconstruct" the structure's "development" "from the reports of critics and readers and judgments and the effect of a given work of art on other works."

Like Wellek and Warren, the Prague structuralists also speak of a text's structure, but they argue that a text makes its own techniques seem natural by treating other techniques as artificial, by distancing the reader from them. Wellek and Warren also acknowledge that the historical reception of a text influences our account of its structure, but they construe the structure as autonomous or self-developing. Its diverse "concretizations" do not denaturalize historical conventions; rather, the readings realize and develop the structure. While the structuralists categorize the devices and forms produced by art's demystificatory force, Wellek and Warren restrict the history of a text to the readings or "concretizations" it has acquired, and its structure, to the development implied by the readings.

Wellek and Warren overlook those discontinuities undermining and disrupting the text's identity. No matter what the changes in what Michel Foucault would call the archive of artistic discourses, conventions, and conditions, the structure assimilates the text's history and preserves an uninterrupted identity. (For accounts of such archives, see Foucault, *Archaeology;* Lentricchia, *After;* and Eagleton, *Criticism.*) The status of a writer, be he a bard of a tribal society, a scribe of a medieval church, a poet of an aristocratic court, a competitor in a bourgeois market, or an employee of a communist writer's union, is unimportant. The position of the reader, be he a ruler of a Greek city-state, a clerk in a medieval church, a prince of an aristocratic court, a consumer of capitalist commodities, or a defender of the working class' interests and powers, is insignificant. And any break in critical modes of reception, be it from the social and political mimeticism of the Platonic academy to the art-for-art's-sake aestheticism of late nineteenth-century England, is minor. By contrast with the capacity of a text's structure to remain "the same throughout the ages," none of these historical differences matters very much.

I am not arguing that historical differences are more important than the similarities which Wellek and Warren acknowledge or that the text fails to establish an identity unifying its interpretations. What I mean is that while Foucault and other poststructuralists take such historical differences to expose the disciplinary frameworks governing interpretations, Wellek represses these differences in order to construct an objective, self-identical text. If history reveals difference and rupture, the structure of the text may be the arbitrary construct of literary institutions, not a universal set of "intersubjective" norms.

Indeed, Wellek and Warren's account of those well-known terms "extrinsic" and "intrinsic" render the social conditions of production and reception irrelevant. Wellek and Warren say that "intrinsic" criticism, which includes everything from rhythm and meter to narrative form and generic type, conforms to a text's structure or "system of norms," whereas "extrinsic" criticism, which includes biographical, sociological or Marxist, and philosophical methods, does not; as a result, the former can provide "criteria of evaluation," but the latter cannot.

In a historical sense Wellek and Warren are right: the Marxist social critics of the 1930s and 1940s did, to a large extent, ignore problems of formal analysis and evaluation, although these Marxists were not very different from their contemporaries, who also ignored such problems. Moreover, Wellek and Warren admit that a social theory of production need not be scientistic, for they commend Max Weber's and Karl Mannheim's sociology of knowledge: it is "less prone . . . to isolate one single factor as the sole determinant of change" (108). Nonetheless, Wellek and Warren go on to insist that "extrinsic" or "causal" study "can never dispose of problems of description, analysis, and evaluation of . . . a work of literary art" (73). Contemporary Marxists like Fredric Jameson dismiss narrow, reductive accounts of literary production and still establish "extrinsic" criteria of evaluation, yet Wellek and Warren never gave up their widely accepted belief that extrinsic approaches cannot provide a "rational foundation for . . . criticism and evaluation" (*Theory,* 108).

Wellek and Warren do not accept Brooks's positivist division of structure and reception, but they still dismiss "extrinsic" approaches and defend the autonomy of the text. They admit past readings but only insofar as these readings show that a text's structure of norms and values enables the reader to transcend his or her subjective biases and historical limitations and to grasp the objective truth.

Scholarly Accounts of New Criticism

My argument is, then, that, to make literary study a professional discipline, the New Critics adopt predominantly empiricist approaches which emphasize a text's figural devices and objective structures. However, many scholars argue that the real opponent of the New Critics is liberal and/or Marxist humanism, not positivist literalism or the critic's subjective responses. For example, Gerald Graff and M. H. Abrams claim that the objectivity of the New Critics conceals their religious and theological hostility to humanism. Abrams argues that the New Critical opposition between scientific and poetic language originates in eighteenth-century romantic thought, whose parallels "between God and the poet, and between God's relation to his world and the poet's to his" undermined humanist rationality (*Mirror,* 272). Similarly, Graff argues that the objectivity of the New Critics stems from their belief that religion should cure us of humanism, not that science should save us from subjectivity. As he says, it is in the name of the "Christian doctrine of Original Sin" that the New Critics destroy "scientific objectivity" (*Literature,* 135), for the humanism which they mean to humble favors both conceptual paraphrase and historical scholarship. Like Abrams, he considers the destruction of conceptual and historical truth characteristic of romantic irrationality. Not only do the romantics summarily reject all scientific, mechanical, or nonorganic modes of discourse, the romantics oppose every rational mode of discourse because they do not distinguish the debased rationality of middle-class empiricism from the true rationality of classical thought (*Literature,* 31–44).

Traditional Marxists also believe that the New Critics' true target was not our critical subjectivity but our literary and historical wisdom, though they emphasize the historian's political commitments, not his liberal "arrogance." Investigating "empty" forms and "insignificant" techniques with "scientific" precision, the New Critics dismiss the social and historical substance of literature and the political responsibilities of the teacher/scholar. Like Abrams and Graff, John Fekete, Georg Lukács, Robert Weimann, and others consider formal analysis an empty exercise of purely "academic" import.

In *The Critical Twilight,* for example, John Fekete elaborates this critique, charging the New Critics with formal insubstantiality as well as political irresponsibility. He too says that the polite formalism of the New Critics fulfills romantic tendencies, but he describes these tendencies as a drive to divorce social life and literary form, not as an unwarranted attack on classical rationality and truth. In Fekete's view, New Criticism doubles the alienation that romanticism imposed upon art. New Criticism's "internal values" increasingly impoverish literary analysis. First, "cultural values" are "isolated from the socio-economic sphere" and subsequently from the authorial subject of "cultural production" and of the "aesthetic realm." In this historical sequence, the artistic isolation begun by the romantics and continued by the New Critics costs literary analysis more and more social substance (17). Because of New Criticism, literary study becomes more indifferent to the totality of life than ever before. Not only do the New Critics stifle their social criticism in order to enter the academic temple; once they get there, they empty literary analysis of even that minimal social import left it by romanticism.

Abrams, Graff, and Fekete rightly claim that the contextual approach of the New Critics fits within the general schema of romanticism, yet the rejection of historical or propositional truth involves more than a romantic disdain of rational thought. In addition, the rejection influences the institutional framework in which the New Criticism establishes itself. In Fekete's account, this framework simply forces the New Critics to commit irresponsible acts—they aid "neo-capitalist oppression." Mid-century American capitalism reorganizes the giant bureaucracies created in earlier periods, repressing trade union organizations and progressive political movements (*Twilight,* xviii–xxiii). The New Critics adapt themselves to this unholy social structure: to do so, however, they stifle the social criticism of their youthful Agrarian period and turn a deaf ear to neocapitalist brutality and oppression. For example, in the 1920s and 1930s John Crowe Ransom led the Southern Agrarian movement. In the *Fugitive* and *I'll Take My Stand,* he published poetic, economic, and political pieces defending the close-knit spiritual communities of the traditional South and condemning the "progress," industry, liberalism, science, wealth, and bureaucracy of the Yankee North. However, after the 1940s, when he taught at Kenyon and edited *The Southern Review,* he gave up the politics of the agrarians and returned to poetry and criticism. Fekete concludes, appropriately enough, that to conquer the highest academic positions the New Critics set aside their conservative politics and advocated a polite formalism (*Twilight,* 85–90).

While Fekete forcefully exposes the New Critics' opportunistic compromises with and concessions to the power structure, he assumes that the bureaucratic rationalization of the New Critical era operates outside American universities, where, to ensure themselves a long and comfortable tenure in academia, the New Critics had only to ignore the evil ways of unholy external forces. However, in the 1940s and 1950s, when the New Critics acquired institutional authority, they made literary study a professional enterprise as well.

Before the New Critics, the serious English professor could dabble in ethics, history, psychology, or linguistics; after the New Critics, s/he had to specialize in literature, for the study of English became a definite discipline independent of the other disciplines. In the 1930s and 1940s, scientific specialists were taking over the sociology, history, psychology, and linguistics that the Victorian man of letters had long considered his own. By caricaturing other disciplines as narrow sciences or "philosophy," by studying literature as "literature and not as something else," the New Critics helped to make literature a distinct discipline with a formal method, a special wisdom, and a distinct object. What Brooks and the New Critics justified was an institutional imperative making the English professor a specialist in literary language, not a dabbler in ethics, history, psychology, or linguistics. The study of English turned into a professional discipline excluding other disciplines. Although the movement which instituted the New Critical approach acquired an enthusiasm surprising to Brooks and other New Critics, the movement accomplished a great deal: as Richard Ohmann points out, at the elite Ivy League colleges and the giant new state universities, the New Critics and their supporters helped to make English a respectable department with its own faculty, students, subject matter, and pedagogy (80). The scientific environment of the burgeoning state universities made and still does make the New Critical stance a successful guarantor of faculty, students, research, salaries, and staff.

Paul Bové claims that the New Critics do not permit radical or oppositional stances: "Fundamentally conservative, even reactionary," practical criticism "cannot be the ground for an oppositional intellectual practice, because it must trivialize history if it hopes to minimize the importance of change so that it can manage and perhaps even encourage the forgetting of social and gender difference" (53–55). However, not only do the New Critics make the study of literary language a successful professional enterprise, they construe literary language as an independent method in a Foucaultian sense: the critics competing for dominance may disavow the doctrines of the founding fathers but remain practitioners of the method. Scholars who reject the tenets of New Criticism may still analyze the import of literary language, including its critiques of ideology or of gender differences. Like a mythological or a psychological approach, a Marxist or a feminist stance is not, by definition, unacceptable or insignificant if it remains contextual or figural. The New Critics wanted to take the humanist down a peg or two; they turned a blind eye to ruling-class brutality and accommodated their era's institutional rationalizations; still, their impact is not all bad, for their commitment to contextual figural analyses admits competing discourses and oppositional practices. Liberal and Marxist humanists concede too much to the New Critics. The romantic insubstantiality and social irresponsibility of the New Critics represent a particular stance or political outlook, not literary formalism as a whole.

Feminist Versions of the Formal Method: Sandra Gilbert and Susan Gubar

The feminist criticism of Sandra Gilbert and Susan Gubar demonstrates the radical potential of formal or New Critical methods, for Gilbert and Gubar show that differences of gender explain the figurative language of a woman's text. In psychological terms, as a matter of hidden or concealed meaning, Gilbert and Gubar preserve the New Critics' apolitical division between literal and figurative language or cognitive and poetic assertion ("The most successful women writers . . . have created submerged meanings, meanings hidden within or behind the more accessible, 'public' content of their works" [*Madwoman,* 72]). Nonetheless, Gilbert and Gubar show that a peculiar psychological or mythical discourse, not absolute values or transcendent norms, distinguishes women's literary language from men's language.

In *The Madwoman in the Attic,* for example, Gilbert and Gubar draw on anthropological accounts of mythology, psychoanalytic accounts of femininity, and even the "paradoxical language of mysticism" to explain women writers' figurative language. These writers do not expound their feminist outlook in a didactic fashion; rather, they dramatize or, to use Gilbert and Gubar's psychoanalytic terminology, "act out" their attitudes by bringing together opposed views—male mythology and rebellious femininity: "In projecting their anger and dis-ease into dreadful figures, creating dark doubles for themselves and their heroines, women writers are both identifying with and revising the self-definitions patriarchal culture has imposed on them" (79). This psychoanalytic language of projection, doubles, identification, and acting out restates Brooks's and Richards's notion of dramatized or realized impulses. The successful text does not preach feminist doctrines; it unifies the dramatically opposed impulses of anger and acceptance, rebellion and submission, creating a paradoxical oneness.

This formal belief that the good text reconciles such opposed impulses pervades Gilbert and Gubar's readings of nineteenth-century women's literature. For example, Gilbert and Gubar argue that Jane Austen's work is divided by a "fascination with the imagination" and an "anxiety that it is unfeminine" (161). This self-division reflects Austen's awareness that, even though adolescent women "experience themselves as free agents," mature women must "acquiesce in their status as objects" (161). Gilbert and Gubar find that in an equally conflicted manner, Mary Shelley takes the "male culture myth of *Paradise Lost* at its full value" but still manages to express "fantasies of equality that occasionally erupt in monstrous images of rage" (220). Similarly, in *Wuthering Heights,* Emily Brontë brings together what Gilbert and Gubar call "the most unlikely opposites," including heaven and hell, dogs and gods, local realms and fairy tales, and Christian names and strange animal names" (259). In addition, Gilbert and Gubar assert that while Catherine's marriage and education trap her in patriarchal roles, fragmenting her androgynous self, Heathcliff turns into a satanic monster, a male female pursuing a murderous revenge against patriarchy (280, 293–94, 296). In their reading of *Jane Eyre,* Gilbert and Gubar consider the meeting of Jane the submissive governess and Bertha the mad wife a "secret dialog of self and soul." The patriarchy imposes hierarchic roles on Jane and Rochester, but they succeed, Gilbert and Gubar claim, in achiev-

ing equality once the death of Bertha frees them from anger, decep-
tion, and disguise (368–69). The fiction of George Eliot shows similar
oppositions, for Eliot's narrator advocates "feminine renunciation"
while the author exacts "female (even feminist) revenge" (491). The
plots dramatize the "anger of the fallen female," the heroine who,
hating herself, seeks that renunciation which "can redeem human life
from suffering" (499).

In "Sexual Linguistics," Gilbert and Gubar also examine female
literary language, but they explore its effects on twentieth-century
writers. Gilbert and Gubar argue that in the nineteenth century
women writers, who were not permitted to learn the arduous Greek
and Latin taught at the male universities, developed a female literary
language whose force and import empirical and psychoanalytic linguists have neglected (522). Empowered by this linguistic "witch-
craft," twentieth-century women writers like Woolf and Stein are
able to create "linguistic fantasies" of their own; however, this female
linguistic practice threatens Joyce, James, Huxley, and other "be-
lated" male writers, who appropriate what Gilbert and Gubar term
the "verbal fertility of the mother" in order to construct vernacular
renditions of the medieval "patrius sermo." To silence their female
competitors, these misogynist writers render their constructions arduous and complex; according to Gilbert and Gubar, "The transformation of the *materna lingua* into a new *patrius sermo*—that is, the
occulting of common language, the transformation of the comment
into the charm—seems to offer a definitive cure of the male linguistic
wound" ("Linguistics," 534).

Gilbert and Gubar, who believe that since the fourteenth and fif-
teenth centuries this "occulting" "transformation" has preoccupied
male writers, neglect the class import of this preoccupation, which
has sharply divided the aristocratic supporters of the scholastic
"patrius sermo" from the middle-class defenders of a national culture. In addition, as Marxists like Lukács and Jameson have noted,
the reactionary attitudes of the modernists include not only hatred
of women but also contempt for working people and for minorities,
disgust with liberal ideals, and attraction to fascist parties and causes.
What is worse, Gilbert and Gubar's accounts of nineteenth-century
women's fiction reduce all rebels—Satan, monsters, orphans, outsiders—to versions of angry women as though women and not minorities or working people have any legitimate reason to oppose the

ruling classes. Still, these interpretations of that fiction and the history of literary language successfully incorporate differences of gender within the empirical, formal approach in which great literature dramatizes opposite views. Critics who condemn Gilbert and Gubar's approach as the "critical method proper to patriarchy" (Lentricchia, "Stevens," 775; Moi, 67) ignore their achievement—to introduce the politics of gender into a formal study that has either ignored the literary import of gender differences or treated literary value in pseudoscientific terms, as objective ideals or transcendent norms.

If the formal method makes this achievement possible, the formal method limits this achievement as well. For example, as Moi points out, Gilbert and Gubar do not explain how a society so oppressed by patriarchy would permit a woman to become a writer (64). *The Madwoman in the Attic* considers sociohistorical conditions so oppressive that women who assert an artistic identity experience terrible anxiety. Indeed, Gilbert and Gubar forcefully detail the pervasive critical metaphors that render the pen a penis conferring on the male writer the power to create and to destroy his female "property" but denying women an equally powerful "organ" of self-expression. However, Gilbert and Gubar argue that while this misogynist practice exploded the tradition of women's writing, the woman writer reintegrates the "dismembered, dis-remembered, disintegrated" pieces of her "precursor's art," establishes "the coherent truth" of the shattered pieces, and achieves an identity and a selfhood. This artistic act, whereby the female artist achieves an identity by unifying her "foremother's" fractured work, restates the New Critical belief that, to achieve coherence, art erases "extrinsic" sociohistorical conditions.

I admit that, following Harold Bloom, Gilbert and Gubar speak of the artist's identity and not of a text's unity. Strong precursors produce anxiety in male and female artists, but female artists experience what Gilbert and Gubar call an "anxiety of authority," not Bloom's male-oriented anxiety of influence. All the same, just as the New Critics assume that a work achieves "intrinsic" coherence and unity only if it transcends "extrinsic" sociohistorical conditions, so too do Gilbert and Gubar assume that a female artist overcomes her anxiety and achieves an identity only if she can escape what they call "male houses and male texts" (*Madwoman,* 85): "The striking coherence we noticed in literature by women could be explained by a common, female impulse to struggle free from social and literary confinement" (*Madwoman*, xii). Here historical conditions appear only in a negative form, as "social and literary confinement" or as imprisoning "male houses and male texts," while artistic achievement takes the positive form of a "common female impulse to struggle free from" that confinement by reassembling the "dismembered" tradition of the literary "foremother." Moreover, Gilbert and Gubar formulate these female artistic practices in mythological and not in sociohistorical terms. For example, Gilbert and Gubar claim that the "traditional male hero" "makes his 'night sea journey' to the center of the earth, while the female artist "makes her journey into what Adrienne Rich has called the 'cratered night of female memory'" (99). Lentricchia rightly says that, by setting up a Manichaean allegory of destructive males and heroic females, such mythic contrasts reduce historically constructed differences of gender to particular instances of unchanging male and female archetypes.

As these mythic constructions of artistic identity suggest, Gilbert and Gubar have not overcome the apolitical neutrality of the formal method whose radical potential they exploit so forcefully. Their figural interpretations of women's literature forcefully demonstrate the formal significance of gender but preserve the ahistorical neutrality of the formal method as well.

Afro-American Versions of the Formal Method: Henry Louis Gates, Jr.

Like Gilbert and Gubar's studies of women's literature, Henry Louis Gates's work on Afro-American literature shows that the New Criticism has radical potential. His work opens Afro-American literature to the formal rhetorical methods that the New Critics reserved for canonical Anglo-American texts. His approach does not escape the apolitical neutrality of the New Criticism, but he successfully exposes the persistent racism of the Western tradition and the figural force of black literature.

In readings of black slave narratives, Jean Toomer's *Cane*, Ralph Ellison's *The Invisible Man*, Ishmael Reed's *Mumbo Jumbo*, and other Afro-American works, Gates shows quite forcefully that Afro-American literature warrants complex figural analysis. His readings do not simply repeat formal or New Critical doctrines in Afro-American contexts; rather, his readings develop structuralist, deconstructive, as well as formal techniques of close textual analysis. For example, in "The 'Blackness of Blackness': A Critique of the Sign and the Signifying Monkey," he describes an elaborate tradition composed of Afro-American myths, tropes, and texts. The myths are those of the Signifying Monkey, whose various incarnations or "figurations" have appeared in West African, North and South American, and Caribbean cultures (*Figures,* 237). The trope is signifyin(g), which does not give information or reveal a transcendental signified; rather, a trope that subsumes other tropes, signifyin(g) is the language of indirection, a matter of technique or literariness (*Figures,* 239). The texts, which include those of W. E. B. DuBois, Richard Wright, Ralph Ellison, Ishmael Reed, and others, form a tradition not because they discuss the "black experience" or describe a metaphysical blackness but because they revise, parody, criticize, restate, or "signify upon" each other, thereby engaging in what Gates calls "rhetorical self-definition" (*Figures,* 242). For example, Gates shows that the title and the prologue of *Mumbo Jumbo* parody those of *Black Boy* and *Native Son.* In addition, he argues that *Mumbo Jumbo* takes up and extends *Invisible Man*'s "double voiced" parody of Wright's naturalism (*Figures,* 247). *Mumbo Jumbo* also parodies "realism as local color," which Gates considers a central Afro-American convention, and detective fiction, especially what Gates, following Todorov, calls the story of the investigation. In fact, Gates interprets the parody of the investigation—an unsuccessful search for the "vast and terrible text of blackness" (*Figures,* 269–70)—as a deconstructive critique of blackness. Not only does this parody celebrate the indeterminacy of interpretation but the parody denies that blackness transcends textual language and represents a metaphysical essence. No more than a mode of signifying, blackness does not escape the play of Afro-American literary language (*Figures,* 274–75).

Gates's commitment to formal figural language and to close textual analysis enables him to produce these rich analyses of Afro-American literature. In "Literary Theory and the Black Tradition," however, he denies any commitment of this kind. Asserting that his "marginal" interest in black literature kept him from "becoming an advocate for any particular theory of criticism" (*Figures,* xvii), he still insists that criticism that means to preserve the dignity of the Afro-

American text and to enter the mainstream of critical debate examines a text's figural language, not its proofs of intelligence (xx–xxi, 54): A "literary text is a linguistic event: its explication must be an activity of close textual analysis" (41). This "activity of close textual analysis" affirms New Critical principles, including Brooks's heresy of paraphrase ("Passages of creative discourse cannot be excerpted and their meaning presented independent of context" [40]) and Wimsatt and Beardsley's affective fallacy ("I have . . . [tried] to avoid confusing my experiences as an Afro-American with the black act of language that defines a text" [xxi]). Despite his "experiments" with French structuralism and poststructuralism and with Russian formalism, he characterizes theory as a prism that he "could *turn* to refract different spectral patterns of language use in a text" (xvii). These scientific metaphors invoke Richards's belief that literary language does not depend upon theory but exists as an independent object. In "Authority, (White) Power, and the (Black) Critic," he grants that readers bring to texts what he calls a "critical gumbo" of "ideological and aesthetic assumptions" and suggests that black critics devise original theories based on the black vernacular, yet he still insists that theory is a "tool" enabling the critic to explain the "complex workings of the language of a text" (32–33). He describes the black literary tradition in structuralist terms, as intertextual relationships; nonetheless, he preserves the New Critical notion that artists construct "coherent, symbolic worlds" (*Figures*, 46) and that mythic structures reconcile "irreconcilable forces" (*Figures*, 51). Last, he complains that traditional Afro-American criticism, which expects black literature to contribute to the struggle against racism, "brought readers and writers into a blind alley" (*Figures*, 41). He parodies this "political" approach as "race and superstructure" criticism and hence as perverse Marxism, attacking it on the aesthetic grounds on which the New Critics attacked their sociohistorical opponents. Consider the following excerpt from his attack:

Form was merely a surface for a reflection of the world . . . ; message was not only meaning but value; poetic discourse was taken to be literal, or once removed; language lost its capacity to be metaphorical . . . the critic became social reformer, and literature became an instrument for the social and ethical betterment of the black person. (*Figures*, 30)

Reducing form to a "surface," denying the figural force of "poetic discourse," treating literature as an "instrument"—this catalog of evils echoes Brooks's and Wellek's attacks on "extrinsic" approaches.

Indeed, in a New Critical manner, Gates dismisses the sociohistorical contexts of Afro-American literature. For example, he documents amply enough the racist views of Bacon, Jefferson, Hume, Kant, and Hegel, who all denied in one way or another that Africans could produce culture and participate in the human community (*Figures*, 5, 15–21), but he does not distinguish the racist assertions of these Enlightenment philosophers from the vulgar racism of the social Darwinians even though the philosophers reveal a colonial ethnocentrism very different from the imperialist apologetics of the social Darwinians. What is more, he suggests that Afro-American literature and criticism arose in response to these philosophers and not to an oppressive social system: "Hume, Kant, Jefferson, and Hegel's stature demanded response" or "Allegations of an absence led directly to a presence" (*Figures*, 27, 26).

He complains that both the racists and the critics have expected black writing to demonstrate black culture and black humanity and not to preserve aesthetic autonomy. In impressive detail he outlines the careers of Phyllis Wheatley, Ignatius Sancho, Wilhelm Amo, and other eighteenth- and nineteenth-century black writers and critics who forcefully opposed the "enslavement and servitude of black people" but readily accepted what the "received tradition of Western critical theory . . . posited"—"the firm relation among writing, 'civilization,' and political authority."

Gates shows that slaves like Phyllis Wheatley wrote poetry in order to demonstrate the humanity of their race and that older critics like Howells and DuBois as well as contemporary critics like Baker and Henderson have preserved the assumption that a race's ability to create culture justifies its claims to human dignity and political independence (*Figures*, 24–28). However, Gates evaluates this moving achievement in aesthetic and not in historical terms: "The documentary status of black art assumed priority over mere literary judgment" (*Figures*, 5); "Black literature and its criticism have been put to uses that were not primarily aesthetic" ("Authority," 28). Writers and critics who expected Afro-American writing to prove that Afro-Americans can be cultured and civilized reduced it to a commodity—literacy (*Figures*, 11)—and dismissed its artistic character. By denying aesthetic principles, these writers and critics, "locked in a relation of thesis to antithesis" with the racist Western tradition, have been complicit with it (*Figures,* 14). Such charges ignore the sociohistorical contexts of these writers.

Gates's implicit equation of John C. Calhoun, the prominent Southern politician who defended slavery, with Alexander Crummell, an accomplished Anglican minister who founded the American Negro Academy, erases sociohistorical contexts in a different way. Gates equates Calhoun, who took the mastery of Greek syntax to symbolize Afro-American humanity, with Crummell, who took the mastery of English to symbolize sociopolitical salvation. Gates treats Calhoun and Crummell as equivalent "metaphors of progress, elevation, and intellectual equality" ("Authority," 37). During the seventeenth, eighteenth, and nineteenth centuries, however, the groups who learned Latin and Greek were very different from those who learned the English language. As scholars have shown, learning Greek was a privilege of white, upper-class males who went to elite scholastic universities in order to enter the church or the government, while learning English was the end of utilitarian, middle-class businessmen and professionals who attended dissenting academies and defended a national language and literature. Gates complains that "unlike almost every other literary tradition, the Afro-American literary tradition was generated as a response to allegations that its authors did not and *could not* create literature" ("Authority," 27). However, the scholastic universities disseminated the international culture of the Greek and Roman classics and condemned and excluded the national language and literature. As a result, the dissenting middle classes had to struggle to establish and to justify a national culture that would bind together the divided classes of the state (Eagleton, *Theory,* 22–30; Doyle; Palmer), for the scholastic defenders of the classical tradition denied that English could match Greek or Latin in subtlety, rigor, or expressiveness (Guillory, 513–15). The Anglo-American tradition did not suffer the terrible racist oppression of Afro-American writers, but that tradition did have to prove that English writing, including the prose fiction of the novel, was genuine literature.

Gates rightly denies that his accounts of "the racist social text" can "be anything *but* political" ("Authority," 33), for these accounts effectively overcome the New Critical faith in objective values and transcendent norms. Although Houston Baker reduces the formal analyses of Gates to those of a "class-oriented professional" ignoring the political struggles that brought Afro-American culture into mainstream universities (88), Baker acknowledges the political value of Gates's criticism, which enables Afro-American literature to enter what Baker calls the "contemporary universe of literary-theoretical discourse" (106). While his mythical figural criticism affirms purely aesthetic principles and ignores sociohistorical contexts, his criticism, like that of Gilbert and Gubar, shows the radical potential of the New Critical method.

Marxist Versions of the Formal Method: The Criticism of Terry Eagleton

In 1963, Joseph Frank could wonder why "the very writers who attack the New Criticism in the name of 'history' should never have tried to interpret its positions in their historical context" (29–30). This comment has subsequently lost its bite, for in the 1970s and the 1980s Marxists reinterpreted the figural language that the New Critics consider purely autonomous or "intrinsic." The criticism of the innovative Terry Eagleton, who develops structuralist, deconstructive, institutional, and formal or figural accounts of literary study, illustrates the achievements and the limitations of this Marxist stance. Like Gates and Gilbert and Gubar, he successfully exploits the radical potential of the formal method, which he construes as a kind of ideological disruption, not as an account of sexual differences or as a justification of a neglected literature. Like the New Critics, Eagleton does not manage to overcome the critical subjectivity of established approaches, but he does succeed in revealing the ideological criticism implicit in "intrinsic," figural language.

In 1961, when Eagleton entered Cambridge, the leading approaches included the formalism of I. A. Richards, William Empson, and F. R. Leavis and the Marxism of Raymond Williams. Eagleton's first literary work, *Shakespeare and Society* (1967), reflects these influences, for it undertakes both practical criticism of Shakespeare's texts and theoretical reflections on our cultural experience. His second work, *Exiles and Émigrés* (1970), shows a similar combination of practical criticism and theoretical reflection. What is more, in

Brooks's manner, this work praises the "symbolic resources" of myth for making available "ways of eliciting, ordering, and evaluating the inner structure of a culture" (139). Yet Eagleton is careful to qualify this praise: the "symbolic resources" of myth reveal only "the inner structure of a culture," not the impossibility of rational paraphrase.

In the 1970s, when Eagleton adopts the structuralist Marxism of the Althusserians, he repudiates the unsystematic empiricism but not the figural language of formal critics. In *Criticism and Ideology* (1976), for example, he restates Richards's and Brooks's formal opposition between emotive, figural language and conceptual, scientific language, but he rejects the inconsistent empiricist modes in which New Critics seek to reconcile "autonomous" literary language with human nature, concrete experience, or objective norms. In fact, he argues that the Althusserian dichotomy of science and ideology overcomes this inconsistent empiricism but preserves the formal opposition of literary language and conceptual discourse. First, ideology and science exclude each other, just as figural and conceptual discourses do. Formal concepts and structuralist science are both systematic kinds of knowledge, while their opposites, ideological and mythical or figural languages, are fragmented and decentered. Second, structuralist Marxism excludes from literary texts what contextual empiricism also excludes—positive scientific knowledge. Richards construes literary assertions as pseudostatements, Brooks condemns paraphrase as a heresy, and Eagleton takes the "signifying" devices of a text to refer to themselves or to ideology but not to history or society (74–75). Why else would he say that the value of Jane Austen's fiction depends upon "the exclusion of the real as it is known to historical materialism" (71)? Why would he say that the "text strikes us with the arresting immediacy of a physical gesture which turns out to have no precise object" (75)? He may not believe that literature warrants the reader's impulses to action or that it dramatizes a writer's ideas; still, he does claim that literature realizes the dreams of ideology, granting it a freedom that history never gives it: "Fiction is the term we would give to the fullest self-rendering of ideology" (77).

Last, while Brooks and Wellek expect formal study to ensure that the text preserves its autonomy and its value, Eagleton acknowledges the place of the reader, whose modes of interpretation realize and produce the value of the text (166–68). The text retains objective values, but those values do not erase the influence of authors or readers. Neither does the established canon or the critical tradition ensure that the critic transcends his subjectivity; rather, texts emerge from distinct conditions that Eagleton calls a literary mode of production. These conditions of production are not extrinsic to the text, for the text inscribes its concept of a reader within it. These conditions are not ahistorical or continuous, for they evolve from era to era, each era revealing a complex hierarchy in which certain modes of production dominate and suppress others. Nor are these conditions of production mere historical facts, for they reproduce the general mode of production in which the literary mode has inscribed itself. In the modern era, for example, literature is, Eagleton writes, "a vital instrument for the insertion of individuals into the perceptual and symbolic forms of the dominant ideological formation" (56). Nonetheless, he still expects Marxist science to overcome the biases of cultural institutions. The critic who possesses a science of ideologies escapes their influence, transcends his own arbitrariness, and perceives the reader's and the text's "true" relationship (96). As Bennett points out, Eagleton considers literary value relational, a matter of literature's contexts and functions, but he still construes literary study as an objective science capable of subverting ideological discourse (*Marxism,* 145–46).

On scientific grounds he abandons the assumption of his early work (and of Brooks's, Gilbert and Gubar's, and Gates's work)—that criticism presupposes a hierarchy in which the literal paraphrases of philosophy mangle the text, while the mythic figures of the text unveil a realm of transcendent essences. Now he assumes that the subject matter of literature includes those ideological tales, customs, practices, and beliefs that Richards considers the special interest of civilized humans. I admit that as a closed, autonomous network of myths, symbols, and signs controlling and manipulating its spokespersons, the ideological discourse that Eagleton examines is much broader than the ideological world that interests Richards. Nonetheless, Eagleton does preserve the autonomy of the text, which, he argues, reworks the signs of ideology, exposing their gaps, speaking their silences. Rigorous literary forms reveal the incoherent ends of ideology. It uses but does not master them. While Althusser's account of science and ideology ignores the autonomy of literary forms, Eagleton's account insists upon it:

Like science, literature appropriates its object by the deployment of certain categories and protocols—in its case, genre, symbol, convention and so on. As with science, these categories are themselves the elaborated product of perception and representation; but in the case of literature that elaboration is not carried to the point of producing concepts. (*Criticism,* 101)

"Object," "categories," "protocols," "concepts"—these terms show that Eagleton defines science in structural and not in empirical terms; all the same, he considers "genre, symbol, convention, and so on" to be as objective as scientific concepts.

Moreover, instead of a unifying or hierarchic coherence, he expects art, thanks to its scientific rigor, to reveal the formal incoherence generated by ideology: "The text disorders ideology to produce an internal order which may then occasion fresh disorder both in itself and in the ideology" (99). Contextual language and interpretive assertion, or literary forms and ideological project do not fully mesh. The discrepancies between the text's announced purpose and its produced form, the contradictions between its various generic models, the incoherence and hesitation in its stylistic devices, the conflicts within its imagery and metaphors, and the weaknesses of its character development and narrative closure all show its lapses and failures. A scientific criticism seeks the text's points of inevitable failure, its lapses into incoherence and disunity, not its experiential grounding or imaginative oneness. In sum, the science/ideology opposition elaborated by Eagleton represents a formalism in which Marxism, not empiricism or phenomenology, overcomes the critic's limitations and reveals the text's true form. However, what the text displays is the incoherence, disunity, or even silence betraying ideology's limits, not the unity or coherence revealing mythology's irrational depths or the text's self-developing identity.

When the poststructuralist era begins, Eagleton confesses that the scientific formalism of *Criticism and Ideology* is "elitist" and abandons it but not the figural language of Richards and Brooks (*Benjamin,* 97). Even though Eagleton considers deconstructive discourse anarchistic and insubstantial, he adopts a poststructural textuality preserving literary language. In the Althusserian work, the lapses produced by ideology's inability to reduce literary language to programmatic ends reveal the text's ideological commitments; similarly, in the poststructuralist work, the gaps induced by figural language's ability to escape the text's "centering voice" reveal those ends. In *Criticism and Ideology,* concrete or "lived" experience is the realm of art, and literary modes of production explain the institutional import of the text; in *Walter Benjamin, or Towards a Revolutionary Criticism* (1981) such experience is the "very terrain of the ideological" (7), and a revolutionary criticism interrupts the linear continuities of literary history, parental authority, and "bourgeois" institutions (66–78).

The differences between *Myths of Power* (1975) and *The Rape of Clarissa* (1982) illustrate the ruptures in terms of which Eagleton preserves and expands the force of literary language. In *Myths,* the text itself accounts for diverse readings. As Eagleton writes: "*Wuthering Heights* has been alternately read as a social and a metaphysical novel—as a work rooted in a particular time and place, or as a novel preoccupied with the eternal grounds. That critical conflict mirrors a crucial thematic dislocation in the novel itself" (120). The unity of the text does not affirm the irrational truths of artistic experience; the unity is a mythical construct resolving the unresolvable—social and political contradictions: "If it is a function of ideology to achieve an illusory resolution of real contradictions, then Charlotte Brontë's novels are ideological in a precise sense—myths" (97). However, in *The Rape of Clarissa,* divergent interpretations show the ideological commitments of the critic, not the thematic dislocations of the text (63–73). In addition, Richardson's conditions of writing, including his incessant elaborations of his texts and his unique circle of female critics, make the text functional, not autonomous. All the same, the disparate voices of the text reveal and preserve formal failure as an ideologically significant disjuncture. Eagleton writes that "the fissuring of 'formal realism' in *Pamela* is determined, in part, by an historical conflict between two essential yet disparate styles: the emergent metalanguage of bourgeois morality, and a still resilient popular speech" (32–33). Literature retains and even expands its figural force; Eagleton asserts that the famous immediacy of Richardson's epistolary method cannot master or efface the "materiality of the signifier."

In short, in both the structuralist and the poststructuralist period, textual gaps induced by literary language ("the materiality of the signifier"), not the subjectivity imposed by discourse, reveal the aims of a writer's ideology. When the structuralist project fails, criticism loses its capacity to define its object or delimit its methods, but this result ensures the "death" of literary theory, not of literary language. In fact, in *Literary Theory: An Introduction* (1983), Eagleton proposes that we abandon the established texts of the canon but not the traditional literary methods, which he wishes to transform by "setting them in a wider context" (177–205). Eagleton's is an impressive and unique achievement: although he evolves from a formal and a structuralist to a deconstructive critic, he does not cease showing that formal literary language has a critical potential forcefully exposing the ends of ideology.

Renée Balibar in France and Tony Bennett in England also rework the formal approach, preserving its independence yet endowing it with an equally critical potential. However, Balibar and Bennett do not unmask the formal lapses imposed by an artist's ideological project, nor do they expect Althusserian science to overcome the critic's biases and limitations. Rather, they examine our critical subjectivity: ideology resides not in the text but in the institutions imposing particular interpretive strategies, preserving the traditional canon, dividing ordinary from literary language, or defining other kinds of literary practice. Eagleton's ideological criticism also exposes our literary mode of reproducing the injustices, inequities, and irrationalities of capitalist life; however, his criticism, like that of Brooks, Richards, and Wellek, does not explore the entrenched interests behind the established canon or the institutional subjectivity of our critical discourse.

Conclusion

To sum up, the New Critics meant to place literary study on solid, disciplinary ground; by defining the text as an empirical object and by excluding scientific concepts, they sought to eliminate impressionistic readings, resist positivist disciplines, and justify literary study. Although they spurned liberal humanism, compromised their political beliefs, and remained arbitrary and subjective, they succeeded in elaborating an institutional politics that lives on despite their decline.

As William Cain points out, "It is not simply that the New Criticism has become institutionalized, but that it has gained acceptance as the institution itself" (*Crisis,* 105). Moreover, far from precluding political analyses, the formal method instituted by the New Critics has come to include the hierarchic conservatism of Brooks, the liberal empiricism of Richards, the liberal phenomenology of Wellek, and the radical feminist, Afro-American, and Marxist criticism of Gates, Gilbert and Gubar, and Eagleton. While humanist and Marxist scholars rightly complain that the New Criticism deprives literature of social and historical force, they overlook the institutional import of the formal method, including these conservative, liberal, and radical divisions. Why do both the proponents and the opponents of the formal method dismiss the institutional subjectivity of literary discourse? The answer lies in their humanism, whose pursuit of transcendent truth forms the subject of my next chapter.

TWO

Humanism and the Politics of Truth

NEW CRITICS OF ALL PERSUASIONS SHARE THE BELIEF THAT LITERARY study concerns itself with artistic forms but not with conceptual truth; authorial humanists, who also divide along political lines, share the belief that literary study establishes objective truths and not interested, partial, or ideological claims. For example, the liberal branch initiated by Matthew Arnold sees in classical objectivity and intellectual free play an ideal of human truth eclipsing the political commitments of politicians, feminists, radicals, nationalists, aristocrats, philistines, dogmatists, subjectivists, or skeptics. The Marxist branch begun by Georg Lukács ranks Balzac, Tolstoi, and other classical realists among the greatest writers because these realists are able to grasp the naked, "objective" truth—that brutal exploitation, callous greed, and self-serving apology infest capitalist society—despite the ideological biases imposed by aristocrats, capitalists, peasants, imperialists, clergymen, chauvinists, Stalinists, or intellectuals. Scholars say that liberal or "pluralist" humanism excludes and condemns monistic, totalitarian Marxism (Erlich, 538; Rooney, 556–57), yet the liberals and the Marxists both assume that great artists escape subjective, "ideological" limitation and grasp objective reality.

This pursuit of objective truth also characterizes the New Criticism, which expects a text's language to uncover the depths of the artist's experience. New Critical humanists take literary works to reveal profound wisdom and to preserve their formal autonomy. By contrast, authorial humanists, who also expect a text to reveal profound wisdom, repudiate the formal autonomy which the New Critics consider so essential. These humanists believe that such autonomy represents an illusory goal that conceals and betrays the ethical or theological beliefs of the critic. Inevitably unsuccessful, the search for independent forms usually reveals the biases and values of the critic. Formal study may hide from but may not avoid politics.

In the 1960s, when I began to study literature, I found this critique of formal study a forceful and a moving defense of historical and even Marxist criticism. Since that time, though, feminist, structuralist, poststructuralist, semiotic, and psychoanalytic theories have revealed a significant inconsistency in this powerful critique: the humanist says that at a formal level apolitical truths are misleading illusions, but at a human or an institutional level such truths remain indispensable. Although the authorial humanist does not wish to avoid the noisy world of politics, he sets the interpretations of a text above the conventions, beliefs, and "politics" dividing English studies. Transcending such divisions, the "right" interpretation gains our acceptance solely by virtue of its truth, not our commitments. Critics following formal, historical, structural, reader-response, or deconstructive methods will ultimately acknowledge the "true" interpretation despite their differences. In other words, the authorial humanist recognizes that formal analysis is political but not that institutional practices and conditions are also political. Less traditional humanists like Gerald Graff, Raymond Williams, or Elaine Showalter untangle formalism's inconsistencies and take forceful political stands. Nonetheless, even these scholars retain the traditional humanist disdain of political commitments and ignore the institutional conflicts of literary study.

The Historical Roots of Humanism

The humanist tradition that these scholars exemplify emerges during the Enlightenment, when, as Michel Foucault points out, the specialized sciences, including physics and chemistry as well as linguistics, economics, medicine, anthropology, and Biblical history, exploded classical hermeneutics, whose exegesis of canonical texts elucidated an enigmatic language printed not only on these texts but on the material world as well (*Les Mots,* 32–59). The sciences challenged the classical notion that the Bible and other canonical texts mimetically replicate a world residing outside themselves. Should this challenge succeed, the mimetic approach would collapse, and the canonical texts would lose authority: literature could not imitate human action or reveal its inevitable results if different disciplines understand action in incompatible terms.

In the eighteenth and the nineteenth centuries authorial humanism emerges in response to this scientific treachery. In coffeehouses, newspapers, and journals, the English middle classes of the eighteenth century fostered a liberal criticism based on taste, wisdom, and rationality and not on social status or arbitrary dictates (Eagleton, *Function,* 9–27; Hohendahl, 46–54). This liberal criticism constructed a canon of vernacular works, including Shakespearean drama and prose fiction, independent of the epics, lyrics, and other genres of Greek and Roman literature. Dissenting academies, mechanics associations, women's boarding schools, and adult schools taught the specialized sciences and the English language and English literature euphemistically labeled "the poor man's classics." The elite scholastic universities, which served powerful, upper-class males seeking posts in the church or the government, excluded these "utilitarian" subjects and fostered a gentlemanly devotion to Greek and Latin (Doyle, 21–22; Palmer, 5–14). In the United States, whose system of education was bound by religious institutions but not by a state church, the conflict between the sciences and the scholastic tradition was less severe. The land-grant colleges established after the Civil War taught the sciences and the languages as well as the women and the African-Americans excluded from the elite scholastic universities. However, in mid and late nineteenth-century England and the United States, several distinct developments provoked an institutional crisis. First, religious faith and traditional morality were declining, while the political strength of the working classes, trade unions, feminists, and other left-wing political forces was increasing. Second, new and spreading technologies undermined the old apprenticeship system and produced a great demand for and expansion of mass public education. As a result, the demand for adult education and for teachers, especially women, also increased greatly (Batsleer, 18–25; Doyle, 24–28; Palmer, 29–78; Bledstein, 80–128).

To resolve the protracted crisis produced by these developments, humanism defended the classical tradition but opened the elite universities to the sciences, the professions, and the national cultures. The classical model still informed the undergraduate education of the elite universities, where the cultivation of gentlemanly pursuits remained the ideal. However, the universities no longer taught only the Greek and the Latin languages and literatures; the humanist fostered the study of English and other contemporary languages and literatures as well. Indeed, influenced by German notions of higher education, supporters of the specialized sciences established graduate levels of English study, where philological approaches to the national literatures dominated (Palmer, 78–79). In other words, humanism resolves the persistent conflict between the classical tradition, now embodied in a liberal undergraduate education and the specialized sciences, ensconced now in departmental majors and graduate programs.

Arnold's defense of culture presents this humanist stance in larger social terms. In *Culture and Anarchy,* for example, Arnold, who was elected Poetry Professor at Oxford and appointed Inspector of Schools, praises the ability of culture to reconcile the social classes and to unify the state. As the pursuit of "sweetness and light," culture brings out the disinterested or "best" self of the aristocratic barbarians, the middle-class philistines, and the working-class populace. Arnold was not a proponent of the sciences, which he condemns as blind machinery; however, to justify this account of culture's power, Arnold turned to the Higher Criticism of the Bible, a specialized science that had been influential in Germany but not in England, where conservative hostility to radical French politics and abstract German philosophy stigmatized the Higher Criticism. Breaking with this parochial narrowness, Arnold argued in *St. Paul and Protestantism* and other theological works that established religion was too rational and too dogmatic to preserve traditional beliefs and to unify the state. Only an empirical, contextual, and literary approach would enable readers who dismiss the literal, dogmatic assertions of outmoded theology to experience empirically or "scientifically" the joy and the truth of religion. Literature as a whole, not just the Bible, would preserve the reader's traditional beliefs and the state's precarious unity. Not only does culture bring out the citizen's best self and unify the state, culture ensures the stability of established values and beliefs (see Baldick, 18–68, 134–56; Eagleton, *Theory,* 23–43; McCallum, 9–67).

Since Arnold's time, scientific linguistics has often opposed but has not destroyed the humanist's unscientific belief that culture can unify the nation and preserve traditional beliefs. Despite such forceful opponents, humanism has consistently acknowledged the force of the specialized sciences and has still preserved what they were threatening to destroy—the classical mimetic tradition. In different ways conservative, liberal, and Marxist humanists admit the sciences yet defend a cognitive mimetic approach. The least congenial to the sciences are the conservatives, who believe that a fundamental group of ideas, forms, and truths underlies and unites the many eras of literary history. For example, Leo Strauss and his students argue that from the Greeks to the moderns the canonical works of literature and philosophy embody the basic truths of an unchanging human nature. Hobbesian empiricists mistakenly rank empirical science above classical political theory, but, as the "highest" kind of wisdom, this theory reveals the spiritual truths hidden from the sciences. Similarly, in the influential *The Classical Tradition* (1949) Gilbert Highet maintains that Greek and Roman genres, including comedy, tragedy, farce, epic, history, romance, pastoral, elegy, lyric, ode, and satire, pervade all of Western literature. As Highet says, "The history of much of the best poetry and prose written in western countries is a continuous stream flowing from its source in Greece to the present day" (545–46). Moreover, while he admits that scientific approaches to the classical era greatly increased knowledge of that era, he condemns the ruinous fragmentation and incoherence fostered by the specialized sciences (499). Last, Northrop Frye also organizes literary works into traditional generic categories, but he favors a scientific criticism that explains the conventions of these genres in anthropological and psychological terms. Not only does he assume that classical genres and forms inform a literary work, but he argues that these genres and forms possess origins in primitive myth and archetypes in the collective unconscious. For example, while historical scholars claim that the novel begins in the seventeenth century, Frye contends that the novel is only one of several fictional discourses whose origins are in the classical era, whose types include the romance, the confession, and the anatomy, and whose heroes have a varying divinity and undertake differing archetypal quests (31–43).

Similarly, liberals from Matthew Arnold to Lionel Trilling, R. S. Crane, and Wayne Booth believe that the classical texts, vibrating with fire and life, define a tradition informing all literature; however, the liberals do not determine a work's place in a generic system or its contribution to our political wisdom; rather, they evaluate the individual insights of a work's author. Canonical texts do possess generic features, such as an invocation to a muse, a description of a character's background, or a hero with superhuman qualities, but these features enable us to grasp the author's intent, not the primitive archetype informing the genre or the basic knowledge deriving from Aristotle and Plato. While the texts in the canon still reveal substantial insight into human affairs, this wisdom, which Arnold termed "the best that is known and thought in the world," represents an insight of individual authors and requires evaluation by psychologists, historians, sociologists, formalists, and other specialists. The conservatives and the liberals distrust "individual" judgments of value and preserve the classical canon, yet the liberals allow the evaluations of these specialists to affect and even to change a work's canonical status. While the conservatives and the liberals defend the classical notion that a text mirrors an "external" world, the liberals follow the postclassical trend toward individual authors, specialized wisdom, and changing values.

The Marxists also accept the mimetic text of the classical tradition and the liberal emphasis on the individual author. They believe, as the liberals and the conservatives do, that the literary text mirrors an independent, external world, but along with the liberals they deny that one continuum of wisdom and form pervades modern and ancient literatures. They too assume that texts possess intentions representing the acts of individual authors; however, influenced by Hegel, Feuerbach, and Marx, they distrust the "abstract" individualism that betrays a liberal faith in a universal human nature; instead, they argue that an author voices his or her social context or "transindividual subject," not an abstract nature. While Matthew Arnold believed that like the classics, great art expresses man's deepest passions and brings out his "best self," Georg Lukács and other traditional Marxists argue that the greatest artists can, by virtue of their political activity, break with their own restrictive ideology and gain an objective insight into their era's social conflicts. In Lukács's famous example, Tolstoi resists the aristocratic ideology of his family, participates in the peasantry's political struggles, and as a result grasps the social conflicts determining Russia's development (*Studies,* 126–205).

Authorial Versus New Critical Humanism

While the liberals assume that a work shows the distinct intention of individual authors, the Marxists consider this intention an objective social insight; nonetheless, the humanists all assume that a text possesses an intentional structure and expresses objective truth, whether it be of a universal, an individual, or a historical type. This broad and rich belief in art's cognitive force divides the authorial humanists from the New Critics, who, influenced by the Arnoldian program, also voice humanist ideals of truth. More precisely, New Critical or formal humanism expects literature to reveal profound truths of human nature but considers literary objects fictive, not real. Scientific discourse alone asserts propositions and cognizes objects; ambiguous "literary" language only expresses attitudes or, at best, cognizes nondiscursive realities. By contrast, authorial humanists dismiss this restriction on language's referential powers as unwarranted and insist that art possesses the conceptual wisdom that the New Critics, like the positivists, restrict to science. The great successes of modern biology or physics do not deprive literature of its classical role—to imitate real life. (See, for example, Graff's critique of positivism in *Statement,* 12–17.)

This defense of art's cognitive force clearly enriches literary criticism. Critics who consider authorial and New Critical humanism the same kind of formal enterprise (Sprinker, "What is Living," 201–2) minimize the value of this defense, which can even make literary study a powerful form of social criticism. Indeed, while the New Critics, who take for granted the narrow positivist view of the sciences, shield literary values from sociohistorical critique, historical Marxists, who have long considered the study of the "human subject" a legitimate science, assume that art depicts the objective truths that the modern social sciences have discovered. The New Critics expect literature to ignore what Marxists require it to reveal—the elitist attitudes of artists, the inequities and injustices of social systems, and the ideologies of social classes.

Marxist and non-Marxist humanism confers on literature the high status of rational knowledge. Not a mere "pseudo-statement" or an empty "dramatic" unity, literature asserts scientific wisdom. Nonetheless, this rich account of literature's cognitive force generates an inconsistency: the authorial humanists deny the formal autonomy of literature but do not abandon the classical ideal of autonomous truth. Their rejecting the New Critical notion of a purely formal language does not keep them from inconsistently affirming an equally formal idea of authorial insight. Textual forms but not authorial insight or social wisdom must be involved, committed, and political.

The Liberal Humanism of E. D. Hirsch, Jr.

The work of E. D. Hirsch, Jr., whom the University of Virginia appointed Kenan Professor of English in 1973, manifests this inconsistency. In *Validity in Interpretation* (1967) he argues that a text reveals the intended meaning of the author, not the empty "semantic autonomy" of the New Critics. He allows different critics to evaluate the "significance" of that meaning as they see fit, but he sternly repudiates the "cognitive relativism" of modern criticism. All critics may evaluate the significance of a text in psychological, sociological, historical, formalist, or even feminist terms, but no critic may reject the true account of a text's meaning. This distinction between meaning and significance opens literary study to the specialized sciences but imposes on it an apolitical ideal erasing institutional differences and methodological divisions.

Hirsch denies the formal notion that meaning is neutral, objective, and ambiguous, yet he makes authorial meaning an equally objective, neutral entity. He argues that delineating the intended meaning of the author enables a critic to overcome the indeterminate character of the formal method. Considered apart from authorial intention, the language of a text displays many irreducible meanings. The advocate of "semantic autonomy" licentiously multiplies those meanings as though written language escapes what Hirsch calls "the subjective realm of the author's personal thoughts and feelings" (*Validity*, 1). Since meaning results from someone's subjective choices and not from an objective, textual realm, Hirsch argues that meaning is determinate and not licentiously plural or ambiguous.

Second, he insists that meaning "logically" precedes "significance":

> *Meaning* is that which is represented by a text; it is what the author meant by his use of a particular sign sequence. . . . *Significance*, on the other hand, names a relationship between that meaning and a person, or a conception, or a situation, or indeed anything imaginable. . . . Significance always implies a relationship, and one constant, unchanging pole of that relationship is what the text means. (*Validity*, 8)

"Meaning" is a "constant, unchanging pole" of the "relationship" between the text and the reader because the critic does not assess a text's "significance" without first establishing its meaning. Similarly, "understanding," which requires a critic to construe the text's meaning in the text's terms, comes before "interpretation," which requires a critic to explain the text's significance in his or her own terms: "It is obvious that understanding is prior to and different from interpretation" (*Validity*, 129).

To say that "understanding is prior to and different from interpretation" is to say that "interpretation" expresses the critic's special interests while "understanding" requires what Hirsch calls "principled agreement." A historical critic may esteem Sir Walter Scott's *Ivanhoe* more highly than a psychological critic does. A biographical critic may value Wordsworth's *Prelude* more than a formal critic does. Critics need not contest each other's "interpretations." However, if critics disagree about the meaning of *Ivanhoe* or *The Prelude*, each one must try to convince the others to accept his "understanding." In short, the practitioners of different approaches must agree on their "understanding" but not on their "interpretations."

Granting such precedence to meaning allows Hirsch to admit and to coordinate the approaches that the New Critics exclude as "extrinsic." The specialized sciences destroying the hegemony of the neoclassical tradition find a place in literary criticism but only if they repress their differences of outlook and accept the priority of "understanding." The propositional forms of the positivist sciences do not preclude literary forms of scientific knowledge. In *Aims,* for example, Hirsch says that analytic philosophy does not deny the "synonymity of meaning" that art requires if it is to possess cognitive force. The propositional assertions of a literary text necessitate only "occasional synonymity," not an absolute identity of meaning (54). Since all approaches can make true or false propositional assertions about a text's meaning, it unites both "extrinsic" and "intrinsic" analyses, both the sciences and the humanities. "Extrinsic" and "intrinsic" approaches coexist under one roof because "understanding" requires objective, public agreement.

To justify this tough-minded realism, Hirsch advocates the phenomenology of Husserl, who believes that individuals intend the same object no matter what their differences of experience, standpoint, or perception. Hirsch provides the following example:

> When I "intend" a box, there are at least three distinguishable aspects of that event. First, there is the object as perceived by me; second, there is the act by which I perceive the object; and finally, there is (for physical things) the object which exists independently of my perceptual act. The first two aspects of the event Husserl calls "intentional object" and "intentional act" respectively. Husserl's point, then, is that *different* intentional acts (on different occasions) "intend" an *identical* intentional object. (*Validity,* 218)

To grasp the "identical intentional object," the critic seeks the object intended by all perceivers, not the object peculiar to one "intentional act." In literary terms, what matters is the meaning shared by all readers, rather than the meaning discovered by one unique reader. Thus, to restrict Swift's satirical object to eighteenth-century British politics, not a common political type, would be to deny that ordinary twentieth-century readers of the satire "intend" the same object. As

Hirsch says, Husserl's dividing the "intentional act" from the "intentional object" "assures the potential sameness of objects in experience over time" (*Aims,* 5).

Indeed, Hirsch considers this "potential sameness of objects" a matter of common sense, not of philosophical method. He assures us that writers and critics of various eras can and do mean the same thing: in Hirsch's terms, "'occasional synonymity' is possible." The Greeks speak of "hubris" and the English, of "pride"—are there any real differences between the two? The tragedies of Sophocles have a moral severity quite unlike the naturalist protest of Henrik Ibsen's tragedies—does that deny that tragedy has one true object? We may neglect the differences between "hubris" and "pride" or Sophocles and Ibsen if the men of all ages possess a basic common sense or human nature, if the opposed revelations of historical or scientific specialists do not divide them. Any man can share the desires and aims of Homer or Shakespeare since the make-up of these writers does not differ substantially from that of ordinary mortals. Psychological, historical, biographical, formal, and other specialized critics can construct a common textual object as long as one universal humanity speaks through writer and critic, one common sense makes itself heard.

Hirsch too readily assumes that a shared "common sense," human nature, or intentional object overcomes differences of history, interpretation, and method. Such differences are more persistent than he acknowledges, for they are not a matter of common objects or human nature but of opposed training and contrary institutions. Although a common nature may unite us, we regularly employ opposed methods of reading or incompatible techniques of understanding. While common sense may obviate our need of special wisdom, common sense does not restrict our strategies of interpretation. The scientists and the humanists employ different discourses with very different aims, methods, and language, yet Hirsch imposes on the scientists and the literary critics a common meaning erasing their differences.

He rightly argues that correct classification, not empirical inspection, tells us which of a text's many implications represent what he calls the author's "willed choice." The critic's inspecting the words "he is brilliant" does not enable him to tell whether their sense is literal or ironic, but his classifying them as irony may give them appropriate qualities, like a sarcastic tone or a double meaning (*Validity,*

3–6). However, to eliminate the infelicitous senses of language, devices like irony must be norms canceling any disjuncture between the strategy of the writer and the experience of the reader. Stamping a generic device genuinely authorial allows the critic to dismiss the meanings and strategies that the device fails to explain. Only the common overlapping labor of readers and writers, not their points of divergence, counts. To overcome the exclusive "intrinsic" approach of the New Critics, Hirsch introduces what they exclude—specialized "extrinsic" approaches—but he imposes on these approaches an equally exclusive entity—a neutral, indifferent meaning, object, or "understanding." Limiting formal ambiguity and admitting the excluded "extrinsic" analyses, Hirsch's distinction between "understanding" and "interpretation" enriches his approach; at the same time, this distinction reinstates the very formal autonomy for which he faults the formal method.

The Marxist Humanism of Lucien Goldmann

The traditional Marxism of Lucien Goldmann, who became director of studies at the École Pratique des Hautes Études, reveals a similar inconsistency. He too believes that objective public "understanding" overcomes methodological differences and as a result precedes and transcends "interpretation." In fact, Hirsch points out that what Goldmann calls "comprehension" has all the scientific qualities that Hirsch requires of "understanding"—public norms, objective validity, and cognitive truth. Moreover, Goldmann's "explanation" is a sociological version of what Hirsch calls "interpretation," for "explanation" assumes that the writer's social context, not his distinct self, gives his work its value.

Goldmann also repudiates formal study, for he insists that literary texts cognize real, determinate objects, not figural devices. The object may be a Hegelian totality, not a propositional assertion or an "intentional" entity, but the text grasps a common, independent world, not a fictive, literary one. However, what explains the cognitive force of art is not the content of a propositional paraphrase or the sameness of an intentional object but the organic unity of part and whole or structure and function. Like the hermeneutic circle, this unity is circular: to characterize the whole of, say, *As You Like It,* the critic must describe the first act; however, to characterize the first act, he must already know the whole. The resulting interplay of part and whole enables him to grasp the object of the text. In later years, when Goldmann added Piagetian psychology to his theoretical repertoire, the dialectic of part and whole gave way to that of structure and function, but the new account of this dialectic preserves the old distinction between comprehension and explanation:

> The two most important intellectual procedures in the scientific study of human facts are comprehension and explanation. Both are purely conceptual procedures. . . . Comprehension is the rigorous description of a significant structure in its relation to a function. Explanation is the comprehensive description of a larger structure in which the structure being studied has a function. ("Structure," 98–110)

In other words, structures make sense if they operate within some larger, "comprehensive" organization; authorial style, a "microstructure," functions within a world view, a "macrostructure" that acts, in turn, within a social context. Moreover, this dialectical interplay of structures gives literary texts "conceptual" force; as "human facts" they too possess a functional structure, for they uncover the organizing activity of what Goldmann terms the "human subject" or the "transindividual other."

Inspired by Marxist, not phenomenological, realism, Goldmann assumes that criticism must reconstruct the historical context of the artist's "transindividual other" because, despite the powers of common sense, time and change alienate the modern mind. Goldmann's assumption is not that the artist lacks free choice but that the alienated modern mind has narrow limits: it does not readily grasp the peculiarities of the circumstances explaining the intention of the artist. Such peculiarities reveal the structuring activity of the practical, active persons who share the artist's socioeconomic position and compose his or her "transindividual other." The social significance of a text comes from the rigorous identity or, to use Goldmann's famous term, "homology" between a text's generic organization and the artist's "transindividual other." In *The Hidden God,* for example, Goldmann argues that Pascal's philosophy and Racine's drama express the self-destructive way in which, to overcome aristocratic dec-

---

adence and royalist repression, the Jansenist religious movement renounces eighteenth-century France. In *For a Sociology of the Novel*, Goldmann maintains that Balzac, Stendhal, and the other great French realists articulate more coherently than other artists the structure of the bourgeois market system (*Roman*, 21–57, 337–72).

Such "homologies" of literary text and socioeconomic position explain the text's significance in forceful, historical terms; at the same time, though, the homologies erase the institutional practices and methods dividing scholars. As a public matter, meaning or "comprehension" counts more than significance or "explanation," for if the artist who shares the socioeconomic position of other professionals is to speak for them, he must deny his artistic contexts and produce a common object.

In different ways, then, Hirsch and Goldmann reject the autonomy of forms but defend the autonomy of meaning. Hirsch believes that the determinate intention of the author both eliminates the semantic ambiguities exploited by formalists and acknowledges the scientific specialists excluded by them. At the same time, he expects the common sense of ordinary mortals to displace the methodological differences of these specialists. Goldmann also rejects the formal critic's exclusion of science and isolation from history, but Goldmann sets the textual "comprehension" of meaning above the historical "explanation" of its significance because he expects artists to voice their social contexts, not their subjective will. Nonetheless, authorial meaning remains autonomous because it eliminates internal institutional differences. Conflicts of "understanding" or "comprehension" give way to agreed-upon meanings and shared objects and purposes.

The Poststructuralist Critique of Authorial Humanism

The humanist might object that this critique fosters an unacceptable relativism. To argue that authorial humanism ignores the institutional conditions and conflicts of writers and critics would seem to deny that truth must transcend particular conditions and points of view if it is to exercise any force. Poststructuralist theory obviates such objections by rejecting transcendental accounts of truth. As Althusser and Foucault say, discourse has its own critical force and need not imitate "external" realities or accept universal or transcendental theories.

The common object and the universal truth that the humanist attributes to literature deny it its unique interpretive procedures and criteria of truth. The "transindividual" other or structured totality in terms of which traditional Marxists explain the value of classical realism imposes on literary critics a self-denying conformity to public norms. Only if critics refuse such conformity and develop their own criteria will they acquire the ability to evaluate literary texts. Should they subordinate their methods to "common sense," "human nature," or social science, they become the unwitting instrument of ideological myths, symbols and beliefs, not the impartial voice of objective truth. The humanist means to reject the narrow technical interests of formal criticism, but his commitment to a "value-free" objectivity imposes nonliterary interests and concerns on literary discourse.

Pierre Macherey, who interprets literary criticism in poststructuralist terms, argues that, to acquire distinct criteria, history, and objects, criticism should distinguish the conditions in which the writer produces a work from those in which the reader receives it. To illustrate the import of this distinction, Macherey draws an analogy between criticism and the detective story. He suggests that two distinct perspectives—the spatial and the temporal—characterize the detective story. Temporally, the crimes in the story make no sense until a sleuth like Sherlock Holmes explains them; they are irrational until the hero-detective uncovers their rationality. In other words, to achieve closure, the story requires the reader to proceed chronologically, the experience of the crimes coming before the explanation of their solution. This temporal approach is different from the spatial perspective, in which the artist produces both the irrationality making the crime a puzzle and the rationality making it perfectly clear. The story must create contrary effects: the crime should seem both inexplicable and well-explained, mysterious and sensible (*Theory*, 18–19). To produce these opposed effects, the artist follows a spatial strategy in which the mystery and the explanation coexist and do not precede each other.

This distinction between the reader's temporal and the writer's spatial strategy means that artistic production follows conventions, rules, and relationships quite distinct from those of artistic reception. Moreover, Macherey argues that to acknowledge these differences between production and reception is not to deny that literature reflects reality. In "Literature as an Ideological Form: Some Marxist Propositions," for example, he and Etienne Balibar suggest that, despite these differences, literature retains its ability to reflect reality, but the reality reflected by it is neither the external world of public life nor the internal world of feelings and responses; rather, it is the divided, ideological world of institutional conventions and conditions. As Macherey and Balibar contend, "The objective existence of literature is . . . inseparable from given social practices [which include] given linguistic practices . . . [and] an academic or schooling practice that defines the conditions for both the consumption and the production of literature" (46).

The humanist neglects the political import of these practices. His commitment to a shared meaning or to a common "understanding" leads him to overlook the divergent conditions, strategies, and conventions in terms of which readers and writers produce meaning. Just as the temporal reader expects the detective to solve the crime, so too does the humanist search for the formal intention indicating the objective insight of a text and canceling the conditions and the conventions of artistic production and reception.

Gerald Graff's Defense of Liberal Humanism

Gerald Graff, who is John C. Shaffer Professor of Humanities and English at Northwestern University, forcefully defends humanist ideals against such poststructuralist criticism but does not question their neutral objectivity. He admits the influence of institutional conditions and takes a more political stand than Hirsch or Goldmann does, but Graff still seeks an indifferent rationality representing "objective" standards and practices and denying the divergent politics of literary study.

Like Hirsch and Goldmann, Graff opposes the apolitical stance of the New Critics but defends an equally apolitical concept of authorial intention. In *Poetic Statement and Critical Dogma* (1970), for instance, he argues that literary language does not preclude conceptual statement; on the contrary, such language requires it if the critic is to have meaningful criteria of value (48–51). Without conceptual objects, our critical standards can only be the empty experience of the poem itself. The New Critics are forced to accept what Graff calls the "non-criterion" of experience as long as they consider "conceptual predication" "extrinsic" (165–66). While both the New Critics and Graff distrust the experience of the reader and favor formal standards, Graff argues that "conceptual predication" would only be "extrinsic" if we mean a logical paraphrase to substitute for the poem. Provided that we do not confuse the paraphrase and the poem, poetic complexity need not thwart conceptual statement (148–49).

Moreover, Graff expects the critic to judge the propriety of the artist's style and attitude as well as the truth of the author's insight. If texts characterize real objects, some attitudes are more decorous than others, and the critic evaluates the text not only as a structure of words but as a good or bad description of its object. If one poem says that unshaven men are exotic and another, that unshaven men are ordinary, not only do they describe the same object but one takes a better attitude toward unshaven men than the other does (156–57).

This theory of poetic decorum even introduces explicitly political standards of judgment, rather than the neutral standards of social history or common sense: as Graff writes, "The concept of poetic decorum . . . is a restatement of the ancient classical principle . . . that poetic style ought to be 'appropriate to a life of courage and self-control'" (*Statement*, 161). As the qualities of the ideal citizen, "courage" and "self-control" represent political virtues, not indifferent truths. Nonetheless, like Goldmann's "transindividual other" and Hirsch's "interpretation," Graff's "poetic decorum" presupposes that knowledge comes before evaluation because the public common context matters more than the subjective literary one. Once the critic grasps the poem's object (but not before he does so), he decides whether or not the poet has treated it appropriately. In *Literature Against Itself,* Graff suggests as much: "We all become value-free objectivists to some extent when we attempt to make sure our value judgments rest on an unbiased understanding of the object" (86).

As I already argued, such "value-free" objectivity and "unbiased understanding" erase the institutional conventions and practices dividing artistic production and reception. In *Literature Against Itself* (1979), Graff acknowledges this "postmodern" objection to objectivity but attributes the objection to the middle classes' harmful influence, not to humanism's limitations. He admits that such artists as Donald Barthelme and such critics as Roland Barthes do not believe that our reasons for appreciating a novel or accepting an interpretation represent intellectual norms binding any rational person. However, Graff says that this disbelief stems from an intrusive political force: the vulgar middle classes, whose narrow notions of objectivity and truth are genuinely contemptible but are not really objective or truthful (*Literature,* 31–62). The commercial middle classes, a social force outside literary institutions, impose a degrading vulgarity on them; in defense of the literary enterprise, artists and critics spurn and abuse the idea of objectivity and rationality, not just middle-class versions of them, and lapse as a result into an alienated and powerless existence (*Literature,* 63–101). If artists and critics did not identify the humanist ideal with the narrow commercial debasement of it, they might overcome the alienation that presently afflicts them and reassume the influential, meaningful lives that they traditionally led. In short, the commercial middle classes foster distorted, ideological notions of truth and reason, to which literary persons react apathetically, unnecessarily alienating themselves from social life.

As an attack on artistic apathy, this defense of the humanist neutrality argument has real political bite, for the defense shows that apathy and alienation are not a universal condition of human life but rather the debilitating effect of literary study itself. However, as a solution to the profession's marginality and complicity, the defense is weak: the return to classical ideals only reinstates traditional humanism. And reinstating humanism means, as I argued in Hirsch's and Lukács's cases, erasing the divergent conditions of literary study.

In *Professing Literature* (1987), Graff goes so far as to admit that institutional conditions limit criticism. In this work he traces the history of American literary practice, beginning with the early nineteenth-century classical college and ending with the late twentieth-century modern university. This history forcefully exposes criticism's hidden but ongoing conflicts, which he characterizes as "classicists versus modern-language scholars; research investigators versus generalists; historical scholars versus critics; New Humanists versus New Critics; academic critics versus literary journalists and culture critics; critics and scholars versus theorists" (14). He rightly shows that, committed to self-regulating fields and to self-revealing texts, critics ignored and repressed the conflicts within literary institutions. Critics who attacked their opponents as narrow elitists or professional dilettantes concealed the institution's conflicts behind a universal rhetoric and, as a result, condemned the institution to repeating them. However, the villain of this forceful history is still the commercial middle classes, who render the "educated classes" marginal and who force the humanists to accept vulgar, vocational aims (34–35).

More important, Graff still defends "value-free" objectivity, for he emphasizes the indifferent neutrality of modern academic policies. The powerful deans of the classical college imposed religious criteria on its faculty, but the modern university, which accommodates feminists and Marxists, is genuinely "egalitarian" (13–14). Graff writes that "literary studies have been no beacon of political enlightenment, but they have not been an instrument of dominant ideology and social control either" (14). Here he acknowledges that literary study has not escaped bigotry but allows ideology to take only the negative form of a manipulative power reducing literary study to an "instrument of . . . social control," not the positive form of political practices justifying social divisions and class privileges. Institutional discourse does not simply reflect middle-class ideals or implement administrative policy.

In addition, such discourse establishes and changes the canon, which is not a neutral, passive entity. Indeed, as many scholars argue, the canonical status of a work stems from an institutional struggle in which the elites of the literary profession strive to impose their concept of a good work, their judgment of a work's status, and their notion of the ruling class' interests (Vernier, *L'écriture,* 25, 50–61; Bennett, *Formalism,* 120–26; Tompkins, *Sensational Designs;* Eagleton, *Criticism,* 83–90). Would Shakespeare's later tragedies have such imposing weight and the more prosaic art of Wordsworth or Tennyson much less weight if the New Critical commitment to ironical, paradoxical language were not so well established? Does not the changing status of Afro-American, third-world, and women's fiction also show that the canon is not a neutral entity? Wayne Booth's discovering misogynist humor in *Gargantua and Pantagruel,* the burgeoning revival of Virginia Woolf's novels, the rediscovery of Zora Neale Hurston—these changes indicate that the canon is not apolitical.

In addition, the canon influences the literary market. For example, it is well known that in the twentieth century the triumph of formalism, including the poetry of Eliot and Yeats, the novels of Joyce and Faulkner, and the criticism of Brooks and Ransom, imposed on artists a sharp division between their popular audiences and the literary elite. Unlike Shakespeare, modern artists can write for one audience or the other but not for both. May not this modernist art have enjoyed such unusual success in American literary circles because in the giant university market, which consumes thousands of novels, anthologies, and collections yearly, the formalist canon exercises an extraordinary power? And does not the formalist canon frequently assert conservative prejudices against women, Afro-Americans, native Americans, communists, and third-world peoples?

Even though literary institutions may not effectively impose their political commitments on the socioeconomic world, they do not passively reflect the "external" impositions of the middle classes or the "egalitarian" policies of university administrators. Indeed, the division between these "external" groups and the "internal" literary world is itself an illusion induced by the humanist belief that "ideological" interests only obstruct the search for truth. In short, Graff's political defense of humanist objectivity forcefully exposes the profession's self-defeating responses to its political marginality and its institutional conflicts, yet the defense ultimately reduces the profession's established discourses to intractable roadblocks barring the humanist quest for truth.

The Marxist Humanism of Raymond Williams

Raymond Williams, who was Professor of Drama at Cambridge University, defends liberal and Marxist versions of humanism, but he is a more political critic than are either the liberals or the Marxists. While he too opposes the formal method and defends a broad authorial approach, he rejects the generic types of traditional criticism and acknowledges the transforming power of literary production. He too repudiates poststructuralist theory, dismisses institutional divisions, and preserves neutral, unbiased truth, but he does so in a unique way, one which is neither formal nor strictly authorial.

A student of F. R. Leavis, Williams never abandons the Arnoldian belief that concrete experience and intellectual flexibility are fundamental virtues, while abstract assertions, a priori assumptions, and static systems are repugnant. Like Hirsch, Goldmann, and Graff, he repudiates the formal approach and admits the specialized sciences; however, he argues that experience, a broader category than the formal critics admit, undermines their elitist values but not humanist ideals. Although the formal critics mean to construe culture as an expression of "life and thought," these critics ultimately reduce culture to the literary tradition and thus to what only a specialized minority can know and appreciate (*Writing*, 187). Such reductive accounts of culture deprive nonliterary disciplines of the ability to record and to preserve significant experience. According to Williams:

> The attachment to culture which disparages science; the attachment which writes off politics as a narrow and squalid misdirection of energy; the attachment which appears to criticize manners by the priggish intonation of a word. . . . The idea of culture is too important to be surrendered to this kind of failing. (*Culture*, 127)

Williams even argues that critics who use cultural practices to exclude the sciences and to improve only a minority destroy the ability of culture to perfect the whole individual and the whole society as well. Coleridge, Arnold, and Leavis, who wish to entrust culture to an educated elite, expect culture to "express a mode of living superior" to the civilized mode. The trouble with this expectation is, as Williams rightly points out, that literature alone cannot regulate "the quality of the whole range of personal and social experience" (*Culture*, 254–55).

Williams's critique of this formal method approximates that of Hirsch and Graff, who also consider the formal method narrowly aesthetic, include the sciences and other disciplines within culture, and expect culture to improve society. In linguistics also he is an objective humanist opposed to formal criticism, among whose worst evils he includes its divorcing literature from philology and hence from social life. Language is a living record of social experience, not an arbitrary list of individual usages or literary contexts, and this record appears in literary and nonliterary disciplines and in popular and in learned speech. *Keywords* (1976) is Williams's most comprehensive statement of this linguistic realism. In this work Williams produces historical etymologies of "art," "culture," "humanity," "objective," and other terms central to literature, sociology, politics, communications, and other disciplines. Although he cannot accept all the meanings of these terms, he means to transcend his subjective differences with other writers as well as the political differences of conservatives, liberals, and radicals. By analyzing the historical origins and development of a word and its many meanings, he intends to establish its common or neutral import, for he considers language an apolitical record of human experience, not the simple tool of any outlook. Moreover, insofar as the unacceptable meanings deviate from and contrast with the original meaning, Williams takes the misusers of words to task for corrupting and degrading our language.

In this way his historical philology embodies a humanist ideal of rationality; not only do the philologist's etymologies describe the neutral origins and development of words, these etymologies transcend the biases of his or her perspective and define standards by which all critics may evaluate and improve language and life. Moreover, Williams's great historical studies also affirm the neutral objectivity of the humanist approach. In *Culture and Society* (1958), his first major work, he constructs a cultural tradition representing a direct, critical, and continuing response to "industrial capitalism." Stemming from Burke, Carlyle, Arnold, and Pater and ending with Eliot, Leavis, and Orwell, this vital tradition provides the terms and the ideals of writers wishing to oppose industrial capitalism and to improve human life. For instance, he says that "what is important in a thinker like [Thomas] Carlyle is the quality of his direct response . . . to the England of his times; to industrialism" (*Culture,* 71–72). Although Williams finds significant weaknesses in Carlyle, he emphasizes the "quality" of Carlyle's "direct response" to industrialism because he considers such responses broader and fuller than traditional political labels would suggest. In general, he insists that the cultural tradition explores experiences richer than the political biases of its proponents, who include the conservative Edmund Burke and T. S. Eliot, the liberal John Stuart Mill, and the radical John Ruskin and William Morris. Scholars who reject these writers on political grounds fall victim to abstract categories.

In *The Country and the City* (1973), Williams produces an equally impressive but equally apolitical critique of the pastoral tradition, including its origins in the classical era, its development into the modern era, and its persistent but mistaken faith in a golden age, happy peasants, and generous landlords. In a masterful way Williams demonstrates that since the classical era successive generations of artists and critics incorrectly attribute such a golden age to the previous generation, callously neglect the poverty and the misery of peasants and workers, and blindly praise the virtues of landlords and industrialists. There is no denying that this work is, as Eagleton says, "one of the most brilliant and seminal he has produced" (*Criticism,* 39); nonetheless, this account of the pastoral tradition examines only the accuracy of artistic descriptions, not their contexts of assumptions and conventions.

In the humanist fashion, Williams's accounts of language and of the pastoral and cultural traditions preserve the neutral ideal of objective truth. What distinguishes Williams's humanism, though, is his belief that the objective truths to which the experience of writers leads are general and historical, not peculiarly textual or uniquely individual. This belief, which persists throughout his work, brings him to cultural versions of Marxist theory as well as to structuralist accounts of artistic productivity. Evan Watkins points out that, to remain true to concrete experience, Williams brings together the structures of literary objects, the types of artistic practice, and the forms of social consciousness (144–46).

The son of a Welsh miner, Williams was a communist militant in his youth, but in the 1930s and 1940s, when he first encountered British Marxist theory, its leading figures—who included Christopher Caudwell, Alick West, and J. D. Bernal—defended an economistic kind of Marxism. They believed that large economic forces in the "base" determined cultural configurations in the "superstructure." Changes in culture tended to reflect and not to influence changes in the economic base. In *Culture and Society,* Williams insists that this passive economism is truly Marxist (273, 279), yet he proceeds to reject Marxism because it interprets literature as a narrow economic force and not as a "whole way of life" (281).

In the 1960s and 1970s, Williams attributes this rejection to the influential Leavis, who complained that the passive determinism led the Marxist to assert abstract, dogmatic formulas and to ignore the detail, structure, and force of particular works (*Writing,* 197). At this time also Williams comes to appreciate Marxism again, but the Marxism that he embraces is the humanist Marxism of Lukács and Goldmann. Like the cultural tradition, which overcomes the formalist divorce of literature and sociohistorical experience, this Marxism penetrates the modern, reified mode of commodity production in order to reveal the true nature of social life (*Problems,* 20–21).

Moreover, this Marxism enables him to emphasize what traditional Marxists and liberals neglect—the productive practices of the author. While economistic Marxism sets up rigid categories dividing base from superstructure and reducing culture to a passive economic reflex, humanist Marxism denies such dualities. In fact, Williams adopts the structuralist assumption that our experience of artistic practices does not allow us to divide the conditions of production from the activity of artists. Such practices create their own conditions and do not presuppose fixed, external conditions to which art and artists must conform. Especially in modern popular culture, which depends on huge technologies, productive processes are central to the creation of cultural value.

I grant that Williams, like Lukács and Goldmann, expects social theory to overcome the abstract concept of an autonomous author: as he writes, "It is only at the . . . [social] level that what seems to be the keep of the concept—his [the author's] individual autonomy— is radically attacked and overrun" (*Marxism,* 193). Literature articulates the world view, "possible consciousness," or "structure of feeling" of those who share the historical circumstances of the author. Just as Lukács says that Tolstoi's involvement with a peasantry struggling to topple an oppressive aristocracy enables Tolstoi to extend the conventions of realist fiction, so too does Williams say that in the nineteenth century the experience of the city's burgeoning life enables Dickens and others to create a new and more powerful kind of novel (*English Novel,* 32). However, the author's concrete practice, not the nature of the relevant genres or the sociopolitical conflicts of the era, inevitably binds the author to his or her audience and hence to his or her society.

In other words, Williams rejects the rigid generic types that Lukács and Goldmann appropriate from conventional authorial criticism: he writes that "form, in Lukács and Goldmann, translates too often as genre or as kind . . . we stay, too often, within a received academic and ultimately idealist tradition in which 'epic' and 'drama', 'novel' and 'tragedy', have inherent and permanent properties, from which the analysis begins and to which selected examples are related"

(*Problems,* 27). The "inherent and permanent properties of genres" lead Lukács and Goldmann to analyze "selected examples" and to ignore troublesome contrary evidence.

Moreover, the "static" academic genres of Lukács and Goldmann neglect contrary artistic practices as well. To explain this neglect, Williams argues that in the romantic era "genre and kind lost their neo-classical abstraction and generality, and lost also their senses of specific regulation. But new kinds of grouping and classification, of an empirical and relativist tendency, became habitual. Indeed these carried, in new ways, prescriptive elements, in modes of response and by implication in actual production" (*Marxism,* 181). Unlike the older, classical genres, the "new kinds of grouping and classification" do not presuppose that an underlying coherence mediates between them and society. In a poststructuralist manner Williams, like Althusser, rejects the dualism implicit in Lukácsian mediation. Just as the superstructure does not reflect the base, neither do literary practices mediate between predetermined literary or social wholes; rather, these practices produce their own meanings and values because cultural signification is a productive activity.

Most important, Williams complains that the historical periodizing of Lukács and Goldmann highlights cataclysmic moments of social change and neglects the smooth continuities of developing social and literary practices (*Problems,* 26). Williams acknowledges discontinuities and breaks in discourse but denies that they disturb its smooth, rational development. No unseemly ruptures overturn this development or reveal opposed and irreconcilable practices and conventions. Eagleton considers this emphasis on continuity decidedly unrevolutionary (*Criticism,* 27). However, the emphasis does not simply restate the traditional humanist belief that a rational account of a phenomenon emphasizes its origins and development and ignores divergent tendencies and institutional differences. In fact, this "reformist" continuity radically undermines the consensual agreement and the intersubjective truth sought by liberal humanism.

Williams argues that literary traditions represent the hegemony of the ruling class, not the truths of common sense or of the transindividual other (*Marxism,* 112). Dominant but not total, the hegemonic tradition is only one among several artistic practices: the residual, the dominant, and the emergent. Residual practices are those which writer inherits from the past; dominant practices represent the established practices of the artist's era; and emergent practices are new, different, unincorporated, or simply avant garde. In these political terms, Williams shows that literary practice may both undermine the coherence of the transindividual subject ("the real relations of the individual, the transindividual, and the social may include radical tension and disturbance" [*Marxism*, 197]) and may expose complex tensions within literary practices. In Dickens's *Hard Times*, for example, Williams finds a disabling inconsistency of theme and character. At a thematic level Dickens satirizes Coketown for the impoverishing uniformity it imposes on its residents; at the level of characterization, he presents a great diversity of personalities and types as though he assumed that character, not environment, determines virtue or fate (*Writing*, 166–67). To explain this inconsistency, Williams argues that the liberal outlook dominating Dickens's era contradicts the residual literary conventions still influencing his Victorian art. This subtle exploration of the novel's incoherence means that Williams's unusual emphasis on artistic productivity makes his criticism more sensitive and more discriminating than the broad epochal criticism of Lukács and Goldmann.

But if Williams succeeds in overcoming the conventional humanist faith in coherence and consensus and the conventional neglect of artistic productivity, he does not by any means repudiate the humanist distrust of institutional discourse. In fact, to undermine Lukács's and Goldmann's static classical genres, he divides what he calls the "real social and natural relationships" from the "relatively organized, relatively coherent formations of these relationships, in contemporary institutions." The peculiarly "literary phenomenon" is, he argues, the artistic "realization of and response to these underlying and formative structures" of feeling, not their organized expression in institutional contexts:

> There were real social and natural relationships, and there were relatively organized, relatively coherent formations of these relationships, in contemporary institutions and beliefs. But what seemed to me to happen, in some of the greatest literature, was a simultaneous realization of and response to these underlying and formative structures. Indeed that constituted, for me, the specific literary phenomenon. (*Problems*, 24–25)

I grant that those "underlying and formative structures" forcefully describe the creative, artistic practices neglected by traditional humanist criticism; still, these structures exclude coherent, formal, academic genres and erase artistic complicity with ideological discourses. While Althusser and Foucault root ideological discourse in institutions that reproduce it at both the formal and the experiential level, Williams considers ideology a property of institutions and abstract systems and not of concrete, individual experience (*Marxism,* 132). He uses the term "structure of feeling," not "ideology," because a structure of feeling represents complex individual experiences and not abstract, institutional systems. Since institutional practices fall between individual experience and abstract systems, this Arnoldian distinction reasserts the neutral character of experience and ignores the inevitable complicity between experience and institutional discourse.

His hostility to Leavis, the formal critics, and Cambridge English returns to haunt him, taking the ghostly form of a criticism that disavows its institutional roots. In fact, Williams, excluded from Cambridge's English Department, believes that literary study can give up the peculiar demands of academic life and serve what he calls "a world of more pressing real choices" (*Writing,* 226). Just as he ignores the ideological import of artistic practices and rigidly separates individual experience from abstract systems and structures of feeling from institutional practices, so he neglects the ideological character of academic discourse. More so than Lukács, Goldmann, or Graff, Williams acknowledges the conditions of artistic production and reception and exposes the political conflicts and divisions within artistic practices. Nonetheless, his account of literary discourse also remains apolitical.

Liberal and Marxist Varieties of Feminist Humanism: Elaine Showalter and Judith Newton

Elaine Showalter and Judith Newton advocate an explicitly feminist politics, yet they too assume that the objective insight of individual (female) authors transcends the misconceptions, stereotypes, and ideologies of established (patriarchal) discourse and reveals the harsh truths of (women's) "real" experience. Showalter's feminism resembles the liberal stance of Hirsch and Graff, while Newton's approximates the Marxist approach of Lukács, Goldmann, and Williams. However, Showalter and Newton both defend the neutral objectivity of the humanist tradition and repudiate the institutional discourse of poststructuralist theory.

In *A Literature of Their Own,* for example, Showalter divides the writing of British female novelists into three stages: a feminine stage, in which the writer accepts family life, self-sacrifice, and artistic endeavor; a feminist stage, in which the writer defends the women's struggle for political equality and social justice; and an aesthetic stage, in which the writer ignores the painful experiences of female life and depicts an androgynous equanimity in her art. No matter what the stage, though, Showalter, like Hirsch and Lukács, expects the good artist to show the objectivity and the commitment of realism. The great feminine writers, such as Charlotte Brontë and George Eliot, successfully opposed the stereotypes and the misconceptions of the male Victorian establishment, which routinely denigrated the intelligence and the ability of women and dismissed their writing (96–99). Indeed, these original writers succeeded in depicting women's true experiences, which include, Showalter contends, the conflict of domestic angel/fleshly devil, the female police of the patriarchy, the illusory solace of opium, the persistent threats of madness, and the ethics of passivity and renunciation. Despite the prejudices of the male Victorian critics, who reduced the writing of women to the supercilious expressions of an insubstantial female sensibility, Brontë and Eliot produced original texts whose influence upon later writers was considerable and whose objective truths have been uncovered only in recent times (103–32).

Showalter praises Brontë, Eliot, and other realists in these lavish humanist terms. Moreover, just as the humanists oppose the formal divorce of art and experience, so she condemns the modernist or "aesthetic" retreat to language and to subjectivity. Refusing commitment, not facing women's harsh realities, the aesthetic writers ignore their female selves and withdraw to the womb (240). For instance, Showalter complains that Woolf represses her female experience and responses and adopts a neutral, self-destructive androgyny. Woolf's art seeks the serene indifference of a unified androgyny, not the "earnest intention" of a committed feminist realism. Indeed, Woolf's art shows the withdrawal of the womb, a return to containment and an escape from reality (296). Lukács characterizes the modernist era in terms of class and not in terms of gender, yet he too argues that in this era the uncommitted artist retreats from history and society and enters a subjective world of decadent sensation and unexamined experience.

As Toril Moi points out, the similarities between Lukács's and Showalter's critiques of modernist or "aesthetic" art reveal her commitment to traditional humanism. However, Showalter does examine what traditional humanists neglect—women's conditions of artistic production and reception. Her accounts of these conditions explain why the feminine writers adopted male pseudonyms or indirectly expressed rebellious feelings. More important, her accounts of these conditions enable her to recuperate the work of forgotten writers, such as Mary E. Braddon and Rhoda Broughton.

However, while she acknowledges the importance of these conditions, she treats them as Graff does, as neutral and apolitical—a matter of contracts and of business sense, not of political conflicts. In fact, she ignores the struggle of the seventeenth- and eighteenth-century middle classes to overthrow the dominance of aristocratic, classical models and to establish the integrity of the national culture, including its language and its art. She grants that educational institutions did discriminate against women; however, she believes that women writers readily overcame this discrimination. Not only did they teach themselves the classics, some even made a pedantic show of their learning (42–43). However, insofar as the women writers who were excluded from the scholastic universities wrote in the "vernacular," their art contributed to the bourgeoisie's struggle to defeat the classical models and to establish and justify the national culture, which sought to match and outdo Latin in stylistic grace and expressiveness. In the late nineteenth century, when women and English literature finally entered the university, culture functioned to reconcile rebellious feminists, workers, and minorities, to build their identification with the national traditions. While Showalter acknowledges the importance of the female writer's conditions of production and reception, she ignores these political conflicts and aims and neutralizes the institutional conditions whose influence she so adroitly describes.

What is more, she seeks a unified, objective account of a women's cultural tradition. For example, in "Feminist Criticism in the Wilderness," she grants that initially feminist critics rightly sought to expose and to critique the chauvinist stereotypes and preconceptions pervading canonical literature. Subsequently, feminist criticism went on to repudiate the "androcentric critical tradition" and to seek "its own subject, its own system, its own theory, and its own voice" (247).

This feminist criticism repudiates not only male-centered literary works but also male critical theory, for such theory is, she argues, "based entirely on male experience and put forward as universal" (247). However, she describes this feminist criticism, which she calls "gynocritics," in fairly traditional terms: "Its subjects are the history, styles, themes, genres, and structures of writing by women; the psychodynamics of female creativity; the trajectory of the individual or collective female career; and the evolution and laws of a female literary tradition" (248). Such a study repudiates the "revisionary pluralism" of Graff and others but still makes room, as their criticism does, for the specialized sciences. In fact, she favors a unified, objective stance in which biological, linguistic, psychoanalytic, and cultural approaches all find a place; as she writes, "But if we wish to ask questions about the process and the contexts of writing, . . . we cannot rule out the prospect of theoretical consensus at this early stage" (246).

Last, and not surprisingly, Showalter too condemns the poststructuralism of Barthes, Lacan, and Derrida. For example, she complains that in *The Rape of Clarissa* "Eagleton's phallic criticism seems like another raid on the resources of the feminine in order to modernize male dominance" ("Critical Cross-Dressing," 129). Similarly, in "Piecing and Writing," she seeks to undermine the French psychoanalytic feminism that ties female writing to the female body and to its unconscious desires. She argues that the "special configuration" of American women's culture lies not in the hidden relationship of creative writing and repressed desire but in a conscious and elaborate analogy between writing and quilting. The issue raised by these complaints is not so much that the male experience of the poststructuralists is "put forward as universal" as that that experience has lost its traditional autonomy and objectivity. Too much of a humanist to deny the cognitive force of art, she reproaches the "scientific" poststructuralists, who deny the "authority of female experience" (244), but she praises the anthropologists, sociologists, and social historians who sought "to get away from masculine systems, hierarchies, and values and to get at the primary and self-defined nature of women's cultural experience" (260). Showalter emphasizes women's artistic conditions, even admitting a tension between the feminist's academic and public selves, but she shares the male humanist belief that legitimate criticism preserves the autonomy and the objectivity of (women's) experience.

Moi complains that Showalter's humanist criticism shows a "fundamental complicity" with "the male academic hierarchy" (78), rightly emphasizing the intimate relationship between Showalter's feminist stance and "male academic" humanism. However, Moi's complaint does not acknowledge the equally intimate relationship between Newton's Marxist feminism and "male academic" humanism. Like Graff and Williams, Newton opposes the formal divorce between literature and history and acknowledges poststructuralist accounts of ideology and discourse; at the same time she too preserves the autonomy of objective truth and ignores or erases the institutional reproduction of ideological discourses.

In *Women, Power, & Subversion,* Newton explains British women's literature in terms of the writer's experience, but she insists that this experience includes class or economic differences as well as gender differences (*Women,* xx). She argues that in the eighteenth and nineteenth centuries middle-class men greatly increased their power, status, and wealth, while middle-class women steadily lost theirs (*Women,* 16–19). George Eliot, Jane Austen, Charlotte Brontë, and other women writers of this period experienced this loss in their lives and depicted it in their fiction. These writers also accepted the ideologies of courtly gentility, women's self-sacrifice and dependency, or women's private influence, and as a result they mistakenly denied that the power of women had anything to do with their economic status. Even Eliot, who grasped the causal connection between women's power and their economic status, felt too strong a corporate loyalty to the community to disavow those ideologies of dependence and self-sacrifice (126–27; 136–39).

Yet Newton does not mean to depict these writers simply as the victims of patriarchal stereotypes. Like Showalter, she sets aside the feminist critique of negative stereotypes and takes up the positive traditions of women's art. She argues that eighteenth- and nineteenth-century women writers did not simply suffer from ideological repression; they also exercised positive force, including the power to define and to control themselves and to achieve success (*Women,* xvi; "Toward," xxii). Moreover, she assumes that this female tradition depicted a realm of positive experience, which, following Williams, she calls a "structure of feeling" (*Women,* 10). The tradition resisted ideology and told the truth but not consistently: the tradition revealed the connection between economics and power and opposed the denigrating ideologies of the patriarchy, yet the tradition also mystified that connection and accepted those ideologies. Newton esteems the positive force of self-definition and individual achievement depicted by these writers, but in a Lukácsian manner she shows that these writers obscure what they experience. They conceal and distort what they describe and protest.

Although these torturous contrasts between accuracy and distortion describe the women's "structure of feeling," the contrasts preserve the humanist faith that the unified world of the text and the unified world of the writer's experience mirror each other. As I have argued, such faith erases the artistic contexts of production and reception. Certainly Newton, like Showalter, fails to mention the place of Burney, Austen, Brontë, or Eliot in the English bourgeoisie's struggle to overcome the privileges of the aristocratic, classical establishment and to make the English language and English literature a unifying cultural force.

Her account of poststructuralist theory reveals a similar neglect of institutional contexts and discourses. In the humanist manner she opposes formalism and poststructuralism on the grounds that they both divorce the study of texts from the realities of history. Unlike traditional Marxism, which sadly neglected differences of gender, Newton's work emphasizes ideological discourse, which shows that gender differences are culturally constructed. However, she dismisses "much" "post-structuralist criticism" as "French fashionableness": in her words, "Rather than elucidating a complex web of relations—social, economic, linguistic—of which literature is a part," such criticism may, like its formal predecessor, "dissociate ideas from material realities" ("Toward," xvi). She praises Althusser's notion that "the work of ideology is . . . to construct coherent subjects" ("Toward," xix) as well as Macherey's notion that literature is not a reflection but a production of ideological discourses ("Toward," xxiii), but she still insists that culture alone cannot ensure justice, equality, or freedom. What explains this inconsistency is her belief that academic life does not limit feminist literary criticism. While Showalter acknowledges a division between the feminist's scholarly and political selves, Newton expects the feminist critic to function as part of a sociopolitical movement: "Materialist-feminist criticism, then, while acknowledging the importance of language and ideas as a site of political activity, is skeptical of the isolation of languages and ideas from other realms of struggle" ("Toward," xxi). Poststructuralism admits the academic "isolation" that Newton, like Williams, means to overcome.

In a similar way, she grants the value of reader-oriented analyses and diverse, interpretive strategies, but she still argues that the liberal pluralism according to which a materialist-feminist view is only one of several readings precludes the commitment and the affirmation demanded by political struggle. While Showalter also opposes the revisionary readings of a feminist pluralism and advocates a unified, objective approach, Newton goes so far as to say that if feminist criticism adopts an "uncompromising complexity" embracing contradictions, feminist criticism can unify text and history, practical action and theoretical analyses, and academic practices and political struggle. I concede that the feminist movement has overcome these divisions more successfully than any other recent movement has; still, Newton's commitment to an "uncompromising complexity" and her rejection of poststructuralist theory preserve the humanist faith that the objective truth overcomes institutional boundaries and asserts a unified, sociohistorical outlook.

Conclusion

I could go on to discuss the distinguished work of Houston A. Baker, Jr., whose innovative accounts of the Afro-American tradition open criticism to new theoretical insights and interpretive stances but preserve its neutral, scientific objectivity. However, I have said enough to suggest that the humanist exposes the unstated political import of what the New Critics consider purely formal truth and uniquely literary language but proceeds, nonetheless, to impose an equally neutral notion of truth—authorial intention, "shared" meaning, or socioeconomic insight—and to erase the divergent historical and institutional aims and conditions of readers and writers. The humanist overcomes the New Critical hostility to cognitive truth and specialized knowledge, but the humanist account of objective truth preserves the apolitical stance of the New Critics. Graff, who takes a more political stance than the traditional humanists do, sharply attacks reductive middle-class notions of rationality and deceptive educational forms of containment and as a result forcefully undermines the apathy and alienation of modernist thought. Williams, who is more political than Lukács, Goldmann, or Graff, dismisses the formal coherence of artistic genres and literary periods and acknowledges the conflicts and divisions within artistic practices as well as the sociopolitical biases and commitments of established linguistic practices and literary traditions. Showalter and Newton expose the sexist biases and oppressive stereotypes of male criticism and reveal the positive strengths of women's literature and women's theory. However, even these forceful political humanists preserve the traditional ideal of neutral objectivity and ignore the ways in which institutional discourses reproduce the injustice and inequity of our exploitative society. By contrast, the theorists of reading whom I discuss in the next chapter go beyond this humanist limitation, for they challenge the humanist ideal of apolitical truth. Some of them repudiate the ideal altogether, while others reassert it in a new form, as potent theoretical critique.

THREE

The Politics of Reading

ALTHOUGH THEORIES OF READING BRING TOGETHER MANY DIFFERENT interests and outlooks, I have decided to examine only the reader-oriented, the phenomenological, and the structuralist approaches, from each of which significant kinds of Marxism have emerged. These theories of reading oppose both the formal neutrality of the New Critics and the apolitical objectivity of the authorial humanists and emphasize the subjectivity of the reader or the critic. However, these theories do not practice a consistent radicalism: reader-oriented theories oppose the formal language of the text and the objective insight of the author but construe interpretation in neutral, objective terms. Phenomenological critics oppose the metaphysical transcendence of traditional approaches but reimpose that transcendence as irreducible literary figures or autonomous theoretical norms. Structuralist critics expose the codes, the conventions, and even the institutions regulating reading but defend a scientific stance that renders interpretation as neutral and as objective as traditional approaches are. These theories of reading rupture with the all too conventional indifference and objectivity of established approaches but still retain the very apolitical forms and neutral truths that they so boldly strive to overturn.

Reader-Oriented Criticism

Terry Eagleton has justly lampooned the radical pretensions of the "readers' liberation movement" ("Revolt," 449–52), for the "movement" challenges traditional methods sharply but inconsistently. Blatantly violating the New Critics' infamous "affective fallacy" (what Stanley Fish calls "the affective fallacy fallacy"), Tony Bennett, David Bleich, Stanley Fish, Norman Holland, Wolfgang Iser, and Jane Tompkins argue that the reader's interpretive activity represents his interests, his discoveries, or his community, not the formal text or the author's intention. Although these critics do not repudiate traditional criticism to the same extent, they all assume that diverse readers produce different kinds of interpretations because reading illuminates the self, the community, or the subjectivity of the reader.

The extent to which these critics repudiate traditional approaches divides them into political camps. Conservatives like Iser and Holland preserve textual forms and authorial truth, restrict the expressive powers of literary language, and retain the referential accuracy of ordinary language. By contrast, liberals like Fish and Bleich grant ordinary language a complexity and a subtlety of expression matching that of literary language and situate the reader in communities regulating his or her activity. Radicals like Tompkins and Bennett also emphasize the expressive power of ordinary language and the interpretive community of the situated reader, but they go on to critique the canon and other literary institutions and to defend the literary value of popular works or of ideological critique. Although all of these critics construe interpretation as positive truth or ahistorical rationality, the conservatives emphasize the reader's private self as though it enshrined the bourgeois distinction of "I" and "You" or "Mine" and "Thine"; the liberals construe the reader as a social construct whose institutional position regulates but does not determine his or her activity; and the radicals expose and attack the institutional grounds or the ideological import of the reader's interpretative practices.

The Conservatism of Wolfgang Iser and Norman Holland

Wolfgang Iser's account of the reader undermines textual and authorial truth in a conservative way. Iser requires the reader to produce interpretations, yet he expects the text to guide him or her and to limit them: "The process of assembling the meaning of the text . . . does not lead to daydreaming but to the fulfillment of conditions that have already been structured in the text" (*The Act,* 49–50). Moreover, Iser argues that language can specify everyday objects precisely, but he refuses to extend this ability—what he calls a "pragmatic function"—to literature. Instead, he, like the New Critics, divides literary from ordinary language, whose "pragmatic situations," "concrete objects," or "determinate contexts" enable it to remain objective; by contrast, literary language does not describe real objects or historical contexts truthfully or falsely (*The Act,* 60–68). Rather, literature "depragmatizes" language, depriving it of its capacity to designate particular objects or to refer to specific contexts. Iser writes that "literary texts do not serve merely to denote empirically existing objects. Even though they may select objects from the empirical world . . . they depragmatize them, for these objects are not to be denoted but transformed" (109). A literary text does not serve "merely to denote empirically existing objects"; rather, the text takes them "out of their pragmatic context" and "shatters their original frame of reference." Nonetheless, literary texts retain language's "pragmatic function," which remains the text's ideal or norm. As a directive, literary language preserves the ideological purity of denotation but not its "pragmatic context" or "original frame of reference"; literary language forces the reader to create what it cannot: a neutral, truthful "description of the object." As Iser says, "Instead of finding out whether the text gives an accurate or inaccurate description of the object, he [the reader] has to build up the object for himself" (109). "Depragmatized" literature can require the reader to produce his or her own objects or contexts but cannot denote them itself; its object represents an ideal directing the activity of readers, not a real, authorial intention or historical context demanding their belief.

In other words, Iser's account of "depragmatized," literary language has the conservative implication that literary language has powers that ordinary language lacks as well as the radical implication that readers can produce what the text cannot—an object, context, or situation. Moreover, in an equally ambiguous way, Iser's account of authorial humanism undermines its sociohistorical import but retains its key distinction between "meaning" and "significance." For example, he describes objective interpretation as a "classical," "absolute" norm concealing "hidden meanings" and stifling the reader's imagination.

> The interpretative norm that sought for the hidden meaning pinned the work down by means of the prevailing systems of the time, whose validity seemed to be embodied in the work concerned. And so literary texts were construed as a testimony to the spirit of the age, to social conditions, to the neuroses of their authors, and so forth: they were reduced to the level of documents, and thus robbed of that very dimension that sets them apart from the document, namely, the opportunity they offer us to experience for ourselves the spirit of the age, social conditions, the author's neuroses, etc. (19)

For the "classical" "interpretative norm," meaning is imposed, history is restrictive (reduced to "testimony" and "documents"), and in representing systems the text is uncritical, if not dogmatic and conformist. But in Iser's "modern" "interpretative norm," the individual himself produces the meaning and experiences the historical "spirit" or the "social conditions," and in representing systems the text is critical and negative.

While Iser repudiates the "classical" norm, he preserves the humanist's key terms: "meaning" (what the author intended to say) and "significance" (the importance of what he said). They take only the private form of the reader's "own" meaning and significance, not the public form of objective meaning and scientific significance, but they preserve the distinction between an author's meaning and the reader's evaluations. More important, Iser still expects the study of the humanities to improve the life of mankind, by which he means the everyday life of the individual, not the potential selves of our common humanity: "Only a work of art . . . enables us to transcend . . . our own lives in the midst of the real world" (*The Act*, 230). Just as the traditional critic expects to overcome his biases and prejudices if he seeks the true authorial intention, so too does the reader who produces the appropriate textual object transcend his ordinary experience. For example, Iser says that in *Joseph Andrews* Fielding imposes distinct moral limits on the characters: Parson Adams can only defend ethical norms, while the other characters can only adapt to "empirical situations." Moreover, Iser argues that because the reader perceives these limitations in the characters, he acquires what the characters lack—insight into his or her self: "The acquisition of this insight enables the reader to unmask the hypocrisy of human conduct, and so to produce the conditions that will enable him to achieve in his own life a balance between norms and empirical situations" (216). Not only does the reader inevitably produce the required insight, a "balance between norms and empirical situations," but the reader also takes appropriate action, ensuring that his or her conduct is balanced and not hypocritical.

Authorial criticism also emphasizes the transforming import of literary study but acknowledges the limits of sociohistorical circumstances. By contrast, Iser takes for granted the conservative fear that causal analyses of social conditions blend readily into totalitarian powers. While the reader's activity shows the individuality and the independence of the Western world, systematic, objective explanation has the uncritical, repressive characteristics of "totalitarian" thought, including a number of nightmarish specters: George Orwell's omnipresent Big Brother, Solzhenitsyn's corrupt state functionaries, or Pasternak's doctrinaire Strelnikov. To express such aversions to Marxism, the New Critics oppose formal "intrinsic" criticism to determinist "extrinsic" criticism, and the humanists set the "common" truth against narrow ideological practices; Iser and other reader-response critics, however, divide "free," "private" interpretation from "public," "dictated" meaning. While Iser means to undermine "absolute," "determinist" explanation, he defends literary language and private significance, affirms a rigid distinction between "my" reactions and "yours," "meum" and "tuum," and imposes individual autonomy, not institutional change, personal improvement, not ideological critique.

Norman Holland shares Iser's inconsistent view of the reader's activity but not his conservative faith in self-determining readers. Like Iser, Holland values the reader's activity yet imposes formal and authorial limits on reading. Holland believes that the reader experiences a text only if he or she interprets it in a characteristic way, yet both the reader and the critic must confirm its truth. In this inconsistent way Holland's notion of objectivity does not preclude but actually requires subjectivity.

Moreover, Holland considers interpretation a function of a reader's identity, which Holland treats as the variations of a theme. While readers' responses to "A Rose for Emily," for example, may show remarkable differences, the well-trained critic readily discerns each reader's characteristic traits, such as defensiveness, indifference, aggressiveness, or vulnerability. At the same time Holland insists that we "distinguish different readings of a text or personality 'objectively,' by how much and how directly they seem to us to bring the details of a text or a self into convergence around a centering theme" ("Unity," 123–24). In this unusually broad usage, the term "objectivity" includes the conformity of details not only with the text but also with the self.

The advantage of this broad usage is that it opens the reader's activity to interesting kinds of psychoanalytic analyses, for objectivity subverts the reader's autonomy and exposes his or her unconscious fantasies. Thus Holland says that once the facts of a text have satisfied the ego defenses of the reader, he readily projects his fears and wishes onto it. In this process, which Holland labels "DEFT" ("defense, expectation, fantasy, transformation"), the text frees the reader to re-experience his or her self-defining fantasies and to grasp their significance (*The I,* 100–106). For example, like many men, Holland does not enjoy Gothic novels because he does not find their characteristic dangers very meaningful. However, as he and Leona Sherman suggest, these novels usually please women because, able to overcome the women's defenses and to win their trust, the novels encourage them to indulge conservative, childlike fantasies, which include a domineering, paternal male expressing unacknowledged sexual desires; an adventurous but submissive female experiencing dangers and threats; a large, dark castle symbolizing the body's limits; and mysterious nocturnal noises and activities evoking sexual violence, fearful seductions, and even violent rapes ("Gothic," 218–27).

While Holland's broad notion of objectivity provides such indepth accounts of the reader's fantasies, this notion also has a serious disadvantage—its scientific reflexivity: just as the reader interprets the text in ways that reveal his identity, so the critic interprets the reader's interpretation in ways revealing the critic's identity. The unconscious self of the reader reflects the impersonal self of the critic. In Holland's words, "The only way one can ever discover unity in texts or identity in selves is by creating them from one's own inner style" ("Unity," 130). However, describing a reader's personality is not an indifferent, classificatory activity that simply opens a text to many interpretations; rather, such description is involved and even critical. Neutral terms like "appearance" and "essence," "unity" and "variations," and "surface" and "depths" conceal but do not efface this involvement. Consider the case of a liberated woman raised in a traditional way but opposed to her submissive inclinations. She would not be pleased to find that Gothic novels affirm the fearful little girl in her. Holland acknowledges the influence of the reader's upbringing but assumes that even though the reader may resist this influence and oppose his identity, the influence of childhood defines the reader as a unified and not a divided type.

At issue here is not the ability of the text to change the reader, as scholars have argued, but the distance and neutrality imposed by the critic's scientific demeanor, for the critic expects the reader's interpretations to cohere around a unified identity if the critic is to interpret and to appreciate them. Describing an identity is, as Alcorn and Bracher suggest, a political act in which the critic commits himself to a unified subject which, like a unified text, regulates interpretations (350–51). The reader loses the autonomy sought by Iser, for the psychoanalytic analyses of the critic reveal the unconscious defenses and fantasies projected by the reader, not her self-determination or her self-improvement; however, the interpretive power of the critic places his scientific objectivity in question, for such power is not neutral but inherently political. While Holland's broad view of objectivity denies the antideterminist autonomy of Iser's reader, the broad view reduces the text and the reader to neutral, unified selves.

The Liberalism of David Bleich and Stanley Fish

David Bleich preserves this neutral scientific stance but not the broad notion of objectivity. Repudiating the text and the author more radically than Iser or Holland does, he values the reader's potential wisdom: "The interpretation of an aesthetic object is motivated . . . by the desire to create knowledge on one's own behalf and on behalf of one's community" (*Subjective*, 93). This pursuit of "motivated," "pragmatic" knowledge violates the humanist ideal, truth transcending personal benefit. Just as the classical empiricist Thomas Hobbes considers a rational person one who responds to experience in personal ways, compares his responses with those of others, and seeks points of agreement and disagreement, so too does Bleich believe that sensible readers articulate ("symbolize" and "resymbolize") their responses, compare their responses with each other, and bargain ("negotiate") over their value. Moreover, just as Thomas Hobbes thought that interest, not reason, rules human affairs, so too does Bleich feel that valuable knowledge or good interpretation satisfies the needs of the community: "The establishment of new knowledge is the activity of the intellecting mind adapting itself to ontogenetic and phylogenetic developmental demands" (*Subjective*, 18). Forbidding scientific terms like "intellecting mind" or "ontogenetic and phylogenetic demands" exude the illusory neutrality of Holland but do not keep Bleich from detailing the benefits that knowledge should provide—it ought to satisfy the individual's "ontogenetic and phylogenetic developmental demands," to enhance the critic's "adaptive capability," and to allow "consciousness" to take "more initiatives" (*Subjective*, 68). By contrast with the traditional belief that wisdom is impersonal and sui generis, Bleich rightly and radically insists that knowledge should benefit the knower.

Bleich also shares Iser's conservative fear that objectivity is dogmatic, intolerant, and determinist. While Norman Holland assumes that objective interpretation subverts the autonomy of the reader but preserves his or her identity, Iser and Bleich insist that objective interpretation is necessarily absolute, categorical, uncritical, and dogmatic. Thus, characterizing objective explanation as "causal" and subjective interpretation as "motivational," Bleich contrasts the two:

> Rather than categorically affirming the existence of an item's cause, the motivational explanation proposes that an item *looks as if* it is motivated in thus and such a way. By consciously aiming for communal validation, the explainer is seeking relative truth value, as opposed to absolute truth. Ultimately, the only criterion of validation is the explanation's viability for the present, where viability refers to communal

negotiation under existing standards of rationality. . . . The success of the explanation derives from its meeting present demands rather than from the certain recovery of past truth. (93)

While negative terms like "causal," "categorical," "absolute," and "certain" describe objective interpretation, positive terms like "motivational," hypothetical, "relative," and "variable" characterize subjective interpretation. Holland considers interpretation both objective and subjective, but Bleich favors only subjective interpretation. He insists, as Iser does, that either the reader's private ends motivate a personal explanation or a dogmatic, "causal" explanation dictates an impersonal meaning. Either apolitical individuals produce and negotiate personal interpretations or readers conform uncritically to "absolute" "categorical" meanings.

As I already noted, a conservative fear of totalitarian communism lies behind this tendentious opposition. Although Bleich shares this fear, he does not insist that the reader preserve his autonomy or accept the critic's analyses. Rather, Bleich adopts a third "liberal" alternative in which communities of readers, not the features of the text or the nature of the truth, validate interpretations and legitimate the subject. The community that accepts his or her interpretations constructs the individual subject who introjects the community's evaluations of him or her ("Intersubjective," 416). In Bleich's terms, not only can the process of negotiation and renegotiation validate a reader's response but the process can legitimate the individual subject whose authority may also "grow or diminish . . . in ever-larger communities" if she shifts her "objectifying capacity from the symbolic object to" herself (*Subjective,* 151).

While Bleich shares Iser's conservative fear of objective explanation, his subjective account of interpretation is social and even institutional. Moreover, unlike Iser and formal critics, he does not divide ordinary from literary language, for he expects all objects, not just the literary, to provoke conflicts and to require active interpretation (*Subjective,* 64–67). He assumes, as Hobbes and other empiricists do, that language can refer to discrete objects and that this ability gives it objective force. The chronological sequence in which the child learns to name and interpret objects marks what Bleich calls the "onto-genetic" priority of naming or "symbolizing." In fact, the sophisticated symbolism of the adult emerges from the failed names of the child. The inefficacy of the original name "motivates" him or her to reinterpret or, as Bleich says, to "resymbolize" the object. While the "use of language as simple denotation" represents the rudimentary symbolizations "first learned by infants," "resymbolization" indicates the mature individual's way of reworking "established symbols in a direction more adaptive to present needs" (65–66).

Just as Hobbes distrusted rhetorical speech and sought a plain empirical language, so too does Bleich interpret literary criticism as a "plain" process of symbolization and resymbolization. Thus he tells us that to determine the status—real or symbolic—of literary texts or other objects, "people" bargain with each other.

> Subjects—or, from now on, people—decide what shall be real objects and what symbolic objects. . . . Most of the important people in our lives are cosubjects of our experience, and we confer reality onto them and then continuously negotiate this reality with them. These negotiations are the ultimate authority for which objects are real and which symbolic. (88)

The critic confers "reality onto" the leading scholars ("the important people in our lives") and negotiates "this reality with them." As a result, the critic establishes their responses and not the text's or the author's as the critic's "ultimate authority for which objects are real and which symbolic." In this way the community of leading scholars acquires the authority and the autonomy that traditional critics attribute to the text or the author.

While this account of how critics in particular and mature individuals in general symbolize and resymbolize objects consistently and effectively displaces formal literary language and objective authorial insight, the account leaves Bleich only neutral scientific terms in which to describe the process of "resymbolization." Hobbes sought a neutral scientific language in terms of which he could describe an absolute monarchy; Bleich seeks an objective, neutral language with which he can describe the symbolic negotiations between readers and critics. He assumes that his account of these negotiations does not exclude "affective" or emotional responses to words. In fact, he argues that the symbolizing and resymbolizing activity of the individual presupposes that he or she engages in a continuous dialogue in which the responses of authoritative figures clarify the emotional import of words ("Intersubjective," 414). Still, to ensure that language does not acquire the "ludic priority" that deconstruction attributes to it ("Intersubjective," 407), he subordinates language to the individual's biological and psychological necessities, whose changes link "simple denotation" and "complex explanation." The mature individual "resymbolizes" names, making them more "adaptive" but not less "affective." Does not this account of linguistic maturity imply that successful symbolizing activity overcomes interpretive conflicts and acquires neutral objectivity? Symbols may initially denote an individual's objects in an objective way because the parent guarantees that the symbols remain efficacious; subsequently, when they lose that power, the maturing individual struggles to reestablish their lost innocence, to recapture the utopian neutrality of childhood.

Not only does Bleich reinstate the objectivity that he so forcefully opposes, but he does not provide critics any means of evaluating the benefits of the knowledge that he forcefully accentuates. What if the critic misconstrues the benefits or mistakes the community's interests? To judge them, the critic does not employ a standard of formal truth, yet the pragmatic grounds of self-interest do not enable him to establish sufficient critical distance to evaluate the benefits. Outside of them, he has no standards; judging them is judging the knowledge. Bleich does not recognize that a discerning critic requires some way to reveal error and illusion or to distinguish ideological notions of interest from true notions. He admits that criticism, like Kuhn's paradigm, has vested interests, including teachers, pupils, technical languages, and experimental techniques, but he does not note science's extraordinary negativity, which can force the dominant paradigm into irrational disarray. For instance, to explain how the gender of the reader influences her interpretation, he suggests that "men and women . . . have interests permanently tied to the biological fact that they are of different genders" ("Gender," 266). The "interests" of men and women do not pose ideological questions or require political analysis because these "interests" are "permanently tied" to "biological" facts, including "different hormonal balances" ("Gender," 235) and not to the ideological constructs of our bourgeois patriarchy.

In sum, more consistently and more radically than Iser and Holland do, Bleich defends the interpretive responses of the reader and opposes the "totalitarian" objectivity of traditional criticism; however, his construing language as a process of symbolization reinstates the neutral objectivity that he so sharply opposes. He considers the reader a social and even an institutional construct, not a determined or self-determining entity, yet he expects language to enable readers to restore their lost objectivity and their failed mastery. He construes all language, not just the literary, as conflicted and interpretive; still, like Holland, he favors scientific neutrality and not ideological critique.

Initially Stanley Fish construes reading in Iser's terms, as the personal responses of the self-determining reader; however, Fish goes on to construe reading in Bleich's social terms, as a situated activity regulated but not determined by the literary community. In fact, he makes an exciting political criticism possible, although he too explains the reader's interpretive activity in a neutral manner, as a matter of the reader's positive beliefs, not of individual self-improvement, unconscious fantasies, or interested negotiations.

In "Affective Stylistics," Fish says that reading is a temporal process in which the reader constructs interpretations and repudiates them in favor of new ones. What readers first read may contradict what they subsequently read, but that contradiction does not invalidate their first or their subsequent reading. If they are competent, such inconsistency only shows that they are experiencing a certain kind of text and not that they are misconstruing its form or its author's intention. Fish writes that "reading (and comprehension in general) is an event, no part of which is to be discarded . . . and when the final discovery has been made and *the* deep structure is perceived, all the 'mistakes' . . . will not be cancelled out" ("Affective," 86). In later work Fish abandons the assumption that competent readers discover one "deep structure" or generic type; here he presupposes such a structure but only to argue that the final experiences revealing it do not destroy the initial experiences suggesting different, even contrary, structures.

In other words, Fish denies what Iser and Holland take for granted—that a reader may read or interpret incorrectly. As an event and not a communication, language naturally induces many different responses, not one true response. Language does not limit response, but neither does anything else. Neither language nor the author functions as a norm regulating and limiting the reader, whose interpretive activity does not suffer constraint. The reader gains a freedom that verges on anarchy.

Moreover, as Fish confesses, this approach does not explain why we read different texts differently. Why do some readers interpret a text one way and others interpret it another? Why are some readings authoritative and others not? To account for this erratic authority, Fish, like Bleich, challenges the formal distinction between literary and ordinary language. Indeed, he frees ordinary language from the literal truth with which Iser and the New Critics burden it. All language, not only the literary, asserts values and expresses attitudes; no language is simply referential or pragmatic: "Ordinary language is extraordinary because at its heart is precisely that realm of values, intentions, and purposes which is often assumed to be the exclusive property of literature" (*Is There*, 108). While Iser assumes that ordinary language lacks values and purposes and only denotes objects or communicates meanings, Fish secures it a wealth of values and aims.

In addition, he assumes, as Bleich does, that the reader is social and not autonomous. What explains the reader's practices is not a free choice or a coherent identity but "interpretive communities"— groups of scholars who accept a common strategy, evaluate performances of it, and, in short, make it prevail (*Is There*, 338–71). New Critics, authorial humanists, phenomenologists, structuralists, Derrideans, feminists, and Marxists break into diverse communities whose discourse institutions disseminate, students master, scholars judge, and journals and publishing houses distribute. In addition, these opposed communities fragment the reader, who cannot belong solely to one community or master only its interpretive strategies. Fractured, diffuse, the reader employs various strategies, resituating them in his or her individual context. Last, insofar as scholars from these diverse communities evaluate the interpretations of readers, those scholars and not the text or the author limit the activity of the reader. Thus, to explain the roots of interpretive authority, Fish does not impose transcendental forms or texts; he exposes the ordinary institutional contexts limiting and fragmenting the reader. Just as the community assembles Bleich's social reader, so these contexts situate Fish's reader, whose interpretive activity expresses his or her positive belief.

Critics object that politically Fish is complacent, conservative, and indifferent, yet, as William Cain points out, his social, Foucaultian approach rejects the antideterminist individualism of Iser and others (*Crisis*, 61–62, 149–64, 195–99; see also Lentricchia,

After, 147; Mailloux, 20–23). Critics also complain that his institutional account of reading affirms established interpretive practices no matter what their political import (Graff, "Response," 115–16; Davis, "Fisher King"; Scholes, *Power,* 157–58). Fish admits that in some instances interpretive authority stems from implicit alliances ("Consequences," 446), but in general these critics are right: he preserves the neutral stance of Holland and Bleich. Although his account of interpretive communities permits what Stephen Rendall rightly calls an exciting radical criticism (56), Fish considers such criticism unprofessional.

The Radicalism of Jane Tompkins and Tony Bennett

Jane Tompkins and Tony Bennett favor a political or ideological version of Fish's social criticism. They consistently dismiss the traditional limits of the reader and steadily acknowledge the institutional contexts of his or her activity and the aims and values of ordinary language; however, more radical than Iser, Holland, Bleich, or Fish, Tompkins and Bennett articulate and criticize the politics, gender differences, or ideologies implicit in these contexts. Like Bleich and Fish, these radical critics remain committed to positive belief, but they open literary study to popular culture, ordinary readers, forgotten writers, and implicit sexual, national, and international ideologies.

To begin with, not only does Tompkins forcefully deny the traditional limits of the reader's activity, she radically opposes the interpretive activity required by formal criticism. In "The Reader in History," she argues that reader-response critics mistakenly adopt the New Critical faith in interpretation. They construe interpretation as a matter of the reader's mental processes, not the text's figures, but retain the formal insistence on interpretation. Tompkins writes that "although New Critics and reader-oriented critics do not locate meaning in the same place, both schools assume that to specify meaning is criticism's ultimate goal" (201). Classical, Renaissance, neoclassical, and even romantic criticism examines the sociopolitical effects of literature, not its meaning; by contrast, New Critics and reader-oriented critics, both of whom confront an isolated reader with an equally isolated text, make the interpretation of literature's meaning "criticism's ultimate goal."

This historical contrast of traditional and modern approaches enables Tompkins to show that New Critics and reader-oriented critics share not only this "ultimate goal" but a whole paradigm. Moreover, she means to rehabilitate the political interests repressed by this paradigm. For example, she complains that it permits only a narrow professionalism inimical to literature's broad sociopolitical interests, which are, she insists, pressing and urgent and not merely theoretical ("Indians"). In addition, she fears that the paradigm renders modern critics unable to appreciate popular literature, for modern critics who esteem "psychological complexity, moral ambiguity, epistemological sophistication, stylistic density, formal economy" demean popular fiction despite and even because of its great popularity (*Designs,* xvii). To recuperate the unfairly denigrated fiction of nineteenth-century women writers, she admits that its plots are "formulaic" and its characters "stereotyped," but she inverts the significance of these faults: a forceful cultural shorthand, the formulas and the stereotypes assert "overlapping racial, sexual, national, ethnic, economic, social, political, and religious categories" (*Designs,* xvi).

For example, while modern critics dismiss the religious sentimentality of Harriet Beecher Stowe, Tompkins recaptures its revolutionary feminist fervor; while they repudiate the stereotypical characters of James Fenimore Cooper, she defends his radical interest in mixed national and racial types. More important, to expose the politics establishing the canon of American literature, she contrasts the forgotten Susan Ashton-Warner with the well-known Nathaniel Hawthorne. In the 1840s and 1850s critics praised both of these writers for depicting idealized childhood, sentimental domesticity, and Christian virtues (*Designs,* 17). What distinguished Hawthorne from Ashton-Warner was not the critics' terms of praise but Hawthorne's position in society. Thanks to his family, his education, his publishers, and his politics, he possessed what Ashton-Warner lacked— close ties to American cultural elites—and he acquired what she lost—a position in the American literary canon (*Designs,* 32–33).

John Guillory complains that this rehabilitation of Ashton-Warner absolutizes literary value, which does not, he says, "always and finally reduce to moral values" (490). Even though Tompkins forcefully undermines the literary language and the complex insight demanded by the entrenched formal paradigm, the pessimistic Guillory assumes that nothing can disrupt the social reproduction of the formal paradigm, whose distinction between, or, as he says, "linguistic stratification" of, ordinary and literary language first emerged in Greek and Roman times and has maintained itself in ancient and modern educational institutions. I grant that Tompkins introduces sociopolitical issues into literary history. She does not interpret the fiction of Hawthorne, Ashton-Warner, Stowe, or Cooper; she describes the historical circumstances and institutional interests explaining the canonical status of these writers. Moreover, if critics like Tompkins do not upset the paradigm's reproduction of itself, the politics of our institutions escape our control.

Tompkins's critique does not conceal reified values or ignore institutional reproduction, but the critique does remain within narrow professional limits. She establishes that the forgotten fiction performed valuable "cultural work within a specific historical situation," that of the original audience; she critiques the textbooks and the anthologies mediating between the original and the modern audience; but she fails to explain the modern value of the fiction's "work." For example, she points out that the sentimental novelists promised but did not produce a theocratic society run by women, yet her explanation of this failure is only that the rhetoric of the novelists could have been stronger (*Designs,* 141). As the social sciences have taught us, there was more to this failure than rhetorical inadequacy, yet a "scientific" explanation, which analyzes the sentimental novelists' social class, political power, and ideological beliefs, would go beyond her professional limit—the positive beliefs of the original audience.

She regrets that "you can't talk about your private life in the course of doing your professional work" ("Me," 169), even admitting that she "hates men for the way they treat women" ("Me," 177), but her "angry" accounts of popular culture stay within neutral professional limits. In short, by attacking literary language and the established canon, she undermines the formal paradigm shared by reader-response critics and New Critics, yet her historical defense of popular culture remains as positive and as neutral as Bleich's and Fish's accounts of interpretive authority. In a Foucaultian manner, she forcefully juxtaposes the past and the present but does not transgress professional boundaries or engage in ideological critique.

Tony Bennett, who develops a reader-oriented kind of Marxism, also opposes literary language and the established canon but does not preclude ideological critique. Like Bleich and Fish, he denies the formal distinction between literary and ordinary language, but he does so on Marxist grounds. In fact, he argues, as Raymond Williams does, that the notion of literature does not have formal, authorial, or any other essential properties; rather, it is arbitrary, historical, a notion that changes in every era as each era reworks and alters the relationships between fictional and nonfictional discourse.

In addition, Bennett shares Tompkins's fear that the established literary canon justifies a purely literary language. To attribute a nonreferential, complex, ambiguous essence to literature is, he says, to valorize the canon and to repudiate popular culture ("Marxism," 142). He faults traditional critics who reduce popular culture's richness of meaning and complexity of form to a mechanically reproduced object or "message." Such simplistic reductions show that these critics remain committed to the established canon and its implicit literary essences. He faults Marxist critics like Lukács and Goldmann for ignoring popular culture and accepting traditional notions of value. These critics explain canonical works in profound sociohistorical terms but do not challenge the established canon. Rather, these critics dogmatically assume that the immanent value of canonical works will become self-evident in the communist era, when a rational subject will finally emerge ("Marxism," 140–41; "Texts in History," 13).

Finally, Bennett consistently denies that texts and authors constrain the activity of readers, arguing that "the literary text has no single or uniquely privileged meaning . . . that can be abstracted from the ways in which criticism itself works upon and mediates the reception of the text" (*Formalism,* 137). The text does not assert a "uniquely privileged meaning" or restrict or contain the activity of "criticism"; rather, the text functions as a passive arena within which the proponents of different "intertextual" strategies make their views prevail. In his terms, "texts constitute sites around which the preeminently social affair of the struggle for the production of meaning is conducted" (*Bond,* 59–60). The "production of meaning" is a "preeminently social affair" because, like Bleich, Fish, and Tompkins, Bennett insists that readers are situated within and constructed by institutional structures or, to use his term, "reading formations." However, Bennett describes the production of meaning as a "struggle" not only because texts do not constrain the activity of readers but also because the methods, outlooks, and ideologies of diverse "reading formations" oppose each other. To interpret a text is to contest its terrain, to vindicate one's methods and beliefs, and, by implication if not by explicit assertion, to debunk opposed methods and beliefs. By construing the text in this military way, as a battlefield and not as a norm or a container, Bennett suggests that the interpretive practices of the situated or institutional reader represent political warfare, not liberal self-improvement or positive belief.

Consider, for example, his forceful account of the way that the figure of James Bond functioned in post–World War II Anglo-American culture. In *Bond and Beyond,* Bennett and Janet Woollacott examine this figure because advertisements, toys, newspaper and magazine serials, cartoons, interviews, novels, and films present such diverse versions of Bond that only this figure unites them (*Bond,* 45). Moreover, Bennett and Woollacott argue that these diverse versions of Bond create "intertextual" networks governing the responses of readers. For example, Bennett and Woollacott suggest that female readers may esteem the figure of Bond not because they adopt the chauvinist perspective of spy and detective fiction but because the romantic fiction in which they are trained routinely depicts a "free" heroine choosing to make love to a handsome stranger (211–28).

Moreover, Bennett and Woollacott argue that the films, novels, serials, etc., do not simply reassert the preexistent ideologies of their readers; rather these works actively shape and reshape the readers' ideologies. To build suspense, the films and novels both shatter the "subject positions" formed by the dominant ideologies and question Bond's ability to reform those positions in acceptable if not new ways (5). In fact, Bennett and Woollacott show that the films, which won the figure of Bond a national and international audience, altered the way that readers responded to the novels (43). Before the films, British male readers, who were trained in British spy fiction and not in American detective fiction, saw Bond as a modernizing figure seeking to reestablish the dominant status that Britain lost after World War II. Unlike the heroes of the earlier spy fiction, the figure of Bond brought together pro-British, anticommunist, as well as chauvinist ideologies. After the films, these male readers saw Bond as an apolitical figure who maintains détente and male hegemony by defeating terrorist threats to peace and feminist threats to male privilege (32–34).

This analysis of the Bond figure involves more than my brief summary suggests, but I have said enough to show that Bennett construes the interpretive activity of male, female, and other readers as an "intertextual" matrix governed by distinct national and even international reading formations. Moreover, this analysis of the Bond figure also suggests that besides a social account of reading, Bennett shares Fish's and Tompkins's belief that, like literary language, ordinary language and popular culture display richness of meaning and complexity of form.

However, Bennett does not grant the Marxist tradition what he so generously bestows on literary works—participation in diverse "reading formations" whose histories, epistemologies, and interests do not overlap. While he argues that the interests and the investments of distinct reading formations, not the transcendent values of artistic genius, explain why a work gets into the canon, what standing the work acquires, and what meaning readers give it, he ungenerously assumes that Marxism, a realm of truth standing above the politics of interpretation, requires only the rational exposition of its insights to win assent. As I will show in the next section, phenomenological Marxists adopt a dialectical methodology that acknowledges what Bennett, along with empiricist, reader-oriented criticism, ignores—that diverse historical contexts explain the differences among Marxist, formalist, structuralist, and other approaches.

Conclusion

The proponents of reader-oriented criticism reject the objective truth and the autonomous text of traditional criticism and emphasize the subjective activity of the reader, whose interpretations may improve him, benefit his community, or justify his interpretive community or reading formation. However, the proponents do not emphasize this subjective activity in the same way or to the same extent. Conservatives like Iser condemn objective interpretation as a kind of totalitarian determinism but retain literary language and authorial intention as implicit norms guiding and elevating the reader. Liberals like Bleich and Fish condemn objective interpretation on similar gounds but describe reading in social terms: literary communities construct the reader, establishing his self-interest and even his identity. The liberals describe the reader as a social but not a unified subject, constructed, divided, and limited by his interpretive communities. While this liberal commitment to a social reader divides Fish and Bleich from Iser and Holland, these critics all accept the empiricist belief that language is neutral and apolitical or that beliefs are positive and not ideological. The radicals, who share the liberal commitment to the social reader, reject this belief but in an inconsistent way: they forcefully defend the values of popular culture or critique the ideologies of the reader yet timidly retain the positive beliefs of past eras or of Marxist theory. In the next section I show that phenomenological critics, who also free the reader from the traditional constraints, condemn this neutral empiricism as blind factuality but affirm the equally ahistorical potency of theoretical ideals.

The Phenomenological Approach

Phenomenological critics also analyze reading, not texts or authors. Like reader-oriented critics, these critics oppose the objectivity of traditional criticism but do not examine the psychological determinants of interpretations or divorce the personality of the reader from the experience of the work. Rather, these critics believe that in our "fallen" condition we can only know the objects that interpreters experience, not those that texts "truly" depict. While reader-oriented critics doubt that literature can refer to objective entities, phenomenological critics question the ability of the whole to divorce itself from its perceivers and make itself transcendent. Immanuel Kant may have thought that experience divides into the appearances (or "phenomena") and the thing-in-itself (or "noumena"), but Edmund Husserl considers the unknowable "thing-in itself" sheer nonsense (*Ideas*, 123). The object does not form an autonomous whole independent of the interpreters who experience it. Interpreter and interpretation inextricably mingle and fuse; we cannot tell the knower from the known, the teller from the tale, or the reader from the author.

While the phenomenologists repudiate the impersonal autonomy of objective truth, they preserve the autonomous whole or the objective truth as normative ideals regulating the interpretation of experience. On the one hand, the phenomenologists readily dismiss "skeptical" poststructuralist critiques of experience in which the individual subject, the transcendent being, or the speculative totality loses its normative force and succumbs to discourse's institutional power. On the other hand, phenomenologists easily retain the humanist belief that classical norms and ideals still regulate the specialized discourses of the natural and the social sciences even though these sciences create independent realms of knowledge.

Moreover, this ready commitment to classical norms and ideals divides phenomenologists into liberal, conservative, and Marxist camps: Husserlian liberals understand classical ideals in optimistic, rational terms, as the subjective result ("synthesis") of empirical observation, interpretive frameworks, and aesthetic and ethical norms; Heideggerian conservatives construe the classical ideal in figural or irrational ways, as language's explosive revelation of autonomous being, not of individual subjectivity; and Frankfurt Marxists understand this ideal in Hegelian terms, as a utopian world implicitly undermining everyday existence. Thus, while phenomenological critics analyze experience or language and not authors or texts, these critics belittle experience, revealing its implicit norms and ideals, and preserve the theoretical pretentions of classical ideals.

Phenomenology and the Philosophical Tradition: Martin Heidegger and Edmund Husserl

The phenomenology of Martin Heidegger and Edmund Husserl illustrates this inconsistency. The objective approach of Heidegger undermines the rationality of the classical tradition, emphasizes subversive, figural analyses of a deconstructive kind, but reaffirms the metaphysical ideals of being and truth. The liberal or "soft" phenomenology of Husserl also subverts the objective truth of the classical era but reconciles the modern commitment to subjective truth with the traditional faith in classical norms and rational ideals. Since Heidegger, a supporter of fascism, repudiates the subjective stance of Husserl, his Jewish teacher, I begin with Husserl's "soft" theory.

In a Kantian fashion, Husserl brings together the famous cogito of Descartes, who argues that the unique impressions of the individual thinker justify his faith in himself and his knowledge, and the equally well-known empirical analyses of Locke and Hume, who believe that sense-perception, not self-consciousness, justifies the individual's faith in himself and his beliefs. Both autocratic Cartesian rationalism and middle-class Lockean empiricism move Husserl to oppose the classical paradigm, which denies individual autonomy in the name of universal truths. Like Kant, he insists that the absolute object ("being") of the classical tradition acquires meaning only insofar as experience manifests it. We can not have a concept of an object distinct from an interpreter's experience of it: "What things are, . . . they are as things of experience" (*Ideas,* 133). Even Kant's unknowable thing-in-itself is absurd.

Despite this strong emphasis on experience, Husserl still preserves the theoretical ideals of the classical tradition. He grants that Locke, Hume, and other empiricists rightfully restrict what we can know to what we can experience, but he complains that they mistakenly limit what we can experience to external material objects or internal psychological feelings. Husserl insists that we can also experience what Husserl calls mental objects ("eidos") whose reality is not purely metaphysical but not material either.

While these objects or "essences" make experience possible, naive everyday "objectivism" obscures or ignores them. Like Descartes, Husserl argues that to describe them the individual turns inward, introspectively examining his subjective impressions. Since they depend upon the individual ego and not upon Aristotle, the Bible, or other authorities, these impressions possess a primacy and an indubitability that such "external" authorities lack. In Husserl's famous terms, we "bracket" the "naturalist standpoint" of ordinary empiricism and analyze our theoretical intuitions, systematically expounding the essences that these intuitions reveal.

Husserl suggests, as Foucault does, that these essences fall into fields the categories and structures of which range from the purely mathematical and scientific to the nonformal and the prescientific (*Ideas,* 232); however, Husserl expects the "pure" intuition of the autonomous ego, not the historical development of entrenched discourse, to explain the essences. As Adorno points out, Husserl rigorously restricts interpretation to what the bare, intuitive data show and to what they logically imply and ignores the terms and the categories mediating between them and the world (*Against,* 6, 36–38). Moreover, bracketing the natural standpoint makes the resulting knowledge of essences subjective, a matter of individual consciousness and not of systematic truth. I grant that descriptions of them evoke a whole (Gestalt), but what Husserl calls "the flux of experience," not the structure of a discourse or a field, induces the observer to synthesize a whole. Describing the essences may impel the observer to recall previous experiences ("retention") and to anticipate future experiences ("protention"), yet the resulting whole expresses the observer's frameworks (schemata) and horizons, not objective truths.

Our knowledge of the essences is subjective and unsystematic, yet Husserl argues that they endow experience with meaning and purpose. They depend upon individual experience, yet he believes that they reaffirm the absolute norms and transcendent ideals of classical "theoria." Indeed, he even expects a grasp of the essences to confer upon philosophy the imperial ability to critique what he calls "all of life and its goals, . . . all the forms and systems of culture" and to produce "a radically new humanity made capable of an absolute responsibility to itself" (*Phenomenology,* 169).

This critique of social life mistakenly suggests that to reconcile the Cartesian cogito with empirical sense-perception is to endow philosophy, the text, literary language, or totalizing thought with a potent negativity transcending the interpreter's subjective standpoint. Nonetheless, the critique has distinct political implications. As Ringer points out, in the early twentieth century, when Husserl joined the German professoriat, the middle classes were steadily eroding the privileges and the status of the great professors. His critique of social life articulates their hostility toward the middle classes. By contrast, Iser, a founding member of the West German School of Constance, takes the critique of social life to affirm middle-class values, while the Frankfurt school, which repudiates both middle-class and communist societies, interprets the critique in broad, sociohistorical terms, as an attack on the Enlightenment's instrumental rationality.

Heidegger, who shares Husserl's opposition to middle-class "technology," construes the theoretical critique as an objective, figural force of the text, not as the subversive import of rational thought. In his later writing especially, the text undermines traditional modes of rationality, exposing their implicit limitations and revealing the disruptive, figural import of language. However, the text also reasserts the presence of objective being whose values and ideals may even animate whole nations.

For example, in "The Origin of the Work of Art," Heidegger assumes, as Husserl does, that if an object fails to reveal its being, the object lacks meaning. However, Heidegger does not expect pure intuitions to reveal the essence of the object; rather, he construes the artistic revelation of the object's being as an event or "happening" that overturns traditional Western frameworks of rationality. Insofar as aesthetic concepts and artistic works imply each other, any account of art moves in what Heidegger considers an inescapable circle, yet to explain the "being" of a Van Gogh painting or a Greek temple, he does not expound his intuitions of abstract essences or bracket the material reality of art; rather, he engages in a self-conscious critique that both affirms and denies traditional approaches and methods. He uses traditional terms to explain the "thingly character of the thing," "the workly character of the work," or "the equipmental character of equipment," but he quickly establishes that the "being" of the work resists such terms. Subject/predicate, form/matter, essence/appearance—these traditional terms subjugate the text "to an interpretation of what is as a whole" (68), denying the text's "pure self-subsistence" (40).

The being of the work does reveal itself but only in terms that do not subordinate the work to this "interpretation of what is as a whole." Traditional views assume that the work's mimetic imitation of reality or its strict conformity with empirical fact reveal its truth, whereas the "being" of the work discloses itself as an original event or a unique happening, not an imitation of facts or realities. Moreover, traditional accounts of truth presuppose that empirical fact or basic reality has already disclosed itself, whereas this very disclosure is what the work, not science or common sense, makes possible (51–52). Most important, these accounts presuppose that if a work conforms to reality, nothing significant is left over. To grasp the truth of the work is to master reality, to establish its identity. However, Heidegger argues that truth both reveals and conceals; it brings some things to light but darkens others. It deceives; it turns untrue.

This critique of traditional notions moves Heidegger to reformulate Husserl's subversion of the "natural standpoint" in objective, textual terms, as the work's revealing and concealing being, its disclosing and hiding truth. "Earth," "world," "rift," and his other unusual words illustrate this sweeping reformulation. "Earth" indicates not only the paint, stone, words, and materials denoted by the traditional "matter" but also a perspective that puts objects into place; as he expresses it, "Earth is that which comes forth and shelters" (46). "World" is not only the meaning of the work but also the coherence and totality achieved by it. "Rift" is the intimate but antagonistic relationship between earth and world. "Earth" resists "world," neither one achieving mastery. As a result, the work cannot disclose being without concealing it. As the "open," being comes into the "clearing" established in the work, yet being also remains hidden, for earth "juts" into world, setting world into itself. Heidegger writes that "the clearing in which beings stand is in itself at the same time concealment" (53).

This antagonism whereby earth disrupts world ensures that the work does not conform to reality, imitate external facts, or affirm an identity. Rather, in a deconstructive manner Heidegger expects the work to disrupt external realities as well as itself and to limit and resist the "preserver's" ability to master it (47). More important, Heidegger also endows literary figures, not rational assertions, with a mystically potent force, for the antagonism of earth and world means that only figures, not themes or propositions, can disclose the truth of the work. He argues that "figure is the structure in whose shape the rift composes and submits itself. This composed rift is the fitting or joining of the shining of truth" (64). The work does not assert conceptual truths; truth "shines" in the "rift" composed by figure or structure.

These figural revelations of truth make language essential, not incidental or constitutive, adventitious or instrumental. Indeed, Heidegger argues that the constitutive force of language undermines the propositional logic of the Western tradition. Language, not the proposition, speaks. That is to say, a proposition like "all men are mortal" can only be true if "mortal" designates a property or an object as unequivocally as a mathematical number designates a point. However, like Hume or Locke, Heidegger considers such mathematical precision an empty ideal. At a level more basic than propositions, language does not restrict a term such as "mortal" to an unambiguous meaning. For example, in theological discourse, the mortality of men may invoke their potential immortality, divine salvation, or eternal life. In literary discourse, their mortality may reveal art's power to free men from death, to preserve them in unchanging life. Far from excluding the contradictory assertion "some men are immortal," "all men are mortal" may, then, restate it in metaphorical terms.

However, despite this constitutive force, language ultimately intimates the presence of "Being." At a metaphorical level, language restores us to those mysterious powers from which logic and factuality have cut us off. They have deprived us of "Being," but by recovering the figural form of our words we can restore ourselves to it. The language of the work resists propositions and facts but not "Being." Heidegger's telling critique of traditional rationality reasserts objective verities, burdening art with an unwarranted theoretical potency. In fact, art becomes what Heidegger considers "an essential way in which that truth happens which is decisive for our historical existence" (80).

As critics point out, this account of art voices a dangerous romantic despotism. A lifelong supporter of fascism, Heidegger endows art with powers that free it from rational restraint (Megill, 169). Moreover, intolerant of individual subjectivity, "Being" subsumes all "beings" in itself, including the reader or, to use Heidegger's term, the "preserver." In the neo-Kantian manner, the figural force of the text elevates him beyond the "commonplace routine" of everyday life (74–75), yet he becomes exceptionally submissive and deferential, abasing himself and venerating transcendent norms so abysmally that Being even sets "the appointed task" of his nation. Nonetheless, Heidegger's account of art does remind us that rationality, like value, fails to transcend its discursive contexts. As de Man points out, Heidegger's figural account of the text does not enable the interpreter to escape his predispositions and depict autonomous truth, for the reader must articulate his dispositions if he is to grasp the forms of the language (*Blindness,* 30–31). More important, Heidegger's account, which grants all language, not only the literary, a figural force, subverts the disciplinary limits of literary study. While Derrida complains that Heidegger reinstates the very "onto-theology" (ontology and theology) that moves him to critique Western metaphysics, Derrida still retains the interdisciplinary notion that "writing" undermines the "autonomous" power of propositional assertions and reveals the determining import of rhetorical figures.

Phenomenology and the Enterprising Reader: Wolfgang Iser

Roman Ingarden, Wolfgang Iser, George Poulet, and many others interpret literary criticism in a phenomenological manner, as a subjective activity with critical potential. The work of Iser is distinctive in that he adopts a Husserlian faith in transcendent ideals, yet he also endows literary language with a figural, Heideggerian negativity. In my discussion of reader-response criticism, I noted that Iser construes the reader's activity and literary language in empirical, antideterminist terms but retains literary language and authorial intention as ideals guiding and improving the reader. Now I would like to add that Iser reworks the Husserlian aesthetics of Ingarden and the figural negativity of Heidegger, repudiating their metaphysical commitments but preserving their theoretical norms. However, Iser's account of literary language does not seek to transform humanity or to reveal the presence of Being; rather, Iser's account preserves the middle-class ideal of the enterprising, self-improving reader.

To begin with, Iser develops the Husserlian approach of Roman Ingarden, who describes the "essence" of the literary text as a polyphonic structure composed of several "strata," including sounds, sentences, and objects. Ingarden argues that readers "concretize" this structure but cannot make it fully evident even though it has no existence apart from their partial "concretizations." In the phenomenological manner, he does not "reduce" literary acts of consciousness to the "psychological" activity of readers and writers. Rather, bracketing such "empirical" concerns, he expects the "ideal meaning" of a text to unify it (17–18).

Iser also construes the text as a many-layered structure concretized by the reader's activity. However, he believes that the interpretive activity of the reader and not the "ideal meaning" of the text unifies it (*Act,* 171). In a subjective, Husserlian manner, Iser describes the experience of readers as a flux through which they wander, constructing projections ("protentions") of new experience and reinterpretations ("retentions") of past experience. Readers produce a transcendent aesthetic whole but only from the distinct "perspectives" and within the particular "horizons" of their "wandering viewpoint." Readers synthesize "perspectives" deriving from the text's narrator, characters, plot, and explicit reader, yet readers still arrive at a transcendent whole. Although textual "strategies" move them to produce this whole, the resulting interpretation of it expresses their personality and not an autonomous structure.

Readers produce their own textual structure or object, but the text still signals, guides, directs, and manipulates them. In fact, Iser insists that literary language is too fragmented for the reader to judge its ends and aims. The text may signal the reader, but the complexity of literary language keeps him from formulating these signals in explicit codes. He may synthesize "perspectives" derived from the text; however, Iser tells us that the "projections of which they [the syntheses] consist are themselves of a dual nature: they emerge from the reader but they are also guided by signals which 'project' themselves into him. It is extremely difficult to gauge where the signals leave off and the reader's imagination begins in this process of projection" (135). Iser cannot "gauge" where the signals "leave off and the reader's imagination begins" because literary language eludes summary and formulation. Unique, "depragmatized," such language does not allow us to tell the subject from the object, to reduce the interpretation to the text, or to change a "potential" structure into the total text.

Nonetheless, Iser believes that, if the resulting interpretation is not too eccentric, it represents a genuine "potential" of the text. Ingarden also speaks of the reader's realizing ("concretizing") the potentials of the text, but, like Wellek and the New Critics, he dismisses accounts of the reader's activity as reductive psychologizing. Both Ingarden and Iser believe that a "potential" of the text admits other readings, which represent other potentials, whereas the "text as a whole" implies one definitive interpretation. However, Ingarden's potentials, which create what Iser calls a "need for determinacy," preserve the "schematic" coherence of the text, whereas Iser's potentials presuppose that indeterminate gaps, blanks, discrepancies, and absences disturb the structure and stimulate the reader's activity (*Act,* 98–99). In a Heideggerian manner, these disturbances undermine the conventional procedures of the reader, moving her to reinterpret the text and, more important, to produce what it cannot—a coherent, affirmative whole (*Act,* 112–14).

While Ingarden's determinate potentials preserve the autonomy of the text, Iser's indeterminate structures acquire a negative force prodding the reader to construct her own text. Moreover, this productive activity changes the reader but only through the text's influence. Although schools, parents, and churches may have taught readers to read, their "controlled observation" of themselves allows them to escape this "fallen" world and to improve their lives (*Act,* 134). Readers who watch themselves reading and who construct their own objects escape the codes and conventions imposed by literary institutions. As Weber contends, to avoid questioning the power of literary institutions, Iser ascribes this negativity to the text's language

("Caught," 200). For example, Iser expects the modern novel to give the reader a direct, unmediated experience of life or the world. As Iser says, "The openness of the world—with Joyce this is everyday life, and with Beckett, it is the world of subjectivity and the end—is transferred in its very openness into the reader's conscious mind" (*Act,* 211). Iser argues that in Faulkner's *The Sound and the Fury,* "the senseless of life is transplanted into an *experience* for the reader" (*Act,* 221). In other words, should a novel characterize the world as open or life as senseless, that characterization is not the ideology of a text or the attitude of an author but a lived experience, an epiphanic truth.

Structuralists achieve critical distance from language by formulating its conventions in systematic terms. Moreover, like Fish and others, structuralists assume that these conventions characterize literary and ordinary language equally well. By contrast, Iser, like Heidegger, esteems the irreducible force of formal literary language. Even though the text signals, guides, and manipulates readers, they do not question its signals or doubt its "good" intentions. The subtleties of literary language keep readers from formulating and criticizing its ends. Its values appear to readers as the positive values of "life" or "the world"; its ideologies, as those of profound experience.

In a paradoxical way, the incoherent negativity of literary language can even force the reader to adopt positive values and redemptive beliefs. For example, Iser argues that the modern novel depicts a deformed, alienated world but demands positive solutions. Unlike earlier novels, the modern novel does not describe an external, predetermined system; tell the reader what to think; spell out the meaning of the plot, the characters, the narrator, or the symbols; and confirm the reader's interpretations. The modern novel negates these features of traditional fiction and frees the reader to produce her own interpretation of it, yet those negations amount, finally, to an assertion of conventional redemptive truths. The absences, gaps, and blanks of the modern novel may imply an alienated world, but that alienation only goads the reader into producing what the text cannot—a redemptive meaning. Iser argues that language cannot "formulate both the deformation of human situations and the remedy in one and the same instant." The "world of the text usually appears in a state of alienation," but this "alienation effect" only shows that the reader must discover its positive "meaning," values, or beliefs.

Iser adds that this meaning awaits "redemption from its potentiality," but he implies that, by redeeming it, readers redeem themselves as well (*Act,* 229).

The Frankfurt school interprets the negative indeterminacy of the text in social terms, as a utopian society undermining middle-class life, not as the reader's disruptive experience of a text's redemptive beliefs. Moreover, while Husserl and Heidegger also ascribe such negative force to the text or to the reader's understanding, they assume that this negative force dissolves the empirical, technological ideals of the middle classes. By contrast, Iser shares the liberal ideals of John Stuart Mill, the nineteenth-century philosopher who argued in *On Utilitarianism* that the pursuit of self-interest enables individuals to improve their lives. Thus, Iser suggests that the traditional determinate text bores its readers because it leaves them nothing to do or, like a communist state, it does everything for them. By contrast, the "modern" indeterminate text, which, like a democratic state, refuses to do their work for them, not only stimulates their intellectual initiative, it allows them to work out their meaning for themselves. In short, Iser's subjective account of literature's unsystematic gaps and absences assumes that the private activity of citizen readers, not the autonomous norms of theory or the objective presence of Being, makes criticism valuable.

Phenomenology and Social Theory: Theodor Adorno

In the phenomenological manner, Adorno, a central figure in the original Frankfurt school, believes that the interpretation implicates the interpreter, that we cannot separate the teller from the tale, the observer from the object, or the style from the thought, but he adopts a Hegelian, not an empiricist, middle-class, version of this inseparability. While the other phenomenologists expose the empty character of abstract being, Adorno repudiates this "reified" condition of intellectual activity. While the other phenomenologists assert the primordial import of immediate experience, Adorno emphasizes the determining influence of concrete social life. While the other phenomenologists expect theory's norms and ideals or language's figural force to transform personal or social life, Adorno expects dialectical thought to exercise such a potent "negativity."

Like the early Lukács, Adorno adopts a Hegelian stance that deepens the sociohistorical insight of phenomenological criticism but extends its theoretical pretension as well. For example, in *Dialectic of Enlightenment,* Adorno and Horkheimer criticize the reified structures of social life, but their version of an instrumental rationality does a good deal more than impose the commodity-form on society. In addition, this rationality justifies a theoretical subjectivity independent of history and society. Adorno and Horkheimer argue that the Enlightenment's opposition to mythological outlooks imposes an equally mythological faith in modern science. Although science assumes that humanity, not the gods, rules nature, both mythology and science presuppose that knowledge enables the knower to dominate nature and people (8–9). In the name of facts and laws, the Enlightenment dismisses magic and fantasy but endows established social structures with a mythical inevitability (27). Moreover, Adorno and Horkheimer show that by construing resistance to these structures as the act of an outsider, Enlightenment rationality effectively diffuses its opponents. Under this rationality, even the socialist movement becomes totalitarian, destroying its opponents in the name of objective history (41).

As scholars point out, this critique of the Enlightenment lapses into an ahistorical, Heideggerian irrationality in which this instrumental rationality dominates the whole Western tradition, not just the capitalist era (Habermas, *Action,* 385). Not only the calculating discourse of instrumental reason but the propositional logic of conceptual discourse also justifies the reified structures of domination (21–28). Even Homer's *The Odyssey,* an epic that Lukács opposes to modern culture, reveals the alienating, irrational forms of social domination (34–35).

Adorno and Horkheimer's influential critique of the culture industry illustrates this ahistorical account of domination. They argue that the instrumental rationality governing the industry's technology, language, and institutions ensures that the industry does not achieve its own ends: it promises to grant wishes, fulfill hopes, and realize desires, but it actually preserves the status quo. While new works advertise their originality and uniqueness, the commodity-form of these works requires them to adhere to rigid mechanical formulas remaining within predetermined forms or generalities and duplicating other products as well as industrial life; Adorno writes, "The constant pressure to produce new effects (which must conform to the old pattern) serves merely as another rule to increase the power of conventions" (*Dialectic,* 128). Offering creativity, independence, and even success, the industry destroys the individuality, the thoughtfulness, and the resistance of the artist and the consumer, both of whom learn quickly enough that anyone could replace them.

These ironic inversions of promise and result insightfully characterize the paralyzing effects of social domination. Moreover, the inversions approximate the equally ironic analyses of Roland Barthes, who also describes the paradoxical reversals and the overdetermined stereotypes whereby the media undoes its promises of equality, creativity, and love and stifles critical thought and rebellious action. However, to explain these ironies, Barthes adopts a structuralist model according to which language acquires the integrity and autonomy of a distinct system possessing equally distinct forms of production and reception. Moreover, like Tompkins and Bennett, Barthes makes room for political resistance and positive action by insisting that the conventions and the ideologies that the media "naturalize" still show an unnatural character. By contrast, Adorno and Horkheimer, who subordinate the discourse of the culture industry to the instrumental rationality pervading the whole Western tradition, erase not only the historical contexts of the media's production and reception but also the very resistance whose absence Adorno and Horkheimer so forcefully lament. In what they call the industry's "mere twaddle," "idiotic" serials, empty laughter, asexual eroticism, untragic tragedy, and other "impoverished" materials, we cannot readily distinguish the debilitating effects of social domination from Adorno and Horkheimer's contemptuous dismissal of the industry's peculiar genres, techniques, methods, and history.

Not only does Adorno construe instrumental rationality in this ahistorical way, he argues, as Heidegger does, that figural language undermines this rationality. His belief that the modernist fiction of Beckett and Kafka undermines the conventional outlook of middle-class readers more effectively than the committed fiction of Brecht does approximates Heidegger's and Iser's faith in literary language's improving negativity. I grant that Adorno does not consider this negativity a pragmatic benefit of an empirical text or a metaphysical effect of Being's presence. I also admit that Adorno rejects Heidegger and Husserl's naïve faith in ahistorical experiences, neutral beginnings, and personal sincerity and forcefully exposes the ideological import of what Husserl considers "immediate" experience and "pure" concepts as well as the intolerant jargon behind what Heidegger terms "shelteredness" and "pure" language. Still, these critiques by no means deny the Heideggerian belief that genuine figural language disrupts the conventions of Western rationality. Moreover, as scholars point out, Adorno's "negative dialectics," which exposes the antinomies and oppositions resisting a discourse's drive for closure, identity, and totality, parallels the deconstructive approach of Jacques Derrida, whose figural analytics frustrates the desperate attempts of classical theory to escape its textual confines and to affirm transcendent realities (Jay, 21–22; Ryan, 73–81). However, Adorno, who construes the classical tradition in social terms, as a subversion of capitalist and communist domination, elevates the theoretical negativity of the phenomenological tradition into a self-conscious, political act: in his words, "True revolutionary practice depends upon the intransigence of theory" (*Dialectic,* 41).

Adorno's Hegelian subversion of fetishism and reification reworks Husserl's and Heidegger's critiques of traditional approaches, forcefully exposing the sociohistorical context ignored by positive reader-response and phenomenological critics. However, just as Husserl, Heidegger, and Iser preserve the metaphysical ideals that they so sharply debunk, so too does Adorno reinstate the ahistorical pretensions of the traditional approaches that he attacks so insightfully. Structuralist critics also adopt the paradoxical belief that figural language disrupts the interpretive practices of the reader but does not keep theorists from escaping the corrosive powers of language and grasping the objective truths of mind, language, or social life. However, the structuralists favor a science that systematizes the forms and the conventions of language, that admits the institutional import of the reader's activity, and that may even expose the ideological significance of his or her interpretive practices.

The Structuralist Approach

The last and the most radical approach to produce a theory of the reader is the structuralist approach, which also analyzes reading but does not seek the personality behind an interpretation or the experiential universe of a text. Rather, structuralist critics understand literary study as a science that names and classifies the conventions and practices governing literary discourse. As the exemplary work of Roland Barthes shows, structuralists argue, as the phenomenologists do, that the aesthetic object or textual whole fails to escape the experience and the perspective of readers, but structuralists go on to say that the discourse of readers, not the norms of the text or the presence of being, accounts for its "objective" features. A systematic account of the codes and conventions employed by readers explains the intelligibility of interpretation.

While structuralists take the codes and conventions of the reader to explain interpretation, they preserve the phenomenological belief that the irreducible figures of literary language provoke readers to break with their conventions and to interpret and reinterpret the text. For instance, Barthes says that readers who fail to write or interpret the text have not truly felt its joy. Jonathan Culler argues that scientific accounts of interpretive conventions do not eliminate the disruptive force of literary language. Jameson construes this disruptive force in Hegelian terms, as an indeterminate totality situating or demystifying the reader's methods. Like Barthes, the innovative Eagleton and Kaja Silverman, Catherine Belsey, and other Marxist feminists even extend this force to ordinary language, whose fashions and myths impose bourgeois ideology on the ordinary reader but not on the scientific interpreter or the literary mythologist. The poststructuralist work of Barthes and of Eagleton preserves this faith in language's disruptive force but trashes the scientific neutrality and the theoretical ideals of the original structuralist project. By contrast, Culler, the Marxist feminists, and Jameson repudiate the poststructuralist outlook and defend the scientific stance and the theoretical ideals of the original structuralist project.

Roland Barthes

The distinguished work of the late Roland Barthes, who brings together the scientific and the phenomenological aspects of structuralism, illustrates the original project as well its subsequent repudiation. Barthes adopts the linguistics of Ferdinand de Saussure, who, to explain what makes speech (parole) possible, brackets the history (diachrony) of language. He construes language (langue) as a formal or synchronic set of conventions explaining why the speakers of a language assume that a certain word or sign associates a certain sound or a phoneme (the signifier) with a certain concept or value (the signified). Breaking language into syntagms (words in sequence) and paradigms (words with similar sounds), Saussure shows that an English word like "cat" signifies a certain value because in the English language "cat" excludes "bat," "hat," "mat," "fat," "rat," and other paradigmatic terms, not because an extralinguistic reality or object motivates the sign "cat." What explains language's signifying force is not its diachronic evolution but a synchronic system or discourse in which each sign defines itself by opposing other signs, not by referring beyond the system. Although the structure of a language evolves, at any one time the synchronic system reveals the formal oppositions of the signs, whose signifieds do not escape the play of difference or represent autonomous concepts. While Pierce says that unlike the sign proper, iconic or indexical signs imitate nonlinguistic entities, Saussure says that language's complexes of phonemes are all historical accidents, not justified necessities. Language's signifiers reveal only its arbitrary conventions, not the "real" nature of the signified.

As a consequence, signification depends upon the arbitrary oppositions and displacements defining a "langue" or system, not upon the speaker's intentions or objective truth; as Culler writes, "If in language there are only differences with no positive terms, it is in literature that we have least cause to arrest the play of differences by calling upon a determinate communicative intention to serve as the truth or the origin of the sign" (*Poetics,* 133). The conventions of a speaker's discourse, not a "determinate communicative intention," construct the objects, establish the meaning of a speaker's activity, and even locate the position of a speaker as a subject. In literary realms, Saussure's bracketing the objective contexts of language uncovers an implicit system of conventions undermining the determinate intention and autonomous text of traditional criticism.

This consequence disturbs the classical realist, who hastens to preserve the world's independence of and the subject's responsibility for his or her speech. This consequence also disturbs the traditional Marxist, who considers the "structuralist paradigm" an insidious means of creating inexplicable or "reified" social structures impervious to theoretical praxis (see Fekete, "Modernity," 233–34). However, the consequence intrigues Barthes, whose structuralism has radical import even though he does not critique established social practices or preserve the world's independence or the subject's responsibility. Barthes's structuralism penetrates the deceptive gratuity of the literary sign, revealing the discourse, ideologies, or mythologies that the self-effacing sign treats as natural and unavoidable and even the social relations that the "seamless" sign renders invisible.

For example, in *Writing Degree Zero* (1953) he argues that writing is a discourse that demystifies the transcendental pretensions of art. Situated between style, which is personal and figural, and language ("parole"), which is social and historical, writing divides into several types: political, intellectual, classical, realist, and blank or white, each of which has its own conventions and requirements. Moreover, while style enables a writer to demonstrate genius or mastery, the conventions of writing establish a historical context constraining the writer. Embedded in the body, style frees the writer; determined by history, écriture limits him. Hence, Barthes argues that the modern writer cannot imitate the classical realism of Balzac, for writing establishes the historical realm of possible and impossible conventions to which the writer must adhere (14–16).

As a historical context limiting the writer, writing undermines the mystifying pretension whereby the styles of artists enable them to transcend their historical contexts. In fact, scholars point out that *Writing Degree Zero* reworks the historical schema of Sartre's *What is Literature?* but rejects its existential defense of an engaged artist's freedom to determine himself. Both Sartre and Barthes consider 1848 a time of historical crisis in which the French bourgeoisie discovers the antagonism of the working class. In fact, Barthes says that this crisis explains why the modern writer, who is torn between his bourgeois status and his artistic vocation, faces a plurality of literary types, not the uniform social world of classical writing. However, instead of a writer who takes a sociopolitical stand, Barthes depicts a writer whose écriture inevitably marks his work as literary and apolitical. Barthes praises the alienating distance of the very modernist writing that Sartre condemns as apolitical withdrawal. Unlike realist fiction, which ignores the alienation of writing and flaunts its literary marks, modern, "white" fiction seeks to destroy them and to reject its bourgeois status. However, even this literary politics inevitably fails: destroying the signs of literature produces a language the imitation and reproduction of which reinstates the complicities of writing (65).

In an equally forceful and ahistorical way, Barthes goes on in *Mythologies* (1957) to expose the bourgeois myths and ideologies that popular culture treats as natural and inescapable. In wrestling, strip-tease, toys, soap ads, cars, food, magazines, and wine he discovers a "parole" (speech) whose signs are the images, gestures, clothing, or phrases of popular culture and whose "langue" is an unacknowledged mythological system. To elucidate the significations of this hidden mythology, he distinguishes the rich historical sense of the signifier from its empty mythic form. Concealing the conditions of the sign's and even the commodity's production, the mythic form distorts the sense and naturalizes the distortion. For instance, detergents which terrify dirt and clean deep enable clothes to experience a profound spirituality (36–38); striptease, which dresses women in exotic feathers or gloves, makes nudity a disappointingly natural state and makes itself, a profession or career (84–87); women's magazines, which count the babies and the novels of female writers, expect women to value motherhood as much as, if not more than, their fiction (50–52). The ordinary reader, who gets the sense of these significations, misses the formal distortions and as a consequence experiences only factual truth or causal necessity; by contrast, the mythologist, who distinguishes the form from the sense, grasps the distortions and their implied myths. Moreover, the mythologist knows what the ordinary reader does not—that bourgeois ideology emerges from distinct historical conditions but refuses to acknowledge its origins or to name itself. The Citroën without seams, the godlike writer on human vacation, the encased brain of Einstein—bourgeois ideology confers mythic status on these fragmentary signifieds by treating their virtues as inherent potencies, not social products: as Barthes writes, "Wine cannot be an unalloyedly blissful substance, except if we wrongfully forget that it is also the product of an expropriation" (61). This scientific knowledge of a myth's historical origins and its systematic character constitutes a "meta-language" enabling the mythologist to expose what the media (the object language) conceals from the ordinary reader—the naturalized myths obscuring the object's conditions of production.

In *Mythologies,* Barthes even suggests that, like science, literature demystifies popular culture. Such writers as Flaubert are not formalists erasing the presence of the author but scientists demystifying the object-languages of popular culture. Kafka's *The Trial* reveals the mythic basis of legal and religious discourse, not the impersonal emptiness nor the irrational suffering of modern life. Moreover, in "Science versus Literature," a classic statement of the structuralist program, Barthes fully dissolves the distinction between science and myth. Writing still provides the "object-language" for which structuralism provides a "meta-language," but writing becomes science, just as science becomes writing (416).

Barthes's accounts of narrative also collapse this distinction between science and literature. In "Introduction to the Structural Analysis of Narrative," for example, Barthes, like Propp, Jacobson, and Greimas, construes narrative as a general syntax composed of horizontal and vertical levels, including functions, actions, and discourse. Horizontal functions are "cardinal points," which elaborate rich, realistic detail, such as descriptions of a Gothic mansion's dark, dusty hallways. Vertical functions are "catalyzers," which connect the main points of the plot. Action or "actants" treat character as a collection of the roles associated with a name, not as a type composed of stable psychological features. Discourse includes the conventions and codes of the reader, who produces the meaning of one level by associating it with another level, as well as the self-conscious reflexivity undermining the reader's codes.

In *S/Z*, however, Barthes disavows this narrative syntax. The "functions" of narrative become "lexias," which are arbitrary sections of discourse, not its universal features. Narrative itself is only one of five codes: the cultural (REF), the symbolic (SYM), the hermeneutic (HERM), the semantic (SEM), and the proairetic (ACT), all of which represent the subjective interests of Barthes, not the true nature of fiction. The discourse of the reader gives way to the "readerly" text, whose signifiers overdetermine their meanings (The villain sells drugs, rapes helpless women, kills innocent people, and aids the Fascists) and render the reader inactive. The reflexivity of language gives way to the "writerly" text, whose "galaxy of signifiers" frees the reader to produce its meanings, not passively consume them.

By reading Balzac's classical "Sarrazine" as a modern "writerly" text, Barthes undermines not only the historical differences between the classical and the modern but also the possibility of a scientific interpretation. His reading of "Sarrazine" still articulates its codes and conventions, but they represent a subjective assemblage, not a concealed mythology. His reading still interprets the text's "galaxy of signifiers," whose plurality makes possible indefinite interpretation;

however, the ostensible objectivity of the interpretation shows only that he favors certain cultural, symbolic, and rhetorical codes, not that he grasps the essence of narrative.

In *The Pleasure of the Text* Barthes draws an equally subjective distinction between "jouissance," which is active, personal, and anarchic, and "plaisir," which remains social, historical, and even ideological. Moreover, he scandalously repudiates the redemptive force that phenomenologists attribute to literary language. While the pursuit of scientific objectivity creates passive "plaisir," active "jouissance" preserves the disruptive force of literary language but not Iser's elevating negations, Heidegger's transcendent Being, or Adorno's theoretical norms.

Critics rightly object that these distinctions between "jouissance"/ "plaisir" and "readerly"/"writerly" render criticism apolitical and ahistorical (O'Neill, 195–99; Lentricchia, *After,* 141). However, the distinctions effectively debunk the illusory objectivity and the reformist ideals of the structuralist project. As Culler suggests, the distinctions, which explain Barthes's earlier contrast between classical and modern writing but reject the contrast's historical framework, destroy the neutrality but not the systematizing practices of the structuralist project (*Barthes,* 31, 89–90). In effect, Barthes demystifies the mythologist, whom he now construes as a subjective, arbitrary reader, not as an objective, neutral scientist. What gives the classical "readerly" text its referential force is the overdetermined character of its signifiers, not the unself-conscious universality of bourgeois discourse. What enables the modern "writerly" text to liberate the reader is the arbitrary, unlimited character of its signs. Although the mythologist can no longer assume that his or her "meta-language" uncovers the sociohistorical conditions that myths refuse to acknowledge, the mythologist can no longer treat such conditions as the effect of a neutral, transparent textuality either.

Pierre Macherey, Terry Eagleton, and Marxist Feminism

While scholars as diverse as Culler and Jameson preserve the scientific stance and the theoretical norms of the original structuralist project, Terry Eagleton, like Barthes, debunks the project's scientific stance and its theoretical norms. In a spectacular way Eagleton adopts and repudiates the scientific criticism of Pierre Macherey. In *A Theory of Literary Production* (1966), Macherey espouses a structuralist approach in which literature and criticism are independent practices. Criticism that defines its object and limits its field attains the status of a science capable of demystifying ideology. Situated between science and ideology, literature reworks nonliterary discourses but does not know or denote sociohistorical reality. Moreover, literature can undermine but cannot know ideology; parodying and deforming it, literature can expose its limits and gaps but cannot condemn it. While the scientific critic explores these gaps and articulates their silence, the ordinary reader falls victim to ideology, whose hidden purposes he inadvertently carries out.

This science of criticism does not rely solely on the text; in that case, the critic would not question the existing canon or distinguish the truly literary from the modern conception of the literary. This science does not rely solely on the reader, either; in that case ideology would succeed in manipulating and victimizing the critic as well as the reader. Rather, to expose the ends of ideology, Macherey isolates the text from the reader's interpretation of it. In a phenomenological sense, the reader's interpretation "realizes" but does not fully grasp the text, whose "true" structure forever escapes him. Absences, gaps, and inconsistencies display the points at which the interpretation of the reader fails because the text eludes him. Macherey assumes, as the scientific Barthes does, that to demystify the ideological ends of the text, the critic needs what the ordinary reader inevitably lacks—an objective metalanguage enabling the critic to perceive the marginal incoherence and gaps that reveal the unstated purposes of ideology (1–14).

In *Criticism and Ideology* (1976), Eagleton complains that Macherey's approach betrays an obscure notion of aesthetic value, but Eagleton elaborates this approach all the same. First of all, Eagleton defines literature as a signifying system situated between science and ideology. To use Eagleton's Barthian analogy, literature, like a man gesturing wildly but pointing to nothing, produces and reproduces its own ideological discourses and does not designate sociohistorical reality. The forms of literature are as objective as scientific concepts are, but ideology frees them from historical constraints. Literature can live the impossible dreams of ideology and puncture them as well. To explain this virulent symbiosis, Eagleton does not say that literature knows what it cannot state; rather, he compares the signifying system of literature to the production of a play. Just as the production may develop the play in various ways, so too can a text rework ideology in different ways. Moreover, by reworking ideology, a text transforms it into aesthetic material, whose complexities and difficulties distance and disturb ideology. The productivity of the text turns ideological conflicts into aesthetic issues, which, in turn, pose new and troubling ideological difficulties. To expose the sociohistorical import of this spiraling development, Eagleton adopts a Freudian stance: just as the manifest content of a dream betrays a latent content, so does the smooth, coherent surface of a text reveal a distorted, partial subtext—its transformed ideological materials.

As Frow points out, Eagleton formulates this Freudian analogy in formal aesthetic language and not in Macherey's epistemological terms, yet he still preserves the scientific epistemology of structuralist critics, whose psychoanalytic insight sets them above the ordinary patient/reader (*Marxism,* 26). Eagleton does not subordinate the literary enterprise to a scientific epistemology or reduce the history of criticism to blind ideological distortion; nonetheless, he believes that ideological discourses "operate" upon unwary, ordinary readers, enveloping them within infinite folds. Eagleton writes that "ideological space is curved like space itself, and history lies beyond it as only God could lie beyond the universe. It is not possible to effect a 'passage' from the heart of ideology beyond its boundaries, for from that vantage-point there are no boundaries to be transgressed; ideology curves back upon itself" (*Criticism,* 95). This all-encompassing ideological space echoes Barthes's self-concealing mythology, which, by refusing to acknowledge its historical origins or to name its class, erases its ideological character. In addition, just as Barthes grants the mythologist a "meta-language" showing him the historical context that myth conceals from the naïve reader, so Eagleton and Macherey expect the "science of ideological formations" to enable a critic to decipher the text's fractured insights into ideology's historical limits and to escape its limitless and inescapable universe (*Criticism,* 96).

Eagleton goes on to disavow the scientific "elitism" enabling the scientific critic/analyst to analyze the repressed unconscious of the ideological patient/reader/text (*Benjamin,* 13). In Barthes's manner, he denies that an interpretive method can achieve the neutrality and indifference of a scientific stance. Moreover, in *Literary Theory: An Introduction,* he explodes the entire theoretical project of structuralist Marxism. Not only do critics lose their ability to escape ideology, but criticism loses its ability to formalize its aims and its methods, for its rhetorical analyses of literary and nonliterary materials destroy its capacity to define its objects and delimit its field. In fact, this destruction of the structuralist project moves Eagleton to proclaim the death of theory and to inaugurate a new realm—a broad cultural or rhetorical criticism (201–6).

By contrast, Marxist feminists admit Barthes's critique of a structuralist science but preserve the original project. They grant that a "science of signs" cannot be complete and noncontradictory but still uphold the possibility of science itself. For instance, Kaja Silverman assumes that the unlimited play of signification fostered by Derrida and Barthes does not by any means destroy the systematic study of codes and conventions pursued by scientific structuralism. Indeed, the work of Saussure, Peirce, Barthes, Derrida, and Benveniste forms a continuum preserving the scientific status of feminist criticism; as Silverman writes, "Reconstruction" complements "deconstruction" (249). Similarly Catherine Belsey contends that the poststructuralist critique of science qualifies but does not overturn Althusserian Marxism. Ideology remains what Barthes and Eagleton say that it is—a self-concealing myth whose ruses the scientific critic, not the ordinary reader, can penetrate. Even though this science does not escape the effects of ideology, scientific knowledge, which, Belsey says, is "never final, always hypothetical," remains possible (*Practice,* 64). Scientific critics may lapse into incoherence, but their high standards still enable these critics to expose ideology's incoherent ends and to disrupt its reproduction of sexual difference.

This Freudian science of ideologies allows structuralist Marxists to turn Lacanian psychoanalysis into a powerful feminist critique of chauvinist ideology. For example, in *The Subject of Semiotics* Silverman takes Lacan's account of subjectivity to explain the divisions and absences of the alienating female identity that patriarchal ideology assiduously reproduces. While the conservative Lacan sets the imaginary realm, where language mirrors the self and its phenomenal world, outside the symbolic realm, the radical Silverman integrates the imaginary realm into the symbolic, where the alienation and the lack imposed by a child's accession to language are cultural or ideological and not biological. She argues that the child's identifying with phallic power is not a biological need but a cultural ideal imposed by the alienated child's needs and the excluded mother's desire. The lack in terms of which Lacan describes women, in particular, and division and loss, in general, represents a cultural and not a physiological condition. Constituted by the desire of the other, the subject imposes on individuals an identity that reproduces the symbolic order of the patriarchy but alienates them from their female being. To demystify this process, Silverman argues, as the Althusserians do, that the discursive practices of patriarchal ideology constitute the gendered and divided subject imposing an alienating identity upon women (215–20).

In *Critical Practice,* Catherine Belsey reworks Lacanian theory in a similar way. The power of the phallus does not show that the law of the father dominates the symbolic realm of language but that ideology reproduces the male and female subjectivities of a patriarchal culture. Accession to language splits the subject into a self that speaks and a self that is spoken or represented (85). By adopting positions that ideology renders intelligible, the speaking self acquires the power of the symbolic realm but betrays and represses the desires of its represented self. Freud and Lacan explain these positions in conservative anthropological terms: because of the incest taboo, the family into which the subject is born imposes on him or her a symbolic system of gender, kinship, and marriage; by contrast, Silverman and Belsey construe these positions in radical Althusserian terms: ideology establishes the symbolic structures of the family and represses the splits and the divisions of the subject (*Subject,* 217; *Practice,* 60–61).

Moreover, Belsey argues that insofar as literature also constructs positions of rational, intelligible truth and conceals the splits and the contradictions in the subject, literature functions in an ideological way (*Practice,* 64–66). Adapting Barthes's and Macherey's critique of classical realism, she says that it constructs positions of intelligibility in terms of which it purports to resolve the conflicting discourses and desires that it depicts. The posing and solving of what Barthes calls enigmas, the creating and rewarding (or punishing) of consistent characters, the diverging and converging of plot, characters, and authorial voice—these devices enable the reader to produce and to accept the intelligible positions that the text depicts as the nature or the truth of the subject. At the same time she argues that the realist text possesses what Macherey calls an unconscious or a "lack" whose divided and opposed discourses reveal themselves on its margin. While this text represses these antagonistic discourses and constructs an intelligible subject, Belsey's criticism exposes these antagonisms and undermines the subject's obvious rationality (103–4). For instance, she suggests that Sir Arthur Conan Doyle's mystery novels depict the scientific rationality of Holmes and Watson in a positive, affirmative way; however, the mysteries of female sexuality disrupt the novels, which do not try to explain female sexuality (109–17).

Such Marxist/feminist defenses of Barthes and Eagleton's structuralism make possible this radical Freudian critique of ideology, but the defense also precludes a historical account of discourse. The unconscious of a realist text may construct and repress sexual difference; however, as Montag points out, the unconscious thereby acquires an autonomy and a universality transcending historical contexts (71). As in a Socratic dialogue, clarifying this unconscious defers history indefinitely.

Jonathan Culler

Jonathan Culler does not adopt an ideological criticism or abandon the scientific structuralism that his *Structuralist Poetics* so successfully presented to American critics. He defends scientific structuralism and preserves the ahistorical, formal analyses and the theoretical critique of traditional criticism. Still, his defense forcefully demonstrates what traditional criticism ignores—the institutional roots of interpretive practices.

Culler argues, as the phenomenologists do, that we cannot make sense of interpretations if we set aside the methodological assumptions of interpreters. However, he insists that if schools and other institutions did not disseminate notions of literature, readers could not distinguish literary from nonliterary prose or judge their effects. The schools' interpretive conventions, including models of reality, cultural beliefs, generic discourses, and formal devices such as parody, irony, and reflexivity, govern the ways in which readers identify, explain, and evaluate literary texts.

Even though Culler believes that the schools disseminate these interpretive conventions, he still argues that literary language ultimately undermines these conventions. He assumes, as Langer, Cassirer, and Wellek do, that formal literary language and objective linguistic science can peacefully coexist in a harmonious universe in which each obtains its own realm. However, the subversive force of literary language disrupts this harmonious state, for, if schools disseminate interpretive conventions, someone must teach readers that literary language undermines what schools teach readers.

To resolve this dilemma, Culler outlines an institutional hierarchy in which interpretation does not matter as much as figural study and literary theory do. For example, in *The Pursuit of Signs* (1981), he allocates the interpretive reading of the "old" New Criticism to undergraduates, who may choose and defend a particular meaning, but requires graduate students, who learn to separate the reader's particular choices from the text's potential figures or conventions, to analyze the possible meanings or the figural potentials of the text. Moreover, he grants literary theory the highest status: an independent, interdisciplinary subject whose ability to challenge the interpretive conventions of the established disciplines surpasses the "defamiliarizing power" of literature itself ("Criticism," 96–97).

This institutional hierarchy preserves the analysis of meaning but places such analysis at a low level—undergraduate criticism—and the study of figural language and its interpretive conventions at high levels—graduate and postgraduate criticism. Inverting traditional priorities in this way, the hierarchy enables the institution to subvert the interpretive practices that it disseminates. However, Culler preserves the institution's traditional power to judge interpretations. The structuralist critic both explains the conventions that readers invoke and evaluates the interpretations that they produce. While Fish denies that reading can be right or wrong, Culler argues that readers may misapply conventions and make mistakes. "To reject the notion of misunderstanding as a legislative imposition is to leave unexplained the common experience of being shown where one went wrong, of grasping a mistake and seeing why it was a mistake" (*Poetics,* 120–21). Culler takes this "common experience of being shown where one went wrong" to mean that critics certify an interpretation objectively, that they establish its truth or falsehood in a scientific way. Just as Noam Chomsky favored a Cartesian rationalism in which linguists verify the verbal competence of speakers, so Culler favors a structuralist rationalism in which literary critics test the formal competence of readers (113–30).

In *The Pursuit of Signs* he restates this Cartesian faith in correct interpretation: the semiotician does not judge interpretations; he describes the conventions implicit in them, the operations enabling the critic to move from statement to statement (68). Even though the interpretations of critics differ, their interpretive practices are not "personal and idiosyncratic acts" but "common and acceptable formal strategies" (72). The mistaken reader, the personal, idiosyncratic strategy—these are excrescences dirtying the bright, shiny science of "common strategies." While Fish and the reader-oriented critics distinguish communal strategies from personal habits and institutional practices, Culler does not allow this Foucaultian distinction; in a narrow Cartesian manner, he takes error and idiosyncrasy to express the blind will of the individual and truth, the universal rationality of the institution.

Although Culler favors a radical institutional hierarchy in which literary theory and figural analyses occupy the highest positions and traditional interpretation, the lowest, his Cartesian stance ultimately commits him to justifying traditional practices. Descartes's cogito legitimates the church and the monarchy of sixteenth-century France; Culler's "impartial" account of interpretive conventions validates conservative practices. As I noted, Tompkins and Bennett repudiate the literary language of the formal critics and examine the practices of ordinary readers and the conventions of popular culture; by contrast, Culler expects structuralist critics to study "those who have mastered the system" (*Poetics,* 120), and literary language and modernist art, not ordinary language and popular culture, motivate this study of the system's masters. Although Eagleton and others announce the death of literary theory, Culler places it at the institution's highest level. Such theoretical disputes imply that the structuralist science of literary conventions is biased, if not conservative (*On Deconstruction,* 38–39). Last, in "Criticism and Institutions: The American University," he praises the innovative style of American universities, which have encouraged structuralist, feminist, and other subversive approaches, but he ignores the internal conflicts that this "innovation" has produced. For instance, while he notes that American departments offer "noted critics" "higher salaries and lower teaching loads" (87), he does not mention that to staff service and introductory courses, these innovative departments overburden and underpay their part-time and one-year instructors. Culler's forceful defense of a scientific structuralism reveals criticism's institutional grounds and inverts criticism's traditional priorities, yet his Cartesian rationalism ensures that this defense remains narrowly formal and apolitical.

The Marxism of Fredric Jameson

Fredric Jameson, the foremost American Marxist, also defends the possibility of a structuralist science, but the philosophical context in which he does so is the Hegelian Marxism of the early Lukács and the Frankfurt school. Jameson assumes that the interpretations of a reader inextricably weave together the reader's commitments and the text's object; in Jameson's terms, "Dialectical thinking can be characterized as . . . the study of an object . . . which also involves the study of the concepts and categories (themselves historical) that we necessarily bring to the object" (*Political,* 109). Like phenomenological and structuralist criticism, this "dialectical" criticism opens the textual "object" to readers' "concepts and categories"; however, this criticism reconstructs or, to use his term, "historicizes" these "concepts and categories" as "representations of desire," "fragmentations of the subject," or "visions of utopia." As Weber suggests, Jameson, like Iser, Adorno, and Culler, acknowledges that literary language subverts formal, authorial, structuralist, archetypal, poststructuralist, and other approaches but seeks to contain the subversion by historicizing its effects ("Capitalizing," 22).

Although this historicizing method endows his criticism with an impressive breadth and depth and returns history to even the most austere authorial and structuralist criticism, this method reaffirms what Culler and the phenomenologists also preserve—the transcendent potency of theoretical norms and ideals. Barthes and Eagleton repudiate such transcendence, but Jameson defends it. In fact, he shares Adorno's and Lukács's pessimistic belief that in the modern era the theoretical norms of the critic and the utopian visions of the artist exercise critical, subversive force, while the reified textual practices, generic types, and institutional structures imposed by the dominant instrumental rationality divide the private individual from sociopolitical life and absorb traditional areas of rebellion and resistance. In what follows I will argue that this Lukácsian commitment to transcendent norms and theoretical ideals vitiates his forceful critiques of authorial, structuralist, and poststructuralist criticism.

Jameson and Authorial Humanism

To an extent, Jameson accepts the humanist belief that rationality exercises a critical force transcending ideologies and institutions. In a negative, paradoxical manner he critiques the traditional liberal humanism of E. D. Hirsch, Jr., and Gerald Graff, as well as the Marxist humanism of Lucien Goldmann and Georg Lukács. Even though he is more political than they are, more open to structuralist and poststructuralist theory, he preserves their humanist faith in objective truth. Indeed, his insistence that, to use his Nietzschean phrase, "the dialectic is 'beyond good and evil'" ("Politics," 62) reasserts the authorial humanist belief that an interpretive stance transcends institutional structures and established discourses and gains acceptance by its own force or, in his terms, its "semantic richness" (*Political,* 10).

He grants what the traditional humanists demand—a textual object and an authorial or transindividual subject—but he does not equate textual objects and historical reality in the realist manner; rather, he considers the common objects, shared meanings, and socioeconomic homologies required by "objective" understanding to be a utopian dream in which, as he says, "the individual subject would be somehow fully conscious of his or her determination by class and would be able to square the circle of ideological condition by sheer lucidity" (283). In the modern world of monopoly capital (but not in the rational world of a utopian future), such self-consciousness is not possible, for the object of perception is not the same for all perceivers nor is the text's meaning the same for all critical approaches. The text and the transindividual subject are, as Goldmann argues, homologous structures, but in the modern world we cannot know that the structure of the one corresponds to that of the other. To identify the one with the other, as Goldmann does, is to arrogantly take for granted what modern society renders impossible—the perfect match of intellectual analyses and historical reality (*Prison-House,* 213–14; *Political,* 43–44).

I grant that, for Jameson as for Lukács, the social conditions implicit in generic conventions and literary techniques give an artist's work its significance. In *Marxism and Form,* for instance, Jameson maintains that only generic conventions can mediate effectively between an artist's work and his society; only these conventions can relate work and social structure in a nonreductive, unmechanical way. However, he goes on to emphasize the productive activity of the artist. Like Raymond Williams, he does not simply extract a kernel of objective insight and dismiss artistic practices as so much chaff: in Jameson's terms, "properly used, genre theory must always in one way or another project a model of the coexistence or tension between several generic modes or strands" (*Political,* 141). Such tensions, which enable a work to repudiate what he calls "the fallen world of empirical being, of reified appearance and of the status quo," show the aesthetic value produced by artistic activity (*Fables,* 19). Moreover, he favors the Althusserian view in which the capacity of the work to distance the reader from its ideologies confers value on it. Distancing the reader is not an intentional act but a peculiar effect which the artist produces by reworking established forms, codes, and ideologies, by shaping them into literary figures (*Fables,* 21–23). While Anglo-American formal critics deny that "extrinsic" approaches can provide a standard of evaluation, Jameson insists that they do so, for he shows that the art's points of rupture with or repudiation of its own "reified" genres and codes reveals a critical social insight.

This emphasis on artistic activity enables him to appreciate an unusually broad range of generic conventions. Unlike the Lukácsian, who seeks the objective relations of text and society, Jameson expects a text to embody a utopian vision subverting reified social structures, not an objective insight depicting revolutionary social processes. As a result, Jameson can find a positive social significance in all generic conventions, not just those characterizing the "true" relations of art and society (*Marxism,* xiv, xv, 306–40). This social significance may be hypothetical and subjective, but it is the possession of all conventions, not the exclusive property of one—traditional realism. In addition to it, romance, fantasy, modernism, comedy, naturalism, and myth also possess a utopian ideal. In *The Political Unconscious,* for example, he argues that the medieval "chanson de geste," which first represents the genre of romance, responds to a historical situation in which marauding bands of violent knights terrorize the countryside. In later eras, when the feudal nobility establishes itself as a class, romance dissolves the social conflicts of the older "chanson" in a utopian manner: romance represents the foreign, evil knight as a mirror image of the good knight (118).

In modernism also Jameson finds utopian ideals. For example, he argues that Wyndham Lewis's integrity of style and rejection of "high" or individualist modernism make Lewis's novels valuable even though Lewis is a fascist and a sexist. Lewis's style has the unusual ability to function as "the impersonal registering apparatus for forces which he means to record, beyond any whitewashing and liberal revisionism, in all their primal ugliness" (*Fables,* 21). Moreover, his art repudiates the psychological individuality or "monadism" characterizing the fiction of James Joyce and other "high" modernists (*Fables,* 14). This impersonality of style and rupture with "high" modernism illustrates Jameson's impressive ability to find aesthetic value in an artist's repudiation of generic codes and conventions and not in the objective conformity of his intention and social structures.

However, his emphasizing the artist's rupture with and displacement of "reified" codes and conventions minimizes the value of artistic conformity and even the institutional politics of literary study. For example, he believes that Wyndham Lewis both accepts and violates the generic conventions of modernism, but it is the violation, not the acceptance, that makes his novels valuable: In Jameson's terms, Lewis "expresses the rage and frustration of the fragmented subject at the chains that implacably bind it to its other and its mirror image" (*Fables,* 61). This esteem of rebellion, rupture, or break denies the value that many critics attribute to works unifying artistic practice and social organization, aesthetic commitments and ideological outlooks. Those critics who believe that oral tales, tribal literature, or handwritten feudal literature identify artistic attitude and social life, or technique and ideology, say that this identity gives the literature value. What would we know about ancient society if we ignored the art of Homer, Virgil, or the Beowulf poet? Would not their work be less valuable if we assumed that they repudiate their generic codes and do not affirm objective truth? Are not these artists too close to the ideologies and conventions of their societies for their works to be valuable in Jameson's sense?

In other words, while literary value may lie in both rebellion and conformity, rupture and solidarity, Jameson confines it to repudiation and nonconformity. Moreover, this limited view of artistic value reinstates the humanist notion that "external" institutional discourse ("ideology") obstructs the pursuit of truth and represses the rebel's negativity. In *Marxism and Form,* for instance, thought congealed into positive systems suffers from what Jameson rightly considers "bad" ideology—hardened dogma; such thought breaks a theory into steps, summarizes the "main points," but neglects the critical processes of thought—the ruptures with opposed theories, the "pain of the negative." In *The Political Unconscious,* however, he extends this forceful critique of blindly positive systems to poststructuralist theories as though their institutional commitments impose equally blind obstacles to critical thought. Jameson takes such theories to represent only the "ideological" level of hermeneutics and to block the "higher levels" of hermeneutics and the "communal" truths of social life (*Political,* 282, 291–93). Not only does he fear that institutional contexts and historical conditions "limit" theoretical negativity, he favors what Paul Ricoeur calls positive hermeneutics. Jameson writes:

> Ernst Bloch's ideal of hope or the Utopian impulse; Mikhail Bakhtin's notion of the dialogical as a rupture of the one-dimensional text of bourgeois narrative . . . the Frankfurt School's conception of strong memory as the trace of gratification, of the revolutionary power of the *promesse de bonheur* most immediately inscribed in the aesthetic text: all these formulations hint at a variety of options for articulating a properly Marxian version of meaning beyond the purely ideological. (*Political,* 285)

Restating humanist ideals, this "meaning beyond the purely ideological" moves Jameson to seek what he terms "a whole new logic of collective dynamics, with categories that escape the taint of some mere application of terms drawn from individual experience" (*Political,* 294). Although he has forcefully analyzed popular culture, third-world literature, and radical political movements, his repudiating such "tainted categories" as the ethical division between good and evil and the Marxist distinction between the progressive and the reactionary commits him to disavowing the "merely" progressive, feminist, Afro-American, working-class, or third-world struggles to alter and to expand the traditional canon and to broaden professional literary study. As an engaged insider, a feminist, an Afro-American, a working-class, or a third-world critic seeks to change and to improve literary institutions, not to rupture with them. Reforming literary study, such scholars ameliorate the "ideological" present and do not map the utopian future; they preserve New Critical, humanist, and other, established discourses but critique their racist, chauvinist, or elitist import. These progressive critiques are not transcendental, but they are not apolitical or uncritical either. Similarly, such structuralist and/or poststructuralist notions as Althusser's ideological state apparatus, Foucault's discursive formations, Bennett's reading formations, and Fish's interpretive communities do not permit the utopian transcendence that Jameson seeks, but do not impose mechanical dogmas or obstruct critical thought, as Jameson charges. Habermas has rightly suggested that to ensure the survival and reproduction of the established disciplines, scholars and critics share a legitimate interest in theorizing and improving their institutional conditions (*Knowledge,* 196–97).

Jameson and the Structuralist Approach

Like Jameson's pursuit of a utopian realm transcending "instrumental" institutional conflicts, his defense of a scientific structuralism preserves the neutrality of the structuralist project but denigrates the subjectivity of the literary institution. Just as Jonathan Culler defends the scientific project of structuralism, so too Jameson upholds its scientific character. He rejects the ahistorical stance but not the scientific neutrality of Saussure, Greimas, and other structuralists. He opens structuralist discourse to history but not to the author's or the institution's subjectivity. In fact, Jameson's version of structuralism condemns the author to mechanically repeating antinomies whose historical origins necessarily escape his or her "conventional mind" and whose resolution inevitably exposes his or her ideological limitations (*Political,* 84–85).

In *The Prison-House of Language,* Jameson complains that Saussure's linguistics restricts language to a positivist framework. The famous distinction between a synchronic or systematic view of language and a diachronic or historical view blinds the linguist to language's historical context. By contrast, Jameson construes structuralism as a scientific "study of superstructures or, in a more limited way, of ideology" and thereby returns the theory of language to society and to history (*Prison-House,* 101). Just as Althusser argued that a scientific Marxism exposes and criticizes ideological practices, so Jameson claims that a properly historicized linguistics describes and evaluates cultural models or paradigms. Embedded in the author's unconscious, these models of interpretation "mediate" between theory and society: as he expresses it, history "is inaccessible to us except in textual form" (*Political,* 35). While Barthes abandons the realist distinction between a model's formal possibilities and its "external" historical context, Jameson retains the distinction not only to bring the repudiated history back into structuralist criticism but also to preserve its scientific character, which is not a matter of a reader's empirically verified competence but of an interpretation's formal, even mathematical, neutrality.

Jameson's defense of a utopian vision escaping the instrumental world of institutions affirms the humanist ideal of transcendent truth; similarly, his "scientific" account of unconscious cultural models mediating between "theory and society" maintains the neutrality of the structuralist project. This account of these models does not dismiss traditional, ethical, or Marxian values; this account reduces the surface of the text, with its embedded interpretations of the author's values and outlook, to merely subjective, private, or ideological attitudes. For example, Jameson reworks A. J. Greimas's structuralist account of narrative in the following way: it defines "internal" limits, which are "nothing more than the total number of permutations and combinations inherently possible in the model in question," as well as "external" limits, in which history "pre-selects a certain number of structural possibilities for actualization, while proscribing others as inconceivable in the social and cultural climate of a given era" (*Prison-House,* 128). This contrast between the model's possible "permutations and combinations" and its preselected and proscribed possibilities implies that at some points the surface of the text and the schema of the possible permutations and combinations will deviate. In fact, Jameson attributes the value of Greimas's model to its ability to register deviations from the surface text (*Political,* 126). Since he argues that the ideological limitations of what he terms the author's "conventional mind" explain these deviations, this historicized version of Greimas's model critiques the author's ideology by discrediting his or her point of view.

His reading of *Lord Jim* illustrates the way in which this emphasis on deviation reduces Conrad's subjectivity to ideological distortion. According to formal critics, Conrad divides the Marlowe of *The Heart of Darkness* into the would-be hero Jim and the contemplative narrator Marlowe and gains, as a result, sufficient aesthetic distance from his characters to make his moral judgments convincing. Conrad's aesthetic devices are, in short, a means of establishing moral standards by which the author judges the characters. However, Jameson says that Conrad's method of characterization is not a neutral device making ethical judgments convincing but an ideological resolution of what are, according to Greimas's semiotics, irresolvable antinomies. Jameson takes Greimas's famous rectangle, which is a four-term variation of a basic structural opposition, to reveal the ideological limits that Conrad's "conventional mind" imposes on the characters' potential development. The rectangle displays possibilities of development that Conrad's ideology will not tolerate.

To describe these possibilities, Jameson cites two theorists: Max Weber, who analyzes the capitalist "rationalization" divorcing instrumental active forms of institutional life from the values of institutions, and Friedrich Nietzsche, who describes the "transvaluation" changing religious objects designed for holy worship into autonomous images available for aesthetic consumption. These theories show that the breakup of the feudal caste system and the growth of capitalist markets produce a divorce between value, which becomes "personal," and action, which remains public or institutional. Moreover, this antinomy between action and value explains the main features of *Lord Jim*'s characters. Thus the gentleman pirate Captain Brown signifies action without value; the religious pilgrims, value without action; the deck-chair sailors, valueless inaction; and Jim, the ideal: action of value (*Political,* 46–49).

In this way the antinomy accounts for the characters' opposed features and satisfies Greimas's rectangle; however, it poses an interpretive problem because, as poles of the antinomy, the pilgrims and the sailors are far more important than most interpretations say. Jameson tries to account for their exaggerated significance by invoking the unseen hand of ideology—it may minimize or understate important figures, as Freud tells us the censor of dreams does. In this case, ideology encourages Conrad to fill out Jim or Captain Brown but prevents him from developing the religious pilgrims or the deck-chair sailors. The trouble is that the ideological constraint explains what the social theory and not Conrad's "conventional mind" suggested—the exaggerated significance of the religious pilgrims or the deck-chair sailors. Ultimately the constraint accounts for only what the social theory produced—the exaggerated importance of the pilgrims and the sailors.

What is more, the social theory is not neutral: in a radical way it criticizes the emerging capitalist markets. Conrad may not share the radical biases of the social theory, but that fact does not make his outlook ideological and the social theory objective. Only if the formal possibilities envisioned by the structural antinomy somehow acquire a transcendent truth does the actual development (surface structure) of the text reveal the merely subjective limitations of Conrad's outlook. Why should the antinomy acquire such elevated status and Conrad's outlook, such degraded status? Is it not because Jameson assumes that even in historicized form the Greimasian antinomy and structuralism generally remain neutral and objective, just as he assumes that the utopian future preserves the neutral objectivity of the humanist ideal? Berthoud rightly suggests that as a consequence of such assumptions, Jameson is "completely incapable of acknowledging Conrad's text as offering . . . a responsible interpretation of the world" (113).

Jameson and Poststructuralism

In general, Jameson believes that the mediating cultural models provided by structuralism, humanism, and other approaches "would remain merely symbolic, a mere methodological fiction, were it not understood that social life is in its fundamental reality one and indivisible, a seamless web, a single inconceivable and transindividual process" (*Political*, 40). This belief that "social life is in its fundamental reality one and indivisible" opposes Althusser's and Foucault's poststructuralist skepticism, for the belief exacts a mystical faith in an "inconceivable and transindividual process," preserves the autonomy of the "transindividual process" and denigrates "subjective" institutional discourses, codes, and practices, what Jameson calls "merely the reality of appearance: it exists, as Hegel would put it, not so much *in itself,* as rather *for us*" (*Political,* 40).

Traditional critics like Jonathan Culler deflate the poststructuralist skepticism of Barthes and Derrida—it qualifies but does not destroy the scientific character of the structuralist project; similarly,

Jameson says that the institutional approach of Althusser and Foucault challenges but does not overturn the transcendental faith of Hegelian Marxism. Culler does not grant that deconstruction has turned the "scientific ambitions of structuralists" into "impossible dreams" (*On Deconstruction*, 219–20); Jameson does not allow that the institutional critique reveals anything more than a limitation of the traditional Hegelian method—it does not respect the autonomy of the levels or the ruptures of historical development.

However, Althusser and Foucault do more than emphasize these ruptures of development or that autonomy of levels; in addition, they repudiate the Hegelian faith in an "inconceivable and transindividual process." They reject the pursuit of a transcendental reality whose underlying or immanent opposition (the famous "unity-in-difference") mediates among different discourses, for, to overcome their reified character, this opposition denies their independence as well as their evolution. In *Reading Capital* (1968), for example, Althusser says that the Hegelian approach imposes a self-identical telos preserving historical continuities and repressing historical ruptures. Echoing Friedrich Engels's fear that the Hegelian method mystically deduces the particular from the universal, Althusser complains that the method constitutes the levels of history from the mind's own substance (15–17, 131–38). He derides the sleight of hand whereby the totality constitutes them out of itself. Like a magician, it extracts them from the hat called spirit, reason, or mind and fails to respect the fields, discourses, or topography peculiar to them. As he says, "And Marx is on his guard, because when he inscribes the dialectic within the functioning of the instance of a topography, he effectively protects himself from the illusion of a dialectic capable of producing its own material content in the spontaneous movement of its self-development" (*Essays*, 148–49). Not only does the figure of a topography undermine the mystical pretensions of Hegelian dialectic, the figure also subverts the Hegelian faith in an "inconceivable and transindividual process" underlying fields, discourses, and disciplines. The critique deconstructs the Hegelian fear of fragmentation and brings Marxism back to discourse's historical and institutional contexts, divisions, and disciplines.

In *The Archaeology of Knowledge* (1969) Foucault states a comparable view: contradiction has many levels and functions within and between discursive formations and does not represent a difference to be resolved or a fundamental principle of explanation (149–56). In *Foucault, Marxism, and History,* Mark Poster explains this claim: as an archaeologist studying the discourse of criminals, the insane, and other dispersed subjects, Foucault repudiates the notion of a transcendental reality underlying and unifying diverse discourses and examines a discourse's history, conflicts, and institutional power (39).

In a sense Jameson anticipates this critique of the Hegelian method, for he argues that, by destroying social isolation and by democratizing culture, such critiques leave the Left no room in which the Left can undertake the traditional Lukácsian analysis of false consciousness. As he writes, "You have to do it from the inside and it has to be a self-critique" ("Regarding," 39). Nonetheless, his several responses to Althusser's and Foucault's critique preserve the methods and concepts of a Hegelian approach.

His first response construes Althusser's critique as an "unanswerable" repudiation of Stalinism (*Political,* 47). I grant that Althusser meant to attack the Stalinists, yet he also repudiated the totalizing approach of Hegel and Sartre. In *Essays in Self-Criticism,* Althusser states clearly enough that the "thesis that 'men' (the concrete individuals) are *the* subjects (transcendental, constitutive) of history . . . not only has nothing to do with Marxism, but actually constitutes a quite dubious theoretical position. . . . You just have to read the *Critique of Dialectical Reason* . . . to be convinced of this point" (98). Here Althusser opposes more than Stalinist versions of Hegelian theory; in addition, he rejects the transcendental subject's ability to mediate between text and history.

Jameson's second response is that Althusser's critique qualifies but does not destroy the Hegelian account of totality. At best, the critique warns us not to forget the differences between the literary, the political, and the economic levels of society, not to reduce one of these levels to another. At worst, however, the critique disperses basic methodological unities. It dissolves the historical narrative in which new periods evolve from the old like butterflies from moths. It fragments that underlying primordial oneness that, because of bourgeois divisions, levels, and disciplines, we see through a glass darkly but will one day discern face-to-face (*Political,* 23–43).

To avoid this fragmentation, Jameson preserves the methodological closure and the conceptual language of a totalizing approach. Why else would he say that the "semantic precondition for the intelligibility of literary and cultural texts" and for their "semantic enrichment and enlargement" stems from three "concentric frameworks"— political events, class struggle, and sequential social formations (*Political,* 78–79)? While these frameworks open interpretation to multiple perspectives, the frameworks also fix the points where those perspectives go astray, the limits beyond which he but not they can go. In addition, while Foucault denies that conceptual distinctions transcend the discursive network in which they are formed and embedded, Jameson assumes that theoretical terms like "class," "value," or "space" escape their disciplinary contexts and acquire a "transcendent" status allowing them to characterize a whole period or to determine political practices or social institutions. How else should we explain that impressive recapitulation of Nietzsche's and Weber's theories enabling Jameson to describe the "antinomies" of *Lord Jim* as an opposition of activity and value? On what grounds but the transcendental can Frye's account of romance and Nietzsche's account of ethics describe the same binary oppositions? How else can deconstruction and Frankfurt social theory both characterize the "dissolution of the subject" in late monopoly capitalism or the literature, painting, film, criticism, philosophy, and architecture of the 1970s and 1980s share a common postmodern notion of space?

Last, in *The Political Unconscious* Jameson says that the poststructuralist critique of the Hegelian method shows the regressive character of a new period—postmodernism. This poststructuralist critique amounts to what he calls "symptoms of and testimony to a modification of the experience of the subject in consumer or late monopoly capitalism." While he grants that the "psychic dispersal, fragmentations, . . . temporal discontinuities" resulting from this critique imply a "dissolution of an essentially bourgeois ideology of the subject," he refuses to endorse the "schizophrenic ideal" projected by poststructuralism. What is more, he argues that only the "post-individualistic social world" of the future can genuinely fragment or decenter the bourgeois subject (124–25).

He acknowledges that criticism is lost in postmodernism's ahistorical present, but he still seeks to transcend its "subjective" contexts and divisions and to characterize the "dominant" features of this era. In several influential essays, for example, he describes postmodernism as a "new cultural logic in its own right" ("Regarding," 29) but assesses it in equally negative terms. He points out that postmodernism, breaking with modernism, which lost oppositional force in the 1960s, develops what Jameson calls an "aesthetic populism" effacing the "older (essentially high modernist) frontier between high culture and so-called mass or commercial culture" ("Postmodernism," 54). Jameson denies that his account of postmodernism represents the sort of "moralizing position" that Lukács takes on modernism ("Regarding," 36), but he sharply condemns postmodernism's integrating culture into "commodity production generally": "The whole global, yet American, postmodern culture is the internal and superstructural expression of a whole new wave of American military and economic domination throughout the world" (57).

Although he clearly distinguishes between the socioeconomic structures of postmodernism and its cultural theories and practices, this condemnation of it extends to and includes poststructuralist theory. His account of postmodernism's features, such as its pursuit of visual and interpretive flatness; its emphasis on intensities, temporal disjunction, difference, and breaks; its construction of a perspectiveless space; its destruction of cultural autonomy and of individual works; its depersonalization of style; and its use of pastiche and collage, describes poststructuralist practices too ("Regarding," 30–33, 37, 45, 51). He grants that postmodernism may also reveal "forms of resistance," but his description of the postmodernist alliance with "military and economic domination" emphasizes what he calls the "cultural dominant" ("Regarding," 36) and minimizes the poststructuralist's radical dimension—its undermining and subverting the conservative, chauvinist subject constituted by popular culture, the canon, and other literary institutions.

In general, his accounts of authorial, structuralist, and poststructuralist criticism imply that the most valuable politics is speculative and utopian, and not institutional or disciplinary. Jameson argues, as Adorno and Horkheimer do, that late monopoly capitalism is too "reified"; "established discourse," too "alienated and fragmented"; and the ruling "realities," too "unshakeable" to permit change. Jameson believes not only that capitalist classes rationalize society, creating reified institutions, but also that this rationalization dominates both external and internal nature, both institutions and the mind, leaving no room for the resistance and the opposition envisioned by Lukács. However, Jameson traces this all-encompassing reification not to the instrumental rationality characterizing the Enlightenment era but to the fragmented subject peculiar to the modernist period. Emerging in this period, the reified structures of modern capitalism have historical, not universal, grounds. During "high realism," Jameson finds the subject unified, and his desire or longing, elevated. In the modernist era, by contrast, capitalist modes of production degrade the desire of the subject and fragment his psyche, for institutional structures formalize and elaborate the rational faculties but impoverish the sensuous faculties. The postmodern era degrades and fragments the subject in a similar way; in addition, this era, which eradicates the division between elite and popular culture, colonizes art and philosophy too, destroying the last vestiges of the psyche's independence. As Jameson writes, "The prodigious new expansion of multinational capital ends up penetrating and colonizing those very pre-capitalist enclaves (Nature and the Unconscious) which offered extraterritorial and Archimedean footholds for critical effectivity" ("Postmodernism," 87).

Insofar as this history of capitalism's reified institutions minimizes the "critical effectivity" of practical or "reformist" action, this history is pessimistic; indeed, the history is too pessimistic, for it denies the value of practical action. Jameson writes that "even the concept of praxis remains a suspect one" (*Political,* 294). Moreover, while he assumes that the reified structures of "high capitalism" obliterate the objective truth of individual life and destroy the possibility of practical action, he preserves the theoretical ideal whereby our constructing a hypothetical whole effectively subverts reified social life. In fact, he defines Marxism in these Hegelian terms: it is "that 'untranscendable horizon' that subsumes . . . apparently antagonistic or incommensurable operations" (*Political,* 10). In this way Marxism exposes what he calls "the 'strategies of containment' whereby they [e.g., the "apparently antagonistic or incommensurable operations"] are able to project the illusion that their readings are somehow complete and self-sufficient" (*Political,* 10).

In short, Jameson's Marxism assumes that the reified state of capitalist social life excludes practical action or, as he says, imposes "structural limits" on "praxis" (*Political,* 91) and permits only a speculative utopian critique preserving theoretical norms and scientific neutrality. At the same time, his approach denies that criticism can meaningfully challenge the dystopia of modern life, merge utopia and reality, or open a path from the existential present to the utopian future. If the rational future but not the dark present may permit change, what can literary critics do but wait and hope for the utopian future to reveal itself? In Jameson's defense, Michael Sprinker says that Jameson's work "cannot be completely evaluated within the present historical situation, since . . . the present . . . must itself be abolished for the future to appear" ("Historian," 347). Jameson has been an outspoken critic of American foreign policy, but insofar as this refusal of evaluation depends upon such an apocalytic future, Jameson's defense of Hegelian theory dilutes the political force of his work. His pessimistic belief that the reified state of capitalist social institutions excludes practical action broadens his literary criticism but weakens his political impact. The institutional approach of Althusser, Derrida, and Foucault opens a rich institutional realm of engaged, formal, historical, and political critique; Jameson's historicization of authorial humanism and literary structuralism broadens and deepens both these methods but ends up almost as neutral and as distant as traditional approaches. Terry Eagleton wisely comments that in this speculative Marxism "the commodity bulks so large that it threatens to obfuscate, not only bourgeois social relations, but a specifically political and institutional understanding in areas of the Left" ("Jameson," 21).

Conclusion

In this chapter, I have argued that the theorists of reading radically undermine traditional approaches but do not consistently develop a political stance. The reader-response critics dismiss the famous "affective fallacy" and rely on the reader's responses, yet even the radical institutional versions of this approach preserve the positive belief and the neutral truth of traditional approaches. The phenomenologists subordinate transcendent truth to the reader's experience; however, the radical phenomenological negativity of Heidegger and of Adorno still imposes on the reader a corrosive self-consciousness reaffirming the potency of classical theory.

The structuralists repudiate the formal text and the autonomous truth of traditional criticism and adopt a scientific stance that exposes the ideological ends or the institutional conventions, not the subjective feelings or the self-conscious ideals, of the reader. However, while Barthes, Eagleton, and other structuralists go on to repudiate the positive beliefs, the theoretical self-consciousness, and the scientific neutrality keeping reader-response, phenomenological, and structuralist criticism apolitical, Culler and the Marxist feminists keep structuralist criticism scientific and ahistorical. Jameson forcefully demonstrates Hegelian Marxism's ability to open structuralism, humanism, and other approaches to sociohistorical theory, but he too preserves the neutral ideals of these approaches and denies the possibility of an institutional politics. Although the poststructuralist approaches that I discuss in the next chapter have provoked widespread indignation, they consistently overturn the apolitical ideals of traditional criticism.

FOUR

Poststructuralism—
The Politics of Skepticism

POSTSTRUCTURALISTS ALSO THEORIZE READING, BUT THEY ARE LESS traditional and less apolitical than reader-response, phenomenological, and structuralist critics are. While the latter critics challenge but preserve traditional notions of literary form, autonomous truth, and scientific neutrality, poststructuralists consistently overturn such notions. Indeed, this uncompromising radicalism has aroused the indignant opposition of New Critics, authorial humanists, structuralists, mythopoetic critics, psychoanalysts, phenomenologists, and others, who fear that poststructuralism destroys established knowledge of society, nature, or self and conventional forms of meaning, including the dénouement of a plot, the development of the characters, the patterns of images and symbols, and the significance of irony and paradox. These indignant critics complain that, emphasizing alterity instead of identity, and difference instead of sameness, poststructuralism dissolves traditional ideals of coherence and unity but does not supply positive alternatives or seek intellectual progress. Indeed, these critics warn us that poststructuralism threatens our moral fabric, undermines our rationality, affirms our existential emptiness, and welcomes artistic alienation and loneliness (Altieri, 71; Krieger, *Theory,* 220–27; Abrams, "The Angel," 425; Said, *World,* 4; Hirsch, *Aims,* 146; Graff, *Literature,* 62; Jameson, *Political,* 35, 53; Fischer, 32, 98, 109; Ellis, 270).

The poststructuralist movement does have such "faults," for it opposes unified texts, determinate intentions, autonomous truths, and self-determining readers; nonetheless, it is broader and richer than these criticisms suggest. In fact, besides figural or textual deconstruction, to which poststructuralism's opponents reduce the whole movement, it includes authorial and reader-oriented approaches, whose commitments are institutional. These approaches all open criticism to an interdisciplinary study whose exciting potential the opponents of poststructuralism deny or ignore (see Fischer, 96). Thanks to this interdisciplinary study, literary criticism does not maintain the boundaries of specialized academic disciplines, each appropriating its portion of the phenomenological universe or organizing its share of a university's curricula and departments. In effect, the traditional compromises between scientific disciplines and literary subjects break down; instead of excluding the specialized wisdom of other disciplines, literary study also stakes a claim to philosophical, psychological, historical, and sociological discourse.

However, the textual version of this interdisciplinary approach favors a purely literary language excluding the "ordinary" language of newspapers, popular fiction, and social history. This approach erases the institutional discourse that, according to Foucault and others, endows "ordinary" language with authority (Foucault, *Archaeology,* 21–50; Bennett, *Formalism,* 131–37; Fish, *Is There,* 268–99; Lentricchia, *After,* 202–3). The institutional critic cannot state or defend the norms structuring his or her criticism, but s/he does explicate a web of authoritative "ordinary" discourses invoked and reworked by the literary text. Moreover, the institutional critic exposes the conflicts and repressions defining traditional approaches but does not destroy their interpretive potential. While feminists and Marxists have shown that the figurative language of the textual approach can generate forceful ideological criticism, this language also ends up saying such a great deal that we cannot tell what it says. It evokes so many contrary meanings that it undermines what the Derrideans consider the metaphysical absolutism of established practices (see Said, "Problem," 12–14, and Cain, "Institutionalization," 19–22). Authorial versions of the institutional approach vociferously oppose this ahistorical critique of established methods; however, committed to transcendent sociohistorical truth, the authorial critics preserve the implicit theoreticism of their textual opponents. Reader-oriented versions of this approach dismiss ideological criticism as unprofessional, but they consistently repudiate the ahistorical critique of the textual stance and the pretentious theoreticism of the authorial stance.

Althusser, Derrida, and Foucault

The distinguished work of Derrida, Althusser, and Foucault illustrates the range and the depth that such differences of approach give the poststructuralist movement. These philosophers preserve the interpretive techniques but repudiate the metaphysical commitments of their parental traditions; however, while Althusser and Foucault go on to critique the institutional power of established discourses, Derrida's phenomenological critique of Western "onto-theology" indiscriminately exposes an empty abyss ungrounding all approaches. These philosophers all elucidate the codes, myths, discourses, and conventions elaborated by a text, but Derrida's elucidation does not escape the ahistorical indeterminacy of the phenomenological tradition that he so sharply critiques.

Derrida restates the skepticism of Nietzsche and Heidegger but struggles against their metaphysical commitments. He develops the Heideggerian belief that language undermines the "autonomous" power of propositional assertions and reveals the determining import of terms and figures, but he considers the Heideggerian notion of "Being" as metaphysical a notion as the autonomous Cartesian proposition is. He also reworks the skepticism of Nietzsche, who denies that the Judeo-Christian tradition asserts universal values. Nietzsche argues that humility, generosity, compassion, and cooperation—the virtues of the Judeo-Christian ethic—do not characterize an absolute "good"; rather, these "virtues" repress their opposites—arrogance, power, playfulness, joy, or idiosyncrasy—and conceal this initial repression. In *Otobiographies*, Derrida admits this skepticism has fearful consequences, including "nihilistic" violence and authoritarian rule (78), yet he still defends Nietzsche's belief that assertions of value conceal repressed conflicts and opposed terms.

In the influential essay "Differance," Derrida elaborates the skepticism but critiques the metaphysical implications of both Nietzsche and Heidegger. He attributes two meanings to "differance," to put off or to postpone and to differ or to be unlike; as he says, "differance" refers to "differing, both as spacing/temporalizing and as the movement that structures every dissociation" (*Speech,* 130). The first meaning, to put off or postpone, restates and undermines Heidegger's notion that language, not propositions, reveals the presence of "Being." While traditional phenomenology treats speech as the expression of consciousness and writing as a mere supplement of speech, both Heidegger and Derrida deny that language serves the ends of thought; however, Derrida goes on to deny that writing supplements and corrupts speech, that phonemes articulate the concept, and that the visible represents the intelligible. While the Heideggerians preserve the privileges of consciousness, including its status as "self-presence" (what Heidegger calls the "onto-theological determination of being"), Derrida undermines those privileges, for he claims that writing, which lies outside Being, generates effects that Heideggerians (mis)construe as the venerable presence of "Being." He writes that "presence is a determination and effect within a system which is no longer that of presence but that of differance" (*Speech,* 147). As "a determination and effect," "presence" stems from "differance" or writing and not from consciousness or being. In Heidegger's aesthetic terms, art brings "what is" "into the Open," but it does so as a "happening," revelation, or "unconcealment" ("aletheia") (36). For truth to "occur" or "happen," this disclosure must blast the reader out of his conventional modes of understanding. Derrida does not deny that art explodes our conventional modes of understanding but that the explosion lets "being" happen or brings it into the open. Instead of manifesting it, writing generates it as a discursive effect or defers it for an indefinite time. In short, both Heidegger and Derrida consider language or writing more fundamental than propositional rationality; however, while Heidegger assures us that language reinstates the metaphysical realities ("Being") obliterated by modern rationality, Derrida insists that writing generates only the illusion of presence, producing the effects of it, casting nothing more than its shadow.

The second meaning of "differance," to divide or to oppose, restates and undermines the skepticism of Nietzsche as well as that of Heidegger. Like them, Derrida doubts the Platonic notion that good and evil or truth and falsehood are absolute terms. Appropriating the theories of Freud and of Saussure he argues that language systematizes itself, economically requiring its terms to destroy their equivalents and obtain a unique space within it. The conflicts of terms define a discourse, whose assertions reproduce their differences, not "Being." As he says, "Within a language, . . . there are only differences"; as a result, "the signified concept is never present in itself, in an adequate presence that would refer only to itself" (*Speech*, 140). Writing repeats terms, yet the repetition does not create a "signified concept" whose "adequate presence . . . would refer only to itself." Writing remains "iterable," but it undermines the traditional desire to affirm autonomous concepts, intentions, being, truth, or virtue. If concepts, intentions, or truth do not escape the contamination of writing, then philosophy cannot be a "pure" discipline, and "differance" establishes an interdisciplinary kind of textuality.

Scholars as diverse as de Man and Spivak rightly say that this account of textuality forcefully undermines and displaces the traditional oppositions between intrinsic and extrinsic criticism, science and poetry, concepts and metaphors, and truth and ideology. By contrast, the opponents of deconstruction fear that Derrida's account of textuality remains as dangerously irrational as Nietzsche's and Heidegger's accounts are. The opponents rightly warn us that Derridean textuality does not escape Heidegger's irrationality. Nonetheless, such criticism simply seeks to reinstate the metaphysical, denotative, or transcendental notions opposed by Heideggerian and Nietzschean skepticism. Critics who debunk deconstruction because it refuses to submit an assertion to "public" criticism or to provide "evidence" supporting it (Fischer, 121) fail to respect deconstruction's "premise," that propositional rationality excludes the metaphorical import of discourse and reproduces illegitimate subject/object divisions. One does not engage in what Ellis calls the "special pleading" of the "insider" (267) if one accepts this Heideggerian assumption.

The Derridean account of textuality does not justify a parasitic negativity or repudiate intellectual progress, as critics say (Margolis, 149; Ellis, 270). Scholars have shown that Derrida struggles against positive metaphysical concepts but that this struggle does not mean that "differance" has, in his words, "fallen from the sky ready made." Even though language is heterogeneous, it is not arbitrary; "differance" includes the "movement by which language, or any code, any system of references, becomes 'historically' constituted as a fabric of differences" (*Speech,* 141; see also Lentricchia, *After,* 174–75; Gasché, *Tain,* 139).

Derrida's work elaborates the "movement" by which a "code" is "'historically' constituted." In "The Pharmacy of Plato," for example, Derrida says that in Plato's dialogue "The Phaedrus" an Egyptian myth about writing generates conflicts between science and myth, dialectics and memory, truth and sophistry, loyalty and democracy, knowledge and mechanical repetition, and speech and writing. Plato trusts speech and memory but not writing, which is too democratic and insufficiently serious. In fact, he fears that, known through myth and not through science or rational knowledge, writing reduces to mechanical repetition external to "living" knowledge. At the same time, though, he admits that writing aids the memory; indeed, Plato expects his writing to enable him to overcome the "sterility" of the philosophical father, Socrates. Thus, writing, which Socrates calls a "pharmakon," stages a series of oppositions (remedy/poison, seductive/harmful, living speech/mechanical repetition, myth/science) that Plato repeats but does not master (*Dissemination,* 94–96). Traditional critics assume that Plato means to produce these oppositions, for, to oppose the sophists, Plato praises speech above writing, knowledge above repetition, science above myth, etc. However, Derrida argues that writing, not the writer, generates them: if Plato is to show that writing repeats without knowing, his famous irony commits him to repeating but not "knowing" the Egyptian myth in which Toth, the god of writing, displaces the god Ra as the moon displaces the sun (*Dissemination,* 73–74).

Derrida also elucidates the historically displaced codes of educational contexts, where unstated conventions constrain what universities call "free speech"; however, I have said enough to suggest that Derridean textuality is more historical and less parasitic than its opponents admit. Nonetheless, Derrida's fear that positive terms will reinstate the metaphysics of Heidegger keeps his account of textuality from fully acknowledging its institutional contexts. As Gasché points out, Derrida can show but cannot properly explain writing—what Gasché calls the "infrastructure"—because Derrida does not wish to reassert the very metaphysical essences that he means to undermine (*Tain,* 148). "Differance" demarcates the grounds underlying the philosophies of Freud and Saussure as well as Nietzsche and Heidegger, all of which show differance's "double gesture," opposing and postponing. Yet Derrida denies that his account of these grounds imposes a "master-word" or a dominant concept. Terms like "differance," whose "a" one can see but not hear, or "trace," that unavoidable mark left by a writer's forgotten discourse, are throwaway words meant only for discourse's momentary flow. In *Positions,* Derrida writes that "the motif of *differance,* when marked by a silent *a,* in effect plays neither the role of a 'concept' nor simply of a 'word.' Since it cannot be elevated into a master-word or master-concept, since it blocks every relationship to theology, differance finds itself enmeshed in the work that pulls it through a chain of other 'concepts,' other 'words,' other textual configurations" (39–40). As a "chain" of "textual configurations," Derridean discourse, intently self-regarding, refuses to assert "master-words" or construct definitive concepts. Only what he terms an "assemblage" or "web," his account of "differance" weaves together other discourses, supposedly giving them a momentary unity but nothing more.

However, his account of discourse has acquired more import than this momentary weaving suggests. Derrida struggles against the "institutionally representative" character of his approach, yet "differance," "trace," "dissemination," "writing," and other Derridean terms have become the familiar phrases of an influential deconstructive movement. As Said writes, "Western thought is something more differentiated, incorporative, and, most important, institutionally representative than Derrida seems to allow" (*The World,* 209). By contrast, Althusser and Foucault also believe that interpretation elucidates sociohistorical myths, codes, discourses, or ideologies, but Althusser and Foucault do not erase the institutional ground of interpretive practice. They undermine but do not abolish the discourse of their parental others, exposing its compromising humanist commitments but preserving its methodological stance.

In particular, Althusser and Foucault deconstruct empirical or scientific discourse, preserving its opposition with unsystematic discourse but undermining its "illusion" of neutral factual objectivity. For reasons that I will clarify shortly, Althusser uses the term "ideology," but Foucault does not; nonetheless, they both believe that the productive force, historical particularity, and critical import of scientific discourse subverts its supposedly factual objectivity.

They argue that such discourse constitutes the object that seems to empiricists to live its own life. Althusser traces the limits of classical political economy not to those conditions of industry and finance that define true economic life but to that complex ("problematic") of practices, discourses, and knowledges in terms of which the political economist produces theories. Similarly, in *The Archaeology of Knowledge,* Foucault reminds us that his subject is the "human," not the exact, sciences; as less formal discourses, the "human" sciences reveal the conditions of their own possibility, not objective truth.

Moreover, the favorite metaphors of Althusser and Foucault, geographical terms like "field," "domain," "terrain," "volume," "mapping," or "surface," emphasize the productive force that Foucault and Althusser attribute to discourse. For example, Althusser says that Marx opens up a new field, history without a spirit, force, or class realizing some predetermined telos, and within this field Marxist historical study acquires its own criteria (consistency, precision, coherence) and need not appeal to universal beliefs or "fundamental" realities. Similarly, Foucault says that psychoanalysis constitutes a new terrain, that of desire and its constraints, and within this terrain theorizing not only takes on a unique form, including a particular technical language and introspective method, but it defines unique rules, such as those regulating the interpretation of dreams or the treatment of neuroses.

Not only do Althusser and Foucault attribute productive force to neutral scientific discourse, but they assume that in significant ways it ruptures with its past. Students of Gaston Bachelard and Georges Canguilhem, two French philosophers of science, Althusser and Foucault develop their professors' notion that a discourse can produce its own science by breaking with the "ideologies" ruling its past. Althusser extends this notion—the famous "epistemological break"—to Marx's rupture with Hegel, while Foucault extends the notion to medical science, classical economics, linguistics, or psychoanalysis. Althusser takes the notion to explain the autonomy of Marxist science, while Foucault takes the notion to account for the rupture dividing modern and classical knowledge ("savoir"). For example, Foucault says that science gave birth to psychoanalysis because the incessant inculcation of taboos upon sexuality, especially "perverse" kinds, ironically generated a strong interest in them; as a result, the theorists seeking a scientific status for modern psychoanalysis had to break down these taboos (*Sexualité,* 25–49). In addition, in *Words and Things* he shows that linguistic discourse did not become a science until it broke with a different obstacle—the realist belief that language provides an unmediated representation of the world (*Les Mots,* 57–59).

Similarly Althusser argues that traditional Marxism absorbed uncritically the classical notion that one homogeneous time pervades economics, politics, legal studies, philosophy, aesthetics, and science; rather, each of these "fields" has, he says, "a peculiar time and history . . . punctuated with peculiar rhythms" (*Reading,* 99–100). Moreover, Althusser insists that at a particular moment an ideological discourse gives birth to its own science: "We have to learn . . . to treat the ideology which constitutes the prehistory of a science, for example, as a real history . . . capable of producing the arrival of a science . . . every science, in the relationship it has with the ideology it emerged from, can only be thought of as a 'science of the ideology'" (*Reading,* 45–46). Marx's relationship with humanism illustrates this symbiotic relationship of ideology and science, for Althusser argues that the mature Marx breaks with his youthful Hegelian humanism and discovers a new, subjectless discourse, an objective science of history.

In *Les mots et les choses* Foucault also argues that a subjectless discourse displaces the humanist subject of the nineteenth century and becomes the new ground of knowledge. Nineteenth-century thought disrupts the representational empiricism of the seventeenth and eighteenth centuries and establishes humanity as the central subject/object of positive knowledge, which can delineate the finitude of the human subject but cannot transcend its limitations. Foucault shows that biology, linguistics, economics, and other positive sciences successfully define the limits of the subject but cannot ensure the subject's transcendence or autonomy. His finitude defines and traps him.

Moreover, Foucault says that in the nineteenth century the field of knowledge fragments; man becomes an object of knowledge but the figure or subject "man" is insufficient to hold together the field, which includes positive sciences, formal mathematics, and modern epistemology. To insert a discourse in this fragmented field, a theorist must adopt mathematical models of truth and repudiate historicism and psychologism (355–59). In other words, a discourse does not possess its disciplinary autonomy from its inception; rather, its proponents, whose reconstructions of it enable it to meet the formal requirements of an established discipline, free it from its eighteenth- and nineteenth-century humanist limitations.

In a similar way Althusser criticizes as illusory the autonomy taken for granted by empirical disciplines but articulates and preserves their implicit opposition of science and pseudoscience as a conflict of science and ideology. In *Pour Marx* Althusser argues that the empiricist commitment to experience grants the perceiving subject a false independence of ideological discourse. While the ability of factual assertions to exclude psychology and rhetoric makes the subject feel autonomous, the subject's perceptions do not escape the influence of the ideologies constituting him or her as a subject. Despite this feeling of autonomy, the subject remains in their grip (238–43). Initially Althusser, who shows a positivist hostility to "psychologism" and "historicism," expects the formal rigor of scientific theory to defeat the "genetic" influences of ideology. To produce a scientific work, a theorist must overcome those influences, but it is the rigorous development of his conceptual apparatus, not strict conformity with fact, which enables him or her to do so (163–97). However, Althusser eventually develops a historical account of this ideology/science conflict: it is not an unpleasant and unavoidable feature of rational discourse but a significant event, rupture, or break within a discourse's history.

In other words, Althusser and Foucault construe the formal or "scientific" reconstruction of a discourse as an event in its history, not as the discovery of its essential truth or of its objective reality. However, Althusser interprets this event positively—by struggling against ideology, a science establishes its formal autonomy, while Foucault interprets the event negatively—by condemning its history, a discourse represses the influence of the institutional complex into which it inserts itself. Modern proponents of a "positive" science may repudiate its history as mere "psychologism," but that repudiation simply represses the discourse's unconscious. As Poster says, to criticize modern discourse, Foucault shows that its ancient versions differ with yet contain its modern version (85–91).

Foucault favors historical, not ideological or metaphysical, critique because he construes a science's emergence from an ideology as a historical rupture, not a formal inconsistency. Since the terms "discourse," or, more precisely, "discursive formation" suggest a historical, rather than a positivist or mathematical, contrast of science and ideology, he prefers those terms to "ideology." As he says in *The Archaeology of Knowledge,* "To tackle the ideological functioning of a science . . . is to question it as a discursive formation; it is to tackle not the formal contradictions of its propositions but the system of formation of its objects, its types of enunciation, its concepts, its theoretical choices. It is to treat it as one practice among others" (187). The relationship of a science and its "discursive formation" does not show itself in the science's inconsistencies and contradictions but in its history, including its discarded theories, "old-fashioned" views, and outmoded practices. The discarded notions and outdated theories uncovered by an archaeology, not the contradictions exposed by logic, reveal the unconscious ("impensé") of a discourse. Despite its facticity, such notions and theories continue to influence and determine a discourse even though it no longer employs their terms.

For example, Foucault says that by bringing the mentally ill into the hospitals originally devoted to the lepers, by separating the sane from the insane, the psychiatrists of the sixteenth and seventeenth centuries break with the classical belief that through the insane the divinities speak to mankind and create the modern "rational" distinction between the "crazy" and the normal, the "mad" and the "rational." In a comparable way, in reorganizing courts and prisons, eighteenth- and nineteenth-century reformers not only conceal punishment and "improve" personality, they establish the modern division between the normal and the delinquent person.

While these historical contrasts effectively critique the scientific pretensions of a discipline, Foucault's account of power lacks critical force. In his early work, he assumes that civil society and the state oppose each other: while civil society grants the individual the freedom to pursue the pleasures induced by the economy, the state takes away the freedom of those whose pursuit of pleasure violates social norms. In his later work he reduces power to an amorphous microstructure disciplining the body. The techniques of this discipline pervade society, which does not control or produce them. As Poulantzas points out, these accounts of power restate the liberal/bourgeois belief that state power is legal or juridical, not ideological. Discourse does not reproduce the apparatuses of the state; discourse articulates an omnipresent microstructure organizing and controlling the actions of dispersed bodies (36, 44).

Althusser, who emphasizes the ideological functioning of discourse, not its historical divisions and oppositions, argues that in a conservative Western society, ideological critique represents significant political action because the continuity of the bourgeois subject depends essentially upon the ideological apparatuses maintained by intellectuals. He mistakenly reduces the history of discourse to blind empiricism, a "theological" mode of reading, but he bolsters the critical import of science, which acquires the ability to resist and to disrupt ideological practices. Foucault, who reduces science to only "one practice among many," forcefully contrasts past and present forms of discourse, emphasizing its ruptures and gaps, but denies the disruptive force of ideological critique.

Derrideans dismiss the Althusserian critique of ideological discourse on the grounds that Althusser construes the economy as the nondiscursive ground of discourse or the "self-presence" of a containing center; Derrideans also complain that the Foucaultian notion of discursive power fails to explain the position of the subject who describes the history of a discourse. Such objections emphasize the parental discourses of Althusser and Foucault and minimize their critical force. Like Derrida's account of writing, Foucault's and Althusser's accounts of discourse undermine and disrupt the idealist/metaphysical pretensions of their parental traditions but do not escape their methodological commitments.

Althusser, Derrida, and Foucault all preserve the established methodologies in terms of which they deconstruct their parental others. The divergent Marxist, Nietzschean, and scientific philosophies influencing the historical and political analyses of Althusser and Foucault lead to substantial institutional studies but not to transcendent realities or to purposeful totalities; however, while the Heideggerian skepticism informing Derrida's insistent exposure of "differance" enables him to unearth the conventions and the discourses erased by entrenched interpretations, he preserves the phenomenologist's contemptuous dismissal of "psychologism" or "historicism"—as he says, "the unsurpassable, unique, and imperial grandeur of the order of reason . . . makes it not just another actual order or structure (a determined, historical structure)" (*Writing*, 36). In these diverse ways Derrida, Althusser, and Foucault establish a rich spectrum of approaches elucidating the figural and institutional roots of discourse.

Poststructuralist Literary Criticism: The Textual Approach of J. Hillis Miller and Paul de Man

Moreover, the poststructuralist movement possesses an equally rich spectrum of literary criticism representing equally opposed textual and institutional approaches. The textual approach, which includes formal, feminist, and Marxist versions, assumes that language is free-floating, arbitrary, irrational, and uninterpretable. Its uncertainty, ambiguity, "indeterminacy," or "aporias" undermine the forms and meanings imposed by traditional interpretive strategies. Its irrationality subverts the neat bounds of interpretive statements and disciplinary boundaries. This subversion opens the textual approach to impressive interdisciplinary studies of feminist, Marxist, Freudian, economic, philosophical, or political works. However, by turning the "heterogeneous" language of writing against the "arbitrary" restraints of interpretive practices, the textual stance erases the institutional discourse reproducing these practices.

J. Hillis Miller, who adopts an empirical outlook quite different from de Man's phenomenological outlook, interprets literary language in these textual terms. For example, in "The Critic as Host," Miller argues that language is not common or public, as M. H. Abrams says; rather, its meanings expand indefinitely and arbitrarily, creating a network that is not clearly inside or outside a text. To illustrate the subversive force of this indeterminate network, he argues that the "labyrinth of words" branching out from the term "parasite" dissolves the boundaries that divide "host" and "parasite," text and reading, and, finally, nihilism and metaphysics (218–22): "The place we inhabit, wherever we are, is always this in-between zone, place of host and parasite, neither inside nor outside" (231).

This "in-between zone" establishes the interdisciplinary potential of deconstruction, whose dissolution of a text's "inside" and "out-

---

side" undermines the practices of literary study as well as the public meaning of a text's language. Without an "inside" or "outside," language reveals so many different chains of meaning that traditional approaches lose their principle, order, or lawfulness. All interpretation becomes arbitrary, if not willful.

Moreover, Miller restates the Derridean notion of "differance" in these subversive terms. This notion involves two kinds of repetition: the grounded, which emphasizes New Critical notions like "similarity," "unity," and "coherence," and the ungrounded, which stresses such deconstructive terms as heterogeneity, dispersal, or differance. The grounded type of repetition permits interpretation but only a conventional kind; the ungrounded type is too diverse and arbitrary to permit interpretation. The grounded type asserts metaphysical truths; the ungrounded type opposes them.

Since the imagery of a text shows both kinds of repetition, we cannot say what a text means. As grounded or ungrounded, repetition undermines the techniques of interpretation but not close textual analysis, which Miller considers an ethical responsibility. In fact, he identifies this uncontainable repetition not with interdisciplinary studies but with the literary text: "The shift back from 'consciousness' to 'language' as the category to be investigated allows in principle a closer look at what is actually there on the page" (*Fiction,* 19). Even though we cannot account for a text's meaning, we can trust the empirical text—"what is actually there on the page." The skeptical Miller considers the "words on the page" an absolute, irreducible plenitude of meaning. The "plain" text fulfills yet stands above all interpretive strategies. Even though one definitive interpretation cannot explain a text's meaning, the text successfully supports incompatible interpretations. For example, in Hardy's *Tess of the d'Urbervilles* Miller faces what he calls an "embarrassment of riches"—"the novel provides evidence to support . . . [a] large group of incompatible causes" of Tess's suffering. He doubts that "there must be some single accounting cause," but he does not question the ability of the words to represent plain evidence. His skepticism extends to consistent interpretation but not to the empirical page, whose sheer white blankness accommodates it to innumerable interpretations. He may oppose heterogeneity and dispersal to unity, coherence, and identity, but he forcefully preserves the New Critics' faith in a literary text's full, burgeoning language.

Although de Man prefers a Heideggerian approach to this empirical stance, he too adopts a deconstructive skepticism in which the subtleties and ambiguities of literary language dissolve interpretive methods, disciplinary boundaries, and institutional discourses. He opens the text to diverse approaches, admitting the insights and the blindnesses of New Critical, authorial, phenomenological, semiotic, and even Marxist interpretations. Formal and authorial interpretations traditionally preclude each other, the first condemning thematic statement as pseudoscientific paraphrase, and the second, subordinating formal techniques to the author's insight or intention. Nonetheless, de Man allows them both to occupy and describe a text. Incompatible, conflicting, these approaches rationalize what de Man considers an interminable scramble for textual power; that is, the text gives itself to formal analyses but does not resolve its ambiguities. The formal closure of the New Critical text no longer constrains literary language, whose free play, intertextual significance, or exuberant "materiality" escapes those inherently "arbitrary" forms of resolution. In de Man's terms, "American formalist criticism" favors a "totalizing principle" but retains only an "empirical notion of the integrity of literary form." This "empirical notion" "could lead to the disclosure of distinctive structures of literary language (such as ambiguity and irony)" but such structures "contradict" the "totalizing principle" (*Blindness,* 32). In addition, even though the New Critics construe intention in psychological terms and neglect the structural intention or "totalizing principle" organizing the text (*Blindness,* 32), the author's intention and generic forms also do not eliminate the language's "figural potential." "Intrinsic" formal approaches; "extrinsic" historical, biographical, or psychological analyses; subjective, phenomenological interpretations; and semiotic readings—de Man allows all of these approaches to scramble for textual power but not to control the language of the text. The language undoes them also, or, as de Man says, forced to acknowledge their insights, it exposes their blindnesses too.

In short, neither the reader nor the author nor the text can successfully address a realm outside literary language. The skepticism of de Man frustrates all such acts of reference, for our interpreting the uninterpretable language of a text brings to light only our presuppositions. In *Blindness and Insight,* de Man adopts a Heideggerian version of this textual metaphysics: interpretation illuminates the text, not "Being," yet the revelation is circular. By giving "poetic language" "form," the critic can reveal his presupposition or "foreknowledge," but he cannot state or "contact" it; he can only show that he is "lucidly aware" of it, for poetic language limits the critic's self-knowledge and imposes its own "being"—the text. De Man writes that "for the interpreter of a poetic text, this foreknowledge is the text itself. Once he understands the text, the elucidating commentary simply tries to reach the text itself, whose richness is there at the start. Ultimately the ideal commentary would indeed become superfluous and merely allow the text to stand fully revealed" (30). Once poetic language has "form," the critic has revealed his foreknowledge and completed the circle; however, the circle closes not on the critic or on his procedures but on the object, the text. In demonstrating "foreknowledge," the critic effaces himself, rendering his methods "superfluous" and the fully revealed text, all-encompassing.

Does not this circle restore the very metaphysical realities in the name of which de Man debunks traditional approaches? Does not the circle turn the text into a transcendental entity overcoming the uncertainties of literary language and repressing the interpretive strategies of the critic? While Derridean deconstruction resists all such returns to metaphysics, de Man, like Heidegger, restores the lost presence of the text itself. The youthful fascism of de Man returns as a text more powerful and more irrational than the empirical text of the New Critics ever was.

Critics deny that de Man's deconstruction is genuinely Derridean, yet in *Allegories of Reading* he goes on, as Derrida does, to resist the encroachments of the text and to defeat this return of metaphysics; now, unlike Heidegger's "Being," which endows its celebrants with transcendent power, de Man's text enervates the confidence of its interpreters, the ultimate "madness" of language paralyzing their grasp of its immanent "form." Thus de Man says that in Shelley's *The Triumph of Life* "the syntax and the imagery of the poem tie themselves into a knot which arrests the process of understanding" ("Shelley," 44). Incomplete, fragmented, such language represents literary art, which cannot realize its own "form," articulate the critic's foreknowledge, or recall a lost wisdom. Uninterpretable, inexplicable, the language of literature blocks the "process of understanding."

For instance, de Man insists that a question can have two irreconcilable meanings:

The grammatical model of the question becomes rhetorical not when we have, on the one hand, a literal meaning and on the other hand a figural meaning, but when it is impossible to decide by grammatical or other linguistic devices which of two meanings . . . prevails. Rhetoric radically suspends logic and opens up vertiginous possibilities of referential aberration. And . . . I would not hesitate to equate the rhetorical, figural potentiality of language with literature itself. (*Allegories*, 10)

The "rhetorical, figural potentiality of language" emerges in those moments when "it is impossible to decide by grammatical or linguistic devices" whether the literal or the figural meaning "prevails." In those moments—elsewhere he calls them "aporias"—the two meanings unhinge each other, opening up "vertiginous possibilities of referential aberration." As Fish points out, literature includes literal, overdetermined moments as well as these uninterpretable moments, yet de Man identifies literature only with this figural potentiality. In *The Trial*, for example, one of the warders who arrests Joseph K. does not have the authority to do so and mistakenly employs the personal pronoun "ja." Clayton Koelb points out that, because of these "misfires," one cannot establish whether or not the warder's statement, "you are under arrest" means that Joseph K. is under arrest (38). Similarly, in *Swann's Way* certain passages about reading defend what de Man calls the "aesthetic superiority of metaphor over metonymy," yet he complains that the text "does not practice what it preaches," for the "assertion of the mastery of metaphor over metonymy owes its persuasive power to the use of metonymic structures" (*Allegories*, 14–15). Such hypocritical incoherence keeps the text from making the claims that it means to make; its assertions lack authority, its acts go astray, and we cannot tell what it means.

Although de Man supported German fascism in his youth and studied romantic literature during his professional life, some critics argue that this exposure of a text's incoherence represents a proto-Marxist critique of ideology (Sprinker, *Relations*, 264). De Man speaks of this inevitable epistemological failure as ideological criticism, but he does not by any means accept the objective or scientific truths in the name of which Marxists critique ideology. Other scholars complain that, if the assertions of a text lack authority, interpretation seals the text off from the world, and criticism becomes socially and politically irresponsible (Said, *The World,* 162; Lentricchia, *After,* 317). However, de Man's rigorous exposure of language's incoherence undermines more than sociohistorical criticism; in addition, the exposure subverts formal, New Critical, phenomenological, semiotic, as well as structuralist criticism. Indeed, the exposure acquires the tragic tone of a peculiarly Platonic wisdom: as he writes, "We end up . . . in the same state of suspended ignorance. Any question about the rhetorical mode of a literary text is always a rhetorical question which does not even know whether it is really questioning" (*Allegories,* 19). Like Socrates, a truly wise critic knows that he or she knows nothing, not even whether or not a "rhetorical question . . . is really questioning." Such a critic devotes himself or herself to literary language but acknowledges what he cannot grasp—the rhetorical mode of a text, the intentions of the author, the responses of readers, the binary oppositions of the language, and the institutional conventions of interpretation. De Man may open the text to what the New Critics exclude from it—plain syntax, referential logic, authorial intention, readers' activity; nonetheless, by calling the moments of figural "aberration" the only literary ones, he tragically reinstates the New Critical dismissal of concepts, theories, institutions, and history. He denies that syntax, logic, intention, structure, and readers control literary language and ensures, as a result, that the text remains as aconceptual and ahistorical as the New Critics wished it to be. He favors Heidegger's hermeneutic circle over Miller's "empirical" principle; nonetheless, he and Miller share a negative skepticism in which literary language overturns conventional approaches and resists substantial wisdom.

The Textual Feminism of Barbara Johnson

When Paul de Man died, Barbara Johnson, who studied with the "Yale" Derrideans, was invited to replace him at a panel where, unlike the other panelists, she would discuss his work and not her own. She complains about the "female effacement" implied by this invitation (*World,* 32), but her work shares the formal or rhetorical stance of de Man and Miller. She assumes, as they do, that the Derridean notion of differance undermines the unavoidable pursuit of unity and identity but not the empirical structures of literary language. In de Man's fashion, she argues that the text anticipates and subverts its readings, exposing their blindness or ignorance. However, while de Man's and Miller's approaches remain apolitical, her approach successfully opens deconstruction to feminist issues, including sexuality and abortion. Her rhetorical approach erases the phenomenological contexts of deconstruction, thereby denying its institutional limits, but she insightfully examines noncanonical texts and raises significant issues of gender and race.

In *The Critical Difference* (1980), Johnson takes for granted the formal belief that literary theory amounts to a sophisticated means of interpreting (but not mastering) literary language. In her terms, "theoretical pronouncements . . . do not stand as instruments to be used in mastering literary structures. On the contrary, it is through contact with literature that theoretical tools are useful" (xi–xii). As "tools," theoretical discourse can be "useful" but not as a means of "mastering literary structures"; rather, useful discourse will, she adds, "change and dissolve in the hands of the user. Theory is here often the straight man whose precarious rectitude and hidden risibility, passion, and pathos are precisely what literature has somehow already foreseen" (xii). In de Man's sense literature acquires the power to foresee and even to undermine the "rectitude," "risibility," "passion," and "pathos" of "theory." However, what confers this subversive power upon literature is her formal assumption that "contact with literature" makes theoretical "tools" "useful."

She believes that deconstruction destroys "the claim to unequivocal domination of one mode of signifying over another," but the formal assumption that contact with literature makes theory useful moves her to read texts as though they transcend their peculiar historical moments and employ the discourse and assert the motifs of contemporary literary theory. Her account of *Billy Budd* illustrates this erasure of historical context. She construes Melville's opposed characterizations of Billy and Claggart as opposed modes of reading. Billy is a literal-minded reader, while Claggart, who personifies "ambiguity and ambivalence," is an ironic reader. Moreover, she interprets these contrary modes of reading in deconstructive terms. Here, for instance, is her explanation of literal minded Billy: "In assuming that language can be taken at face value, he excludes the very functioning of *difference* that makes the act of reading both indispensable and undecidable" (84). Does not her describing the illiterate Billy as blind to "the very functioning of *difference*" imply that Melville has characterized him in contemporary terms? Her explanation of the ironic Claggart implies a similar equivalence between Melville's language and contemporary discourse: "Claggart meets his downfall, however, when he attempts to master the arbitrariness of the sign for his own ends" (85). What does the statement that "he attempts to master the arbitrariness of the sign for his own ends" do but restate in poststructuralist language what traditional critics would call a character's tragic flaw? In de Man's Platonic manner Johnson goes on to argue that the "opposition between the literal reader (Billy) and the ironic reader (Claggart) is reenacted in the critical readings of *Billy Budd*" (85) but deconstructed by the story: as she says, "in studying the plays of both ambiguity and binarity, Melville's story situates *its* critical difference neither within nor between, but *in the relation between the two* as the fundamental question of all politics" (106). This conclusion so thoroughly assimilates the story's characterizations and its readings into Derridean discourse that not only does the story undermine established readings of it, but the story discusses difference, which it situates in the "relation between" ambiguity and polarity and which it turns into a dramatic but ahistorical issue—"the fundamental question of all politics."

In *A World of Difference* (1987) Johnson raises forceful issues about gender, race, and the canon but preserves this textual stance. She complains that Miller's defense of deconstruction construes difference as a "cancerous femininity" (35) and that de Man talks about the philosophical tradition as though it were a "men's club" (38–39), but she continues to defend the Derridean approach. For instance, she translates the empirical structures of Poe's "The Raven" into Derridean discourse; as she says, "The Raven" "dramatizes the theoretical priority of the signifier over the signified" (98). She acknowledges critics' vehement objections to de Man's belief that language has "random effects," but she still emphasizes the usefulness of this belief. In her terms, such criticism requires us to determine what "we do with the knowledge that we cannot be sure that any given language pattern isn't random" (6).

Her earlier work also asserted feminist views but did not label them feminist. For example, she points out that in Mallarmé's "The White Waterly," the poet's wishes to ignore the "worldly, conversational head" of the lady and to "become one" with her "unconscious." Johnson condemns such an act as "fragile, unauthorized, fantasmic" (19). In addition, she objects, as feminist Lacanians do, to the biological interpretations of the phallus. It does not signify the presence or absence of the penis, as Derrida says; rather, the phallus is the sign of sexuality as difference (140). Where *A World* opens new territory is not in its bold feminism but in its treatment of the canon. Instead of questioning the boundary between literature and philosophy, as de Man and other Derrideans do and as she did in her earlier work, *A World* investigates the barrier between canonical and noncanonical texts, especially what she calls "the lies, secrets, silences, and deflections of all sorts . . . taken by voices or messages not granted full legitimacy" (31). Even though the determination of what "voices or messages" are not "granted full legitimacy" is an institutional and not a rhetorical question, she rightly argues that her rhetorical analyses of such voices and messages reveal the "literary ramifications" of a feminist politics (31). She still erases deconstruction's institutional structures, which she condemns for making the "radically innovative thought" of the Derrideans simplistic, dogmatic, and conservative (11), but her boldly challenging the boundary between canonical and noncanonical discourse effectively renders the Derridean notion of "undecidability" a political issue.

Her sensitive interpretation of Mary Shelley's *Frankenstein* shows the forceful manner in which she opens the formal de Manian framework to this feminist politics. Her interpretation reworks the formal reading of Gilbert and Gubar but preserves a Derridean stance. Like them, Johnson says that Mary Shelley's "struggle for authorship" defines what is specifically feminist in her work (145). Mary Wollstonecraft, Shelley's (fore) mother, moves Shelley to become an author, for Shelley must "prove herself worthy" of her parentage; at the same time, she must kill her mother if, as an author, she too gives birth to a destructive monster. Johnson argues, as Gilbert and Gubar do, that such matricide explains Shelley's supposed fear of success (152). However, Johnson denies Gilbert and Gubar's formal belief that the text unifies its opposed outlooks—the chauvinist myths of

Paradise Lost and the repressed feminist "monster." Shelley's repressed femininity lies not in the rebellious monster but in her self-contradiction, which appears, Johnson says, "in the gap between angels of domesticity [e.g., Frankenstein's murdered sister and dismembered bride] and an incompleted monsteress" (153). Moreover, while Gilbert and Gubar treat Shelley as a temporizing feminist who reconciles rebellious womanhood with Miltonic mythology, Johnson considers Shelley a radical feminist who "fictively transposed her own frustrated female pen envy into a tale of catastrophic male womb envy" (151).

Although such forceful feminist readings justify her belief that carrying an analysis to the point of undecidability does not exclude "political engagement" (11), her deconstructive approach limits and even undermines this engagement. In both works, she argues, in de Man's Platonic fashion, that deconstruction becomes effective and remains surprising if it reveals the ignorance repressed by our claims to know (*Difference,* 108; *World,* 16). As a consequence, she treats rhetorical devices as neutral entities escaping the play of political conflicts. For instance, in "Mallarmé as Mother," she construes the maternal role as a rhetorical structure independent of gender: as she says, a male who questions "the determinability of meaning, the separability of binary opposites, the search for self-identity—would somehow appear to fill the maternal role better, more effectively, than a woman" (*World,* 141). While this rhetorical account of the "maternal role" permits men as well as women to function as mothers, the rhetorical view renders motherhood a genderless role as well. Similarly, in "Apostrophe, Animation, Abortion," she treats apostrophe as a neutral device independent of politics. As she says, "What I would like to emphasize is the way in which arguments for and against abortion are structured through and through by the rhetorical limits and possibilities of something akin to apostrophe" (*World,* 191). Like her repeated complaint that binary oppositions oversimplify complicated literary structures, this insistence that "something akin to apostrophe" structures political stands restates de Man's and even Heidegger's phenomenological belief that opposed values and conflicting beliefs presuppose yet resist figural structures; however, Johnson ignores what Derrida has acknowledged—the irrationalist and even fascistic politics implied by this Heideggerian dissolution of propositional truth.

Marxist Versions of Deconstruction:
Terry Eagleton, Michael Ryan, and
Gayatri Chakravorty Spivak

While Johnson opens deconstruction to feminist concerns, she does not censure its anarchic irrationalism; by contrast, Eagleton, Ryan, and Spivak do condemn this "anarchic" negativity, yet they still develop a Marxist version of deconstruction in which figural, textual, literary language undermines established approaches.

For instance, in *Walter Benjamin* Eagleton complains that, violently evasive, deconstructive skepticism ("a death drive at the level of theory") reveals the dissipated state of contemporary liberalism and not the abyssal negativity of Derridean theory. The liberal outlook of de Man or Miller, not the Nietzschean or Heideggerian roots of their method, moves them to dismiss closure and identity, sacrificing "the reality principle" to the "pleasure principle" and the "homogeneous self" to the "logic of multiplicity." The liberals even disperse the subject, rendering it politically "impotent" and imposing "quietism and compromise" (138–39).

Attributing the "evils" of deconstruction to its liberalism enables Eagleton to establish a Marxist poststructuralism that remains textualist. He praises Benjamin's prophetic articulation of what Eagleton terms "the current motifs of poststructuralism . . . in a committedly Marxist context" (*Benjamin*, ii). In this "committedly Marxist context," he preserves the skeptical method but not the "liberal" politics of de Man and Miller. For example, de Man faults the New Critics because they employ a "totalizing principle" opposed to literary language's "distinctive structures"; similarly, Eagleton reproaches traditional formalists like F. R. Leavis or T. S. Eliot because they wished to enslave the "materiality of the signifier" to the artist's voice or "ideological" presence (7). Moreover, Eagleton, who means to free the "signifier" as thoroughly as de Man and Miller have, discovers that in Benjamin's work the "carnality" or "materiality" of language resists the impositions of traditional approaches as effectively as de Man's "figural potential" and Miller's "repetition with difference" do. In Benjamin's account, the style of the baroque *Trauerspiel* possesses, Eagleton says, a "complex carnality," a "display of substance," a "self-delighting purely sensuous residue over and above the meaning with which all written language is inexorably contaminated" (5). Unlike the romantic symbol, which unites concept and sound, signified and signifier, and erases the sign's materiality, this enigmatic baroque sign conceals its meaning in innumerable images and sounds and undermines the interpretive practices of Eliot, Leavis, and others (5–8).

Moreover, Eagleton also assumes that literary language repudiates the history and the traditions of the literary institution. Hence, he argues that, like Harold Bloom, Benjamin expects the critic to reject the authority of his parental discourses, breaking violently and decisively with the "linear historicism" ("tradition") of established literary practices (47–48). In *The Function of Criticism* he praises the classical tradition of the literary institution, but here he insists that Benjamin is right—"tradition belongs to the oppressed and exploited" (48).

Eagleton rejects the "liberal skepticism" of de Man and Miller, yet, as Sprinker suggests (*Relations,* 243), his interpretive practice affirms what theirs affirms—the text's irresolvable conflict of language and sense, figural potential and interpretive strategy, critical insight and institutional practice. However, while the "liberals" lament or embrace the Platonic state of ignorance in which literary language leaves them, Eagleton attributes a "positive" socioeconomic import to literary language. For instance, he draws parallels between language and the commodity: just as literary language opposes interpretive statement, so the commodity undermines its socioeconomic roles. The metonymic substitutions of language void the sign's interpretive significance; similarly, the economic exchanges of the commodity empty its functions of value (25–30). In other words, Eagleton means to infuse the literary language of the textual approach with the speculative insights of Hegelian Marxism; nonetheless, like the textual critics whose liberalism he condemns, he affirms the irreducible powers of literary language; it does not voice an instinctive ideology or a debilitating liberalism, affirm the romantic symbol, or admit "homogeneous" history, but neither does it permit concrete institutional insight either.

While the innovative Eagleton has gone on to produce valuable historical and institutional studies of literary criticism, Ryan and Spivak turn Eagleton's Derridean stance into a formidable Marxist methodology. Like him, they reject the conservative philosophical terms in which de Man and Miller interpret deconstruction but retain their rigorous commitment to literary language as well as their erasure of institutional discourses. In *Marxism and Deconstruction,* for example, Michael Ryan says that the deconstructive account of language implies a positive social theory even though Derrida confines his analyses to "concepts and to language" (35). While Derrida remains content to analyze philosophical texts, none of his critiques "is simply philosophical; each also engages political questions" (63). Like de Man and Miller, Ryan assumes that deconstruction may affirm or undermine established approaches, but he extends this power to social theories and established institutions: as he says, "To affirm the abyss deconstruction opens in the domain of knowledge is politically to affirm the permanent possibility of social change" (8). This pursuit of "permanent social change" leads him to draw extensive analogies between Derrida's views and those of Marx, Sartre, and Adorno, on the basis of which he argues that deconstruction forcefully undermines the ideological commitments of social, political, and economic discourses. In his words, the deconstruction of "bourgeois philosophy and social science" suggests an "analysis of the social constitution of consciousness through the unconscious," including "the part played by logocentric operations and procedures in the everyday pursuit of race, sex, and class oppression" (35).

Ryan's undertaking such powerful ideological critique moves his deconstruction far beyond a purely formal textualism. However, he fails to escape the literary/philosophical tradition that he repudiates in this radical way. For example, if social theory is to reside "outside" philosophy, deconstruction would have to admit a realm "outside" metaphysics, yet Derrida repeatedly contests this distinction between an "inside" and an "outside." More important, while Derrida does not wish to elevate his terms into metaphysical concepts, Ryan, who says that "concepts are forces" (140), gives them quasi-Platonic status. Not only do the analogies and similarities of diverse discourses treat alterity, iteration, heterogeneity, difference, supplementarity, writing, etc., as positive concepts, these analogies turn those Derridean notions into imaginary sociopolitical ideals and endow them with critical force. In other words, just as Plato argues that the rational soul generates the ideal republic, so Ryan says that deconstruction implies a radically feminist, democratic, and egalitarian socialism, by contrast with which the liberal democracy, bourgeois patriarchy, and hierarchic communism of established political institutions pale into inferior oblivion.

In fact, in the name of this radical, socialist, and feminist democracy, he condemns institutional forms of Marxist discourse. For instance, with Cold War animus he reduces Lenin's theory of the state to a Stalinist affirmation of hierarchy, (logo)centrism, and dictatorship. Moreover, even though communist leaders in France, Spain, England, Italy, Japan, and the USSR have repudiated the Stalinist commitment to hierarchic, centralized practices, including the dictatorship of the proletariat, he maintains that Lenin's theory denies communist parties the ability to reform themselves: "What will be privileged or marginalized in a practice of socialist construction derived from Lenin" is "anything that contradicts state centrism. . . . Marginalized will be such inessential things to the central state as the 'antagonism . . . against the state power,' 'really democratic institutions,'" and so on (175). Last, Althusser rigorously distinguishes the object of theory from the objects of real, practical life and forcefully deconstructs the empiricist and the humanist commitments of classical Marxism, yet Ryan, who equates Althusser's approach with "communist party diamat," argues that both of them "apply founded systematic constructions to the world" (45). Ryan's deconstruction opens Derridean theory to forceful ideological criticism, but his Platonic stance does not avoid that theory's indiscriminate dissolution of institutional discourses.

While Spivak takes an equally pessimistic and indiscriminate view of institutional discourse, she develops a cogent and compelling type of Derridean Marxism. Her sensitive account of the Derrida/Searle debate explains and justifies this Marxism. As she points out, Derrida objects to Austin's belief that literary or metaphorical discourse is "parasitic" upon literal discourse. Like the misfires that show that Austin cannot stipulate all the conditions of an illocutionary act, literary discourse is an inherent but excluded possibility of speech-act theory. Since the intelligibility of writing depends on an "iterable" or repeatable explanatory code, not on an author's intention or on historical circumstances, writing does not construct self-identical concepts capable of functioning in propositions. Like de Man and Miller, she takes this notion of writing to break down the traditional distinction between logic and language, concepts and metaphors, or intrinsic and extrinsic forms; however, she extends the distinction to Marxist social theory, whose "clear cut oppositions between so-called material and ideological formations" also break down. She rightly concludes that even a "rigorous" science of logic cannot exclude writing, metaphors, or ideology: "If a reading such as this were to be translated to the social text, . . . clear cut oppositions between so-called material and ideological formations would have to be challenged as persistently as those between literal and allegorical uses of language" ("Revolutions," 39–40). She too assumes that this challenge opens literary study to interdisciplinary discourses, but to escape "idealist" notions of literary study, she examines the social text, whose political, sociological, or historical discourses cannot exclude ideology: as she says, in this text "the sedimentation and investment of history as political, economic, sexual 'construction' would be seen as irreducible" (40).

As a consequence, she develops a notion of textual "practice" at odds with literary deconstruction. Unlike Johnson, she acknowledges that a Derridean sort of ideological critique develops out of but differs from Heideggerian phenomenology, which undermines the conceptual truth of propositional discourse yet reasserts the metaphysical presence of "Being." What she calls Derrida's "regional" commitment to Freudian theory enables him but not Heidegger to describe the structural unconscious as the "other" and, as a result, to characterize language as a structural unconscious resisting metaphysics (42). To produce a radical version of this Derridean strategy, she does not construe concepts as Platonic forces; she simply substitutes her own "regional" commitments—feminism, Marxism—for Derrida's: as she says, "If the 'other that is not quite the other' were to be conceived of as political practice, pedagogy, or feminism— simply to mention *my* regional commitments—one might indeed look for '"revolutions" that as yet have no model'"(47).

I suspect that she speaks of "political practice" and not of "Marxism" because she understands this practice in radical terms: more elliptical than circular, writing exposes the "hypocrisy" of a text's assertions and undermines the traditional quest for transcendent meaning and absolute grounds. Still, like Eagleton and Ryan, she refuses to limit deconstruction to a corrosive Platonic irony (47). She does not admit that deconstruction, which confronts the "other as such" and not just the "philosophical other," represents a philosophical stance

(46, 48), yet, as political practice, writing preserves the phenom-enologist's heady theoreticism. Writing remains self-divided, but writing overcomes all the oppositions that Lukács expected the working class to overcome, including the opposition between subject and object, theory and practice, Being and history, and subjectivity and objectivity (42).

Moreover, in the textual manner, she attacks the literal language of empiricist thought and erases its institutional import. Her provoca-tive accounts of feminism and Marxism illustrate this dismissal. First of all, while Elaine Showalter and others have argued that feminist criticism should examine women's linguistic, social, psychological, and literary practices, Spivak objects that such empiricist approaches mistakenly construe women's experience as an independent subject. This objection insightfully suggests that this autonomous construc-tion of "woman" depends upon but does not acknowledge the his-torically prior, male way of constructing "woman." However, the objection also questions the legitimacy and the achievement of independent women's studies departments, which those whom she calls her "positivist feminist colleagues" ("Feminism," 135) managed to establish despite determined opposition.

In a similar way her account of Marx's *Capital* preserves its critical force but undermines its institutional discourses. She says that to ex-plain the evolution of capital, Marx adopts Hegel's account of a con-cept's self-development, substituting the notion of capital for Hegel's notion of the idea and its alienation ("Marx," 237–38). To show that Marx does not, as a result, blindly protest what his system renders necessary, she proceeds to argue that capital, which is "radically im-proper" and not simply contingent and evil, can appropriate labor because "it too can be im-proper to itself" ("Marx," 239–40). Marx protests the fact that capital can "be capable of consuming and realiz-ing the potential of the human body as a commodity" ("Marx," 242), but his protest still shows what Lévi-Strauss's privileging of speech over writing also shows—"a longing for transcendence that makes us posit a proper situation of self-proximity or self-possession against which to measure our fallen state" ("Marx," 229). This Derridean reading of capital forcefully restates the Lukácsian belief that the de-velopment of capital entails a division of labor fragmenting the worker, depriving him of his "self-proximity or self-possession"; however, the reading does not acknowledge that Darwinian biology also influences Marx, who, when *The Origin of Species* was published, wrote Darwin a letter of congratulations. Marx elaborates the evolution of capital in Darwinian as well as Hegelian terms. Not only does capital develop, it evolves. Its qualities emerge by accident but its superior capacities keep them in place. Besides a metaphysical nostalgia for a lost wholeness or self-possession, Marx's account of capital reveals the "struggle for survival" to which capitalism commits its workers. They may resent the loss of wholeness, but they create militant unions and radical political parties because of the life-threatening dangers—collapsing mines, poisonous fumes, exploding machinery, pointless wars—to which capital exposes them. The Frankfurt school explicitly debunks Marx's belief that working-class unions and parties can overthrow the capitalist system; by contrast, Spivak's deconstruction silently erases this "empiricist" belief.

Her Derridean critique of Marx's commitment to traditional logic and to classical economics illustrates the evangelical zeal with which she means to save Marx from such empiricist discourses. She argues that although Marx's analyses of money and of capital attack their intolerance of heterogeneity, Marx inconsistently adopts a method—the idealist method of "capital"—which also excludes heterogeneity. As a result, she fears that Marx does not readily admit what Derrida shows—that capital appropriates not only the mind and the body of the worker but also the methods of theory, including its commitment to logic. While she praises Marx's and Althusser's critiques of Hegel, she complains that, unlike Derrida, Althusser and Marx preserve the science of logic. To get Marx out of this "idealist" camp and into the Derridean camp, she returns to "the thematics of im-propriety," which locate "in the Marxian text the wherewithal to undermine its own traces of traditional metaphysics" ("Marx," 243).

The trouble is that this textual critique of metaphysics ignores the power of established discourse, in general, and classical British economics, in particular, to impose its terms and its methods on its opponents. As Foucault, Althusser, and Marx himself say, Marx does not initiate the field of classical economics; he elaborates a radical version of Smith's and Ricardo's theories. His participation in this field ties him to capital, yet he still subverts capital in forceful and influential ways. As Althusser points out in unusually Derridean language, Marx shows that the insights of "bourgeois" classical economists turn into blindnesses as well, especially when these economists discuss the sources of profit. To reduce this powerful critique of capital to collaboration with it is to dismiss the internal subversion which the collaboration makes possible and to ignore the power of established discourse to force its opponents to dispute its assertions in its terms.

Spivak might object that this emphasis on established discourse reinstates what Foucault means to undermine—the traditional subject. However, to undermine the subject is not to escape or to transcend it, as the phenomenologists assume, but to expose its incoherence, inconsistencies, and gaps and thereby to weaken its political force. In sum, Spivak may not consider deconstruction a literary stance or a philosophical tradition, but her belief that writing is a textual practice presupposes what the youthful Lukács also presupposes—that practice can abolish the traditional philosophical distinctions—and erases what Lukácsian theoreticism also erases— the determining influence of entrenched discourses. In sum, while de Man and Miller preserve a purely formal kind of textual criticism, Johnson, Eagleton, Ryan, and Spivak, who also set language against meaning, writing against identity, and ideology against system, expose the sociopolitical import of this subversive procedure. These radical critics forcefully repudiate the literary language of the formal critic, extend the critical techniques of textual deconstruction to social, political, economic, and feminist theory, but do not overcome the Derridean dismissal of institutional discourse. Indeed, even though Derrida has acknowledged the fascist import of Nietzsche's and Heidegger's skepticism, Johnson and the Derridean Marxists ignore such political inflections of established discourses.

Poststructuralist Literary Criticism: The Institutional Approach of Stanley Fish, Frank Lentricchia, and Edward Said

Unlike the textual approach, the institutional approach, which includes both authorial and reader-oriented criticism, does not divorce literary language from institutional practices; rather, this approach situates discourse in historical "archives," "networks," or "communities" concretely mediating between text and society. Lentricchia and Said, who represent an authorial kind of institutional criticism, argue that this historical approach retains the intertextual, heterogeneous force that the textual critic attributes to language but does not erase the institutional practices that explain the force. These authorial critics explicate a web of "ordinary" social, political, economic, or literary discourses reworked but not contained by a text. In addition, these critics argue that this approach undermines the humanist faith that the insight of the author transcends its era and reveals objective truth. Caught within a discursive web, the author's insight, like the text, does not escape historical determination. However, this determination does not obliterate the theoretical autonomy of the critic, who retains the "freedom" to "affiliate" with established or with oppositional criticism. Just as authorial humanism permits the forceful political criticism of Lukács, Graff, Williams, and Jameson but neutralizes their political force, so too does Said's and Lentricchia's commitment to autonomous theory vitiate their forceful institutional politics. By contrast, Fish, who defends a reader-oriented version of the institutional approach, takes literary discourse to reveal the strategies of the reader's interpretive communities but not their politics. He treats ideological criticism as unprofessional, but he consistently repudiates the figural analyses and the theoretical pretensions of humanist, phenomenological, and Derridean approaches.

The authorial approach of Lentricchia and Said assimilates institutional discourse to the humanist tradition promoted by Arnold, Trilling, Hirsch, Lukács, and Williams, but preserves the theoretical independence of the author and the critic. For example, Lentricchia argues that although Derrida and Foucault both undermine the autonomy of the author and the objectivity of truth, Foucault does not permit the arbitrariness and subjectivity imposed by the Derridean abyss. This loss of autonomy and of objectivity does not preclude what Hirsch and other "traditionalists" seek—"genuine" knowledge of history and society: as Lentricchia says, Foucault "would agree with traditionalists that unless we deploy . . . some form of the principle of determinacy, criticism cannot offer itself as a cognitive activity, for the refusal of determinacy is the refusal of knowledge" (*After,* 190). While the Derrideans and the Foucaultians both admit that an author's work does not escape the discourses and conventions of its historical era, this admission limits the Derrideans, who refuse the "principle of determinacy," but not the Foucaultians, who recuperate the "determinacy" and the "knowledge" of the "traditional-ists."

To illustrate this surprising benefit, Lentricchia reconstrues the traditional notion of a historical period. Instead of limiting a period, as formalists do, to a major theme or a dominant progenitor, the Foucaultian critic examines both the major and the minor contem-poraries of an artist, thereby revealing the "archive"—discourses, conventions, forms—taken for granted or forgotten by the artist (200–202). This construction of an archive does not simply describe the influences on or the backgrounds of great individual authors; the archive brings to light the politico-literary oppositions in terms of which an author's work may acquire, retain, or lose its institutional status. Literary disputes over what an epic or a tragedy discusses or what counts as a novel or a poem reveal the institutional politics de-termining this status. In fact, such disputes can amount to ruptures heralding what Lentricchia, following Foucault, calls the "emer-gence" of a new archive (203–5).

In a similar way, Said assimilates the work of Foucault to the his-torical criticism whose long-standing opposition to sacred texts and hermetic interpretations justifies what Said calls a "secular" stance. Deriving from Arnold, Auerbach, Lukács, and Williams, this secular stance emphasizes the historical situation of the writer as well as the positive, affirmative character of culture. In the traditional view, cul-ture enables authors or critics to rise above their social "affiliation," to defend the basic truth of human life, and to obtain the state's ap-proval of their insight and their values. Foucault's work allows Said to add that not only does culture affirm the values and the truths ap-proved by the state, but culture distorts and represses the state's alienated "others," including third-world peoples, liberated women, rebellious workers, homosexual love, or unusual religions. In Said's terms, Foucault has shown that "the dialectic of self-fortification and self-conformation by which culture achieves its hegemony over soci-ety and the State is based on a constantly practiced differentiation of itself from what it believes to be not itself" (*The World,* 12). Here Gramsci's notion of hegemony, which says that the culture of the rul-ing class dominates the opposed cultures of the state's subordinate classes, fuses what are hostile approaches—traditional humanism and Foucaultian discourse. On the one hand, although this humanism claims to characterize the universal passions of mankind, Said allows it to describe only "the dialectic of self-fortification and self-conformation by which culture achieves its hegemony"; on the other hand, even though Foucault treats political structures as a discursive effect of disciplinary practices, Said subordinates disciplinary discourse to the autonomous state, whose "constantly practiced differentiation" of itself "from what it believes to be not itself" reproduces culture.

Moreover, like Lentricchia, he denies that this new historical criticism simply studies the influences upon and the backgrounds of the great authors; rather, such criticism brings to light an era's archive or discursive formations, including what he calls a "range of circumstances: status of the author, historical moment, conditions of publication, diffusion, and reception, values drawn upon, values and ideas assumed, a framework of consensually held tacit assumptions, presumed background, and so on" (*The World,* 174–75). Unfortunately, this comprehensive list of the archive's impersonal components undermines the traditional autonomy of the author but not the traditional privileges of the critic: as Said adds, "Here is the place for intentional analysis and for the effort to place a text in homological, dialogical, or antithetical relationships with other texts, classes, and institutions" (*The World,* 175). This affirmation of "intentional analyses" and of "homological, dialogical, or antithetical relationships" reinstates the theoretical autonomy undermined by the historical archive.

As this affirmation suggests, even though the new authorial approach has led to powerful historical studies, including Said's influential *Orientalism,* the approach remains committed to transcendent truth and to limited institutional criticism. For example, in *After the New Criticism,* Lentricchia acknowledges that in Foucault's work the discourse of medicine, grammar, and political economy "constituted its object and worked it to the point of transforming it altogether" (194). However, he suggests that even though discourse has this transforming force, we are not entitled to assume that its objects lack autonomy or, as he writes, that "there are no objects for consciousness to mediate" (*After,* 207–8). However, to opt for a positive objectivity and historical neutrality is to align one's self with the humanist tradition, whereas to defend the constitutive force, particular history, and critical import of discourse is to repudiate the humanist's neutral objectivity and to favor, as Althusser and Foucault do, an institutional politics. As Bové suggests, Said and Lentricchia cannot have it both ways: either Foucault's account of discourse is constitutive or that account mediates positive "objects of consciousness"; either we adopt the institutional politics implied by Foucaultian discourse or we return to the traditional politics defended by humanist Marxism.

To an extent, Lentricchia favors the traditional ideal of neutral truth, for he praises Foucault's "general impatience with the idealism of" Gramsci and Althusser ("Reading," 61); they examine what Foucault wisely rejects—"the refashioning of potentially resistant minds, . . . the creation of both active and of unthinking consent to ruling class power, values, and ideas" ("Reading," 43). This Foucaultian "impatience" with ideological critique ("idealism") weakens the political import of Lentricchia's new historical approach. Consider his account of Wallace Stevens's poetics. Lentricchia says that Stevens, who accepts the "American ideal" of the independent, masculine man, sees poetry as ladylike, unmasculine, and self-renouncing but does not display chauvinist arrogance. Rather, this apparent chauvinism protests the triviality and marginality of modernist art ("Patriarchy," 751). This interpretation preserves the historical but not the feminist import of Stevens's views. Gilbert and Gubar rightly object that this interpretation blithely translates gendered language into gender-neutral terms ("The Man," 389)

By contrast, Said, who favors political critique, wisely complains that Foucault obliterates "the role of classes, the role of economics, the role of insurgency and rebellion" (*The World,* 243–44). However, Foucault's failing to appreciate "insurgency and rebellion" does not entitle Said to add that Foucault "pretty much ignores the whole category of intention" (*The World,* 186) and "falls victim to the systematic degradation of theory." Such complaints only show that in the traditional manner Said reduces institutional discourse to blind dogmas threatening to destroy thoughtful, critical individuals. Nor does Foucault's failure to appreciate "insurgency and rebellion" entitle Said to insist that resistance "cannot equally be an adversarial alternative to power and a dependent function of it" (246). Here Said's humanist repudiation of theological and institutional "dogma" comes back to haunt him as a spiritual resistance piously refusing to admit any complicity with ("dependent function of") its oppressors. Said and Lentricchia mean to show that Foucault advances cultural or historical criticism beyond Marxist humanism, yet their accounts of Foucault's politics ultimately reassert the humanist's apolitical autonomy.

Fish, who also develops an institutional approach, does not favor a political or ideological criticism, but he consistently and forcefully repudiates the theoretical pretensions of humanist historicism and phenomenological deconstruction. To explain the roots of interpretive authority, he does not reaffirm the transcendental objectivity of authorial humanism or the figural analyses of textual deconstruction; rather, he denies that the richness of literary language necessarily impoverishes ordinary language, whose wealth of values endows literal moments of literary experience with the interpretive significance which Derrideans confine to indeterminate figural moments. Indeed, Fish says that the abyssal heterogeneity that makes language uninterpretable stems from the Derridean's exclusion of ordinary language (*Is There*, 101–2). Literary critics may still produce irreconcilable interpretations, but that irreconcilability simply forces the reader, who experiences the conflict, to produce a resolution. Moreover, Fish argues that the "interpretive communities" embedded in literary institutions and constituting and regulating the reader's activity subvert the theoretical autonomy of the critic, who loses the freedom to choose between the establishment and the opposition. In fact, Fish complains that literary theory pretentiously seeks an inappropriate, if not impossible, power over the communities' interpretive practices. Such an imperialist practice blurs the differences of theory and practice. As a Wittgensteinian language game, literary theory has rules and ends that are not those of "practical criticism"—it plays a different game. Fish considers the gap between theory and criticism irreducible because, defined in formal terms, theory must but cannot produce invariably valid interpretations. And if it seeks to foster ideological "self-consciousness," it does not exert any special force and cannot guarantee change ("Consequences," 448). Distinct internal interests and not independent theoretical norms explain the changes and the history of institutions.

Critics object that this attack on theory mistakenly locates conflict and division in interpretive assumptions, not in the institutions governing interpretation (Weber, "Capitalizing," 17). However, Althusser and Foucault also locate conflict in discourse and not in institutions alone. Moreover, Althusser and Foucault also divide theory from practice, deny that theory has consequences, reduce theory to its own practices (forms of production), situate the subject within his institutional contexts, and, most important, preserve the authority of ordinary propositional discourse.

The differences among Fish, Foucault, and Althusser lie not in theory's position (above or within practice) but in its aims: Althusser expects theory to preserve the standards of intellectuals, while Fish wants it to confess its irrelevance. In an empiricist manner, Fish divorces theory from everyday life, whose discourse does not permit necessary causal relations or autonomous theoretical standards; in a Kantian manner, Althusser considers the critique of presuppositions—what Kant calls the "synthetic apriori"—a genuinely theoretical operation enabling disgruntled critics confronting the repressive, intolerant ideologies of capitalist life to defend their formal standards and to conserve their institutional integrity.

Tompkins and Bennett, who also repudiate the autonomy of theory, assume that interpretive communities impose class and gendered values on readers; by contrast, the serene Fish disdains such political criticism. In fact, he complains that radical critics who reject the narrow professionalism of literary studies and raise questions about capitalist ideologies ignore the situated character of the reader, whose activity expresses his positive belief, not his self-improvement or his intellectual standards. Like Hume, who believed that reason, a servant of the passions, cannot undermine the habits, customs, and predispositions of the mind, Fish affirms the positive truths of the situated reader and denies the political value of negative thought. He consistently repudiates the theoretical pretensions of humanism and phenomenology, but he affirms the apolitical authority of institutional conventions and dismisses the rebellious power of the negative, the irrepressible force of critique.

This opposition between neutral or conservative institutional and traditional approaches, on the one hand, and radical theoretical or figurative approaches, on the other, has long characterized the American reception of poststructuralist theory. However, the poststructuralist movement is broader and richer than this opposition suggests. Not only do the poststructuralists refuse to accept metaphysical appeals to transcendental terms and predetermined frameworks or to ignore the internal divisions and conflicts repressed by established criticism, the poststructuralists also open literary criticism to forceful historical, philosophical, psychoanalytic, feminist, ideological, and rhetorical analyses. I admit that the textual critics emphasize the arbitrariness of literary lang uage and the impossibility of interpretation, whose strategies "inevitably" mistake the language of the text. Although the textual critic develops an exciting kind of feminist and ideological criticism, the textual critic preserves the New Critic's hostility to conceptual and historical insight and dismisses the institutional "archive" of established discourses. However, institutional versions of poststructuralism open the established discourses of the text or the interpretive community of the reader to concrete historical and political critique. These institutional approaches rework established strategies, revealing their results, not their impossibility, emphasizing their potential, not their failure. The next and last chapter, which discusses formal, authorial, reader-response, structuralist, and deconstructive accounts of Thomas Hardy's pessimism, provides a "practical" illustration of institutional criticism's ability to expose the metaphysical commitments, repressed contexts, and erased discourses of established approaches but preserve their interpretive potential.

FIVE

A Practical Example
Hardy's Fiction and the Politics of Pessimism

THIS POSTSTRUCTURALIST ACCOUNT OF LITERARY STUDY HAS SHOWN that Marxist and established criticism implicate each other. New Critical, authorial, reader-response, phenomenological, structuralist, and poststructuralist approaches reveal political divisions that include Marxist or radical stances; at the same time, Marxist criticism reworks but does not escape these established approaches. Moreover, I have argued that, while deconstruction dismisses interpretation as a metaphysical quest for absolute truth, an institutional approach preserves the interpretive force but not the conservative stances of established approaches. Now I would like to suggest that this institutional approach gives rise to a "practical" criticism in which particular readings betray the political commitments of their parental methodologies. A reading does not simply apply a method to a text; rather, a reading presupposes a nexus of methods whose commitments the reading may affirm or repudiate. The aim of my "practical" criticism is to expose and to critique these commitments.

The pessimistic fiction of Thomas Hardy is a peculiarly apt subject because critics representing the whole spectrum of approaches acknowledge that a gloomy, irrational distrust of self, nature, and society pervades the mature work of Hardy, but not his early work, which affirms optimistic religious and liberal discourses (Lerner, 49; Webster, 51; Howe, 24; Schwartz, 125; Zabel, 35, 40; DeLaura, 396; Merryn Williams, 84–85; Miller, *Distance and Desire*); however, no one has satisfactorily explained why he becomes a pessimist. The New Critics praise his "artistic imagination" and literary devices but dismiss his didactic pessimism as "extrinsic" to his art. This stance shows the value of his artistic techniques but neglects the ideological critique implicit in them. The authorial humanists rightly say that the pessimism of Hardy approximates that of Woolf, Faulkner, Joyce, and other modern writers, but the humanists dismiss his "melodramatic" plots because they ignore the institutional conditions in which Hardy produces pessimistic fiction and the conventions and discourses with which his art breaks. Reader-response critics insightfully argue that the discrepancies between the narrator and the characters impel the reader to interpret the fiction and improve himself. However, these critics turn the pessimism into a conservative attack on immature, irresponsible individuals, not an ideological critique of social relationships. In addition, the "indeterminacy" permitting this reversal abstracts readers from their social conditions. Structuralists, who also construe the pessimism in these conservative terms, as a critique of individual failures, explain the complex functions of the work's form, especially the techniques affirming its values. Like the formalists, though, the structuralists erase the ideological critique implicit in the text's formal devices.

Last, textual deconstruction considers the pessimism ultimately inexplicable. For example, J. Hillis Miller tells us that in *Tess of the d'Urbervilles* the repetition of the images changes them, falsifying our accounts of her suffering. Miller is right: the language does falsify interpretations of her suffering, but this falsification is not the whole story that poststructuralism has to tell. In addition, it situates the fiction within four conflicted historical discourses: the theology of pastoral fiction, the liberalism of Victorian realism, the sensationalism of daily newspapers and detective mysteries, and the pessimism of modernist art. Situated in this framework, the fiction's language reworks sensationalist discourse, breaking with Victorian liberalism and pastoral theology and developing toward but not reaching twentieth-century modernism. Even though the language of the text undermines established accounts of the pessimism, interpretation remains possible. Decentered, fragmented, interpretation is New Critical, authorial, reader-response, and deconstructive, but it is viable.

Formal Reading

The formal critic appreciates Hardy's artistic devices but displaces his pessimism and his artistic context. Like Barbara Hardy and others, Albert Guerard, for example, considers Hardy a weak novelist (Guerard, 60; Hardy, 41; Mizener, 193; Forster, 94). His didactic pessimism ruins what his artistic imagination enables him to achieve; as Guerard says, "We must also recognize that his rich and human imagination accompanied a plodding and at times even commonplace intellect" (1–2). In the intellect Guerard includes everything that Hardy absorbed from Victorian conventions and institutions, especially the pessimistic theories about art, society, religion, morality, and marriage. In the imagination, Guerard includes "creative energy" and "artistic sympathy." In short, the "intellect" invokes "extrinsic" matters, while the "imagination" refers to "intrinsic" forms and devices. For instance, Guerard says that "Hardy's sympathy, which was the great source of his creative energy, proved more powerful than his clearly defined intentions; his characters did not escape him but they did escape his didactic view of them" (70). Freed from the intellect's "clearly defined intentions," the imagination's "creative energy" rescues the fiction but loses historical, social, or "extrinsic" value.

Critics like Tony Tanner and Peter Brooks successfully trace the "creative energy" praised by Guerard to the imagery and symbols unifying the fiction (Tanner, 407–31; Brooks, 233–53). In *Tess,* for example, the images of "red" associated with Tess's dress, lips, and mouth and with Alec's strawberries invoke Tess's vibrant sexuality; the red of the dead horse's gushing blood, of the returning Alec's scratched cheek, or of the murdered Alec's spreading blood suggest the indifferent powers of the universe (the "immanent will"), while the red of the wounded pheasants Tess mercifully kills or of the trapped rats and mice the farm workers relentlessly destroy characterize Tess as the sacrificial victim of a metaphysical hunt. The image of the mist that unifies the scenes of dancing, drinking farm workers, and of Tess's tragic rape suggests the brutally sensual, "pagan" nature repressed by social mores. These analyses of the images powerfully explain their import; however, even though the critic may go on to construe these images as unconscious mythopoetic or artistic symbols rather than philosophical statements or didactic assertions, this construal denudes them of "extrinsic" significance as effectively as Guerard's "creative energy" does.

Indeed, critics like Brooks or Tanner are so comfortable with the New Critical attack on "extrinsic" interpretation that they treat this attack as an inherent feature of Hardy's art. By contrast, Guerard, who initiates the formal reading of Hardy, works out this attack in detail. For example, Guerard acknowledges that Hardy organized his fiction according to the "architectural principle" and the "cultivation of unities and exactitudes" required by late-Victorian editors and critics; nonetheless, Guerard complains about Hardy's indifference to "the major concerns of form: timing, control of tone and attitude, the distribution of energy and creative impulse" (60). Moreover, to ensure that only the well-to-do sections of the Victorian reading public could afford to buy, not just borrow, novels, the giant lending libraries forced Victorian writers to produce expensive, three-volume novels; all the same, Guerard objects that Hardy wrote to "roughly predetermined length" (56). Even though Hardy did manage, as a result of his financial success, to crack the power of the lending libraries and produce an expensive but profitable one-volume novel, *Jude the Obscure,* Guerard still regrets that Hardy "did not take his craft seriously in the way that James, Proust and Gide were to take it seriously" (158) and wrote novels "that would sell easily," rather than those that were finely crafted. Furthermore, Hardy could not have become a novelist without the advice and assistance of friends like Horace Moule and editors like Sir Leslie Stephens, yet Guerard faults Hardy for conforming with their views: "The manifest prejudices of the novel-reading public, as well as the cautionary admonitions of editors" affected Hardy more than "contemporary fiction itself." In fact, even Hardy's nonconformity irritates Guerard, who wishes that the "stupidity of Hardy's critics" had not driven Hardy to take up "radical positions," such as disgust for the Victorian compromise or sympathy for rebels (30).

While Guerard explicitly dismisses the "extrinsic" influence of editors, readers, friends, publishers, and teachers, later critics assume that the language of the fiction itself excludes such influences; nonetheless, both versions of the formal approach dismiss the artistic conditions governing Hardy's production of his texts. The opposition between didactic narration and literary devices displaces the historical contexts in which Hardy produced his fiction. The uncompromising modernism in the name of which the formal critic faults Hardy had already achieved its autonomy; by contrast, Hardy still sought to free art from the compromises imposed by sociopolitical institutions. Enamored of Fielding and other British realists, he adopted their liberal strategy for achieving this independence: the story's turn of events reveals the artist's subjectivity (what Hardy calls his "impressions"), not the triumph of the divine will. In his hands, this strategy preserves the objectivity but denies the optimism of traditional fiction. Like George Eliot and D. H. Lawrence, Hardy accepted the realist's faith in objective causal forces operating invisibly but not the belief that such forces operate for the good. Chance remains a causal force, but reason, virtue, justice, and truth do not prevail.

For example, the story of Tess alludes to two popular plots, the marital quest and the marital dilemma. In the quest, a bumbling but good-hearted mother sends her naïve daughter to seek a husband among wealthy, upper-class relatives. The visit may embarrass the daughter, but ultimately rationality and propriety prevail, for her eventual marriage combines wealth, status, passion, and virtue. In *Tess* Hardy deploys this pattern but repudiates its ideological optimism. Tess's parents arrange for her to introduce herself to her wealthy, aristocratic relatives, the D'Urbervilles, but Alec immediately reveals a desire to seduce Tess, not marry her. Tess's red mouth and lips, the red strawberries Alec places in her basket and her mouth and on her hat and bosom, the red flowers she wears with her white dress—these and other sensual red images unify the fiction but undermine the older fiction's treatment of desire.

Not only are these images intensely sexual, they are disturbingly violent. The gushing blood of the punctured horse, the cut cheek of the rebuffed Alec, the spreading stain on the landlady's ceiling, and the wounds of the crippled pheasants suggest brutality, violence, and death. In Hardy's fiction, sexual desire is both positive and threatening, sensual and irrational. Nature intensifies the conflict of desire and convention, maddening, not soothing, aroused passions. *Tess*'s allusions to the ancient Greek satyrs, the images of the sun's inflaming rays, the mists uniting the sensual dances of the farm workers with the seduction of Tess, the ancient pagan rituals of the peasants, the pagan monuments like Stonehenge or road markers, the magical power of a fiddler's music to tame a raging bull invoke what traditional fiction denies—the irrational violence of compelling desire.

In the dilemma, the second kind of plot undermined by Hardy, the shrewd heroine must choose between two prospective husbands, the sensual employer intent upon her seduction and the hypocritical minister seeking her salvation. For example, in *Jane Eyre,* Jane's irreverence helps her to win the love of her employer, whose sexual desire she keeps in check quite easily, and the wildly passionate Rochester reforms himself, moved by his blindness and his mad wife's suicide. By contrast, Tess's physical beauty, not an irreverent spirit, attracts Alec, who rapes her even though she struggles to restrain his desire. Subsequently, Alec converts to Reverend Clare's religious fundamentalism but, to satisfy his desire for Tess, abandons his newfound religion. More important, just as Jane must choose between an immoral landlord and a devoted missionary, Tess must choose between the decadent Alec and the idealist Angel. While an unexpected inheritance and an independent spirit enable Jane to make a rational decision, Tess's resources do not allow her to do so.

For example, her family's discovery of its noble origins marks the further dissolution of her family's income, motivates her introduction to the seductive Alec, and stifles Angel's last-minute impulse to forgive her "trespass." Moreover, her unconcealed origins become a symbol of repression and death. Her family's only horse dies because her father celebrates their newly discovered status too much, the carriages in which Angel and Tess ride after their marriage were the d'Urbervilles' funeral coaches, and the tomb to which the sleepwalking Angel carries Tess is an ancient d'Urberville monument. Last, in traditional fiction, the heroine's proximity to nature is a resource: not only does it give her self-control but it makes her independent. In Hardy's fiction, nature only mirrors the heroine's feelings; at

Talbothay's, for example, the "juicy grass," "thistle milk," "crackling snails," and "slug slime" echo her rekindled passions, while at Flintcomb-Ashe, the hard earth, freezing winter wind, and strange Arctic birds confirm her oppressed, disillusioned state of mind. Despite Tess's loyalty to Angel, Alec can impose his will on her because nature does not grant her a stoic independence.

In short, to combat the older plot's ideological commitments, Hardy invokes these two plot forms, the marital quest and the marital choice, but chooses images and symbols that undermine the older faith in wealth, status, origins, nature, morality, and reason. While the New Critics appreciate the aesthetic value of his images and symbols, the New Critics neglect this ideological critique because they consider the narrator's pessimism only the didactic imposition of "extrinsic" interests.

An Authorial Reading

Authorial humanists acknowledge the ideological import of Hardy's pessimism but not the significance of his artistic productivity. In Hardy's later fiction, the humanists find a sensitive grasp of modern anomie and alienation. Like James Joyce and William Faulkner, Hardy depicts the deleterious impact of modern industrial life, which ruins traditional social ties and undermines our political and religious beliefs. Hardy's uneasy pessimism characterizes modern life. At that same time, however, the humanists neglect the artistic labor enabling Hardy to produce the pessimistic fiction. Despite their grasp of the pessimism's historical import, they overlook its artistic roots.

Irving Howe's account of *Tess of the d'Urbervilles* and *Jude the Obscure* illustrates this approach to the fiction. Howe considers these novels modern because they depict the anomie and alienation characteristic of Joyce's *Ulysses* and Woolf's *Mrs. Dalloway*. As Howe points out, such novels emphasize a character's inner psychological tensions and denigrate the external dramatic development of the typical Victorian plot (144–45). Since Hardy's plots are Victorian, Howe is unhappy with them, and he voices a common feeling—the plots have too much improbable metaphysical weight; too many bad things happen in too short a time. For instance, he says that the plot of *Tess* "seems in isolation a paltry thing, a mere scraping together of bits and pieces from popular melodrama: a pure girl betrayed, a woman's secret to be told or hidden, a piling on of woes that must strain the resources of ordinary credence" (114).

While Howe grasps the modernist dimension of Hardy's pessimism, this appeal to "ordinary credence" erases the artistic context of *Tess,* for it divides the alienation and other modern effects from the ill-wrought plot. What Howe assumes is that Hardy's work on the Victorian plot has nothing to do with the effects of anomie and alienation, that classifying the works as modern on the basis of those effects allows one to ignore the plot and to dismiss its Victorian attitudes. However, while the conventional Victorian plot bonds the reader and society, Hardy's plot destroys this bond and generates alienation and anomie. For example, in the plots of Fielding and Dickens characters who possess innate virtue, industry, and ability usually overcome the debilitating impact of poverty and orphanhood and acquire the social position to which their virtues entitle them. This result justifies the sense of belonging and confidence of a Tom Jones or a David Copperfield and confirms the reader's identification with his community. In *Tess* and *Jude,* however, the opposite is the result: society undermines virtuous and able protagonists, whose collapse alienates the reader and justifies anomie, rather than community. George Eliot, who assumes that the plot reveals the community's benevolent but invisible influence on the characters, fosters that positive bonding that Hardy must dissolve if he is to produce the modern sense of alienation. Hardy modeled his first novels on Eliot's fiction, as George Meredith and other editors advised him to, but when critics attributed *Far from the Madding Crowd* to her, an angry Hardy grew critical of her work (Florence Hardy, 98). *Tess* and *Jude* show his ruptures with Eliot. For example, *Adam Bede* parallels the plot structure of *Tess,* for the relationship of the impoverished Tess and her seducer, Alec d'Urberville, the wealthy owner of a large farm and estate, approximates the relationship of the poor Hetty and her seducer, Squire Donnithorne, also a rich landowner. However, while the squire arrives in time to save Hetty from hanging, Hardy's narrator regrets that no one can save Tess from rape or hanging. Moreover, for abandoning her unwanted baby the community punishes Hetty, whose suffering is severe and just; by contrast, the suffering and execution of Tess, who is a virtuous and able woman, is unjust. That is to say, the fate of Hetty illustrates the action of a just community and confirms the bond of reader and society, but the fate of Tess represents the opposite effect, the disintegration of that bond.

The plots of *Jude* and of Eliot's *Middlemarch* have an equally conflicted relationship. In *Jude,* Arabella and her friends and family trap Jude into a destructive marriage; the community and the clergy harass the unmarried Jude and Sue; the loss of status, income, and employment compel Phillotson to undertake a cruel remarriage to Sue—these incidents establish the community's malevolent character. In *Middlemarch* the community initially acquires a similar character: it almost prevents the marriage of Dorothea and Ladislaw, and it destroys the theoretical ambitions of Lydgate the doctor. Yet Dorothea does manage to run off with Ladislaw, and Lydgate's smug personality, aristocratic taste, and hypocritical friends do justify his loss somewhat. By contrast, the suffering of Jude and Sue has no such justification: the unwarranted death of Little Father Time and of Sue's children, Sue's destruction of her intellect and personality, and Jude's fighting with Arabella and resorting to alcoholic oblivion show what Hardy calls life's "horrors," nothing more. In short, filled with improbable events, the fiction of both Eliot and Hardy illustrates the Victorian melodrama that Howe deplores; however, it is by inverting the import of Eliot's optimistic melodrama that Hardy produces the alienation that Howe praises.

Of course, the humanist might grant that the plot alienates the reader from society but still claim that it does a bad job. This complaint is just but unfair, for it neglects Hardy's compromises with his editors and publishers. Since a number of editors rejected *Tess* on moral grounds, Hardy had to eliminate "imprudent" scenes, especially those describing the passion of Tess and Alec. With a black mustache, a big cigar, and a fast buggy, Alec becomes more of a melodramatic villain than the high-living playboy that Hardy initially created. Faced with similar complaints about *Jude,* Hardy changes Little Father Time into the offspring of the married Arabella, rather than the unmarried Sue, and adds a tragic motif tying together the house of Atreus and the family of the Fawleys. Because of these compromises, the novels generate a sentimental compassion and benevolent despair inseparable from modern alienation. Such feelings "ruin" the fiction if one judges it abstractly, not contextually, if one considers only its intentional norm, not its artistic conditions.

Reader-Response, Phenomenological, and Structuralist Readings

Reader-response, phenomenological, and structuralist critics do not dismiss Hardy's "didactic" pessimism or assimilate it to modernist fiction. They open the text to the reader, who produces the pessimism, imbuing it with a conservative import. It does not attack social institutions or lecture the reader; it criticizes the shortcomings of rebellious, immature characters. However, this account of the reader's activity abstracts the reader from his or her sociohistorical context.

Thomas Hardy: Distance and Desire by J. Hillis Miller represents a phenomenological version of this stance. On the whole, Miller's account of the fiction remains objective; however, to explain the pessimism, he "brackets" the objective, naturalist standpoint of the practical man. Miller says that as a youth Hardy must have thought himself abandoned and the world unsatisfactory, for in his maturity he withdraws from the world, giving up the possibility of committed action. The fiction reflects this withdrawal: not only do the characters watch themselves watching things but the narrator poses as a dead man telling his story as though it took place long, long ago. Moreover, this pose generates what Miller calls a "complex superimposition of perspectives" that the reader grasps only if he pauses to reflect upon the "apparently . . . realistic narrative" (3–7, 56–58). Why does the reader pause to reflect if the narrative is realistic? Is it not that, like a phenomenological skeptic, Miller doubts the objectivity of realistic narrative? Clearly, the reader constructs a "complex superimposition of perspectives" because Miller challenges the objectivity of the authorial text. It is Miller's skepticism, not the narrative, that frees the reader to reflect upon these "perspectives."

In *Working with Structuralism,* David Lodge also construes the narrators of Hardy's fiction as uninvolved observers, but Lodge considers this form of narration a cinematic technique shared by modern film and classic realism. Metonymically digressing from "the plot to the characters and from the characters to the setting in time and

---

The Politics of Literary Theory

space," the realist author employs a visual, cinematic language that "suppresses overt reference to the conventions employed" (95–96). Lodge rightly considers Hardy's use of this language his greatest achievement. However, insofar as Lodge insists that "Hardy's ability to make concrete the relationship between character and environment," rather than his storytelling, his insight, his philosophic wisdom, or his "melodramatic" plots and characters, "makes him such a powerful novelist" (97), Lodge's account of Hardy's art, like the formal and authorial accounts, erases Hardy's conditions of production and reception. Indeed, in the traditional manner, Lodge expects literary form to reinforce predetermined values. For example, in *The Return of the Native* Hardy's depicting "a little speck of human life in a vast expanse of nature" expresses the "vulnerability of the individual human life" (99). In a similar way, Lodge insightfully argues that in *Jude* the "complex cross-referencing of symmetrical incidents creates a tragic sense of an inescapable destiny" (109). However, he takes this "profound pessimism" to comment upon the weakness of the characters, not the conditions of society. Only the "margins" of the novels portray the socioeconomic forces working against Jude and Sue or the limitations of the marriage institution. To dismiss such concerns as marginal is, however, to deny the ideological import of Hardy's pessimism.

Dale Kramer's *The Forms of Tragedy* represents a more consistently skeptical, reader-oriented account of Hardy's pessimism. Kramer assumes, as Wolfgang Iser also does, that readers produce redemptive meanings and improve their lives; thus, in Hardy's profoundly pessimistic fiction Kramer discovers a conservative optimism representing this reformist potential. Kramer argues that the narrator, like the characters, expresses just another point of view, not an objective or a didactic authorial voice. The narrator describes the point of view of the characters or distances himself so much that his views do not matter. Moreover, the resulting discrepancies in perspectives and values free the reader to judge the characters for himself. In Iserian terms, the gaps between the narrator's and the characters' perspectives do not express the intention of the author; rather, the gaps stimulate the reader's interpretive activity. When the narrator complains about the indifference of the universe, the quagmires of sexuality, and the degradations of married life, the formalists assume that these complaints express the despair of a didactic author;

by contrast, like Lodge, Kramer feels that the narrator describes the characters' outlooks or says little that matters (138–43). The characters, not the narrator, are pessimistic.

As the author's voice, the narrator's pessimism represents negative social criticism; as an account of the characters, however, the pessimism becomes conservative exposés of their private failures. For example, when Jude discovers that by himself he cannot easily master Latin and Greek, the authorial narrator complains about nature's indifference to human desires, but Kramer's narrator points out Jude's self-indulgent despair (146). Similarly, when the liaison of Jude and Sue collapses, the authorial narrator satirizes the intolerance of the clergy, the landlords, the schoolmaster, and the townspeople, but Kramer's narrator emphasizes the emotional resources provided by the countryside but neglected by Jude and Sue (158). In short, instead of sensitive personalities rebelling hopelessly against a conventional, cruel, and unjust society, the characters are independent, enterprising individuals whose inability to exploit all their resources brings on their doom. Society is not to blame; Jude and Sue defeat themselves. Their failure is tragic, but it is their own fault. Despite their tragedy optimism prevails because in Kramer's view stronger, smarter characters could have done well easily enough.

While the formalists condemn the novels for the narrator's liberal attacks on the church, the schools, the family, and the state, Kramer praises them for their conservative critiques of individual immaturity and weakness. In addition, he elevates social conventions above criticism or change, rendering them unimpeachable. The narrator's social criticisms represent the characters' immaturity, not legitimate protest, because convention is eternal, rational, and just. For example, when the narrator of *Jude* satirizes the religious hypocrisy of Farmer Troutham, Kramer considers the satire an irrational defiance of agriculture. When the narrator deplores the sexual oppression of Sue's fellow students, Kramer sees only an immature resentment of motherhood's burdens. Repulsing critics and destroying rebels, conventions acquire an ahistorical permanence.

Kramer does not attribute his conservative interpretation to this ahistorical view of convention; rather, he shows that the indeterminant, Iserian text admits both his conservative and the traditional liberal views. Nonetheless, its ability to do so poses a dilemma: why is the text both conservative and liberal? both descriptive and didactic? We intuitively assume, in other words, that the two views are not compatible, but this assumption may show the historical limits of our reactions, rather than the contradictory character of the text. The modern reader may simply feel the conflict of the two more sharply than the Victorian reader did.

I grant that in the 1860s, when Hardy felt the inspiring voice of John Stuart Mill, the Victorian reader would have sensed a sharp conflict between the conservative and the liberal attitudes expressed by the novels. At that time, the progressive liberal movement, which sought political, intellectual, and sexual equality, fought against conservative restrictions on family life, political activity, and sexual choice. In the 1880s, however, the liberals and the conservatives formed an alliance; in particular, moved by an "evangelical revival," English feminists, who had supported liberal ideas of equality, adopted conservative restrictions on sexual "immorality" and "license." As Jeffrey Weeks says, the feminists and the conservatives found that they both hated the Victorian double standard, and the feminists, to form an effective alliance, accepted a conservative sexual ethics (86–88).

Robert Gittings, Hardy's biographer, points out that Tryphena Sparks, who is definitely one of Hardy's cousins and may well be one of his mysterious women as well, introduced Hardy to the nonconformist feminism of the 1860s. By contrast, the sexually conservative Florence Henneker, whose writing Hardy edited, may have initiated him into the conformist feminism of the 1890s (*Young,* 165–81; *Older,* 104–10).

Not only did Hardy know the changing attitudes of the feminists, his novels comment on their changes. For example at first Sue Fawley defends a nonconformist, sensual love and personal chastity, but she subsequently adopts a loveless, asexual family code. Similarly, Jude believes at first that his unsuccessful marriage to Arabella blackens any new relationships with women. Under Sue's tutelage, though, he adopts a more liberal view. Similarly, Tess fears that sinful, unnatural sexual activity dooms unmarried mothers to a life of suffering. Influenced by Angel Clare, however, Tess comes to accept liberal views of sex, religion, and men. The accidental meeting of Tess and Alec emphasizes this change: while the repentant Alec has momentarily adopted fundamentalist religious views, the liberated Tess has seriously taken up Angel's agnosticism. In *Jude* also, the characters' development crisscrosses: while Jude grows staunchly fundamentalist, Sue gets ardently liberal and agnostic, but when Sue turns conservative, Jude stubbornly defends his liberal agnosticism.

In other words, the novels are Bildungsromans whose contrasting characters emphasize their intellectual growth; however, Hardy's characters never discover any positive insight indicating personal maturity or social progress. Instead, they find themselves in an untenable condition: social conventions do not allow them the roles their enlightenment requires. Despite Tess's intellectual growth, her "circumstances"—the "bad" reputation, the low-paying jobs, the family's poverty—leave her little choice but to become what Alec urges her to be—his mistress. Even though Sue and Jude maintain a loving, spontaneous relationship, the towns, the churches, the landlords, and the schools oppose it, allowing them only loveless, coercive ties with the coarse Arabella and the repulsive Phillotson.

When Little Father Time hangs his brothers, his sisters, and himself, he gives the social intolerance tormenting Sue and Jude a palpable form. Indeed, Sue and Jude turn this intolerance on themselves, tormenting and maddening each other. Not only does Sue marry Phillotson even though he disgusts her, she destroys the sparkling intellect that distinguished her. Similarly Jude remarries the vulgar Arabella and drowns his intellectual impulses in alcohol. As Kramer argues, these endings are tragic, but the tragedy shows the limitations that social convention imposes on the characters' lives, not the fruitlessness of immature rebels. Just as we modern readers assume instinctively that conservative and liberal views oppose each other, so too do we take for granted the conventions allowing women to occupy independent professional roles and to choose their own lifestyles. Kramer successfully opens the text to the reader's activity but, to preserve the Iserian commitment to individual reform and improvement, he interprets the pessimism as the characters' immaturity and weakness and ignores the historical differences between modern and Victorian readers.

A Deconstructive Reading

Deconstructive critics also open the text to the reader's activity, but they deny that the reader can produce satisfactory interpretations.

For example, in *Fiction and Repetition,* Miller argues that the tragic yet undeserved suffering of Tess makes the reader want to know why she suffers while the figural language of the text keeps the reader from figuring out the reasons why she suffers. In the formal manner, Miller takes red things, the sun, copulation, writing, and other chains of imagery and patterns of repetition to express Hardy's pessimistic faith in the immanent will, but he argues that these chains repeat with a difference, undermining the explanatory power of established interpretations. In the Iserian manner, he expects the reader to interpret these chains and patterns, but the resulting interpretation can never reach "a sovereign principle of explanation" because the novel justifies what he considers "multiple incompatible explanations of what happens to Tess. They cannot all be true, and yet they are all there in the words of the novel" (126–27). Miller rightly emphasizes the interpretive activity of the reader, but he mistakenly assumes that the novel itself refutes established explanations of Tess's suffering and hence of Hardy's pessimism. If we situate the novel's language in its historical context, we may not provide a "sovereign principle of explanation," but we can suggest that Hardy's productive activity, not the novel itself, undermines established interpretations of his pessimism. It emerges from but does not reduce to the conflictual discourses moving Hardy to rupture with the ironic, totalizing style of Fielding and Eliot and to anticipate the neutral but alienating style of Faulkner and Joyce. Influenced by newspapers and mystery novels, the fiction's language, like the images, symbols, conventions, and plot, shows that Hardy undermines traditional liberal and theological optimism and approximates modernism's isolating, pessimistic effects.

Hardy's pessimism emerges from his artistic labor and not from his parents, who taught him to be religious. In fact, as a young man he studied religious treatises, attending Bible classes and reading the Bible every week (Gittings, *Young Hardy,* 15–45). *Far from the Madding Crowd* and his other early novels are distinctly optimistic: in them, ancient rituals bind characters into a just community working out the fate each one deserves. The stoic strength, theological commitment, and social responsibility of characters like Gabriel Oak justify their good fortune and vindicate society and God.

Influenced by Horace Moule, who wrote several positive reviews of *Under the Greenwood Tree* and *A Pair of Blue Eyes* and published them in the liberal *Saturday Review,* and by Sir Leslie Stephens, who edited the equally liberal but more powerful *Cornhill Magazine* and who encouraged Hardy to write *Far from the Madding Crowd,* his most successful early novel (*Young Hardy,* 244), Hardy gave up his religious faith. He became instead an enthusiastic liberal and worked into his fiction the discourse of John Stuart Mill, the *Saturday Review,* and *Cornhill Magazine.* In *The Mayor of Casterbridge,* for example, the success of Farfrae's innovative methods and impersonal policies justifies the liberal faith in enlightened self-interest and rational calculation, while Elizabeth-Jane's "minute forms of satisfaction" satirize it.

In his later fiction, however, Hardy does not affirm traditional Victorian religion or this liberal optimism. Human action comes to seem impulsive, blind, and unprincipled, guided by an unconscious will, not a divine vision or a rational spirit. Scholars assume that his reading the philosophy of Arthur Schopenhauer, not his personal development, made him a pessimist (Miller, *Distance,* 16–17). However, the "Immanent Will" and the other terms coined by Schopenhauer figure prominently only in Hardy's last work, *The Dynasts,* published more than twenty years after *Tess* and *Jude.* In fact, in a letter to Helen Garwood, whose doctoral dissertation (1911) examined Schopenhauer's influence on him, he insisted that he developed a pessimistic view of life himself (Pinion, 106). The notes that Hardy and his wife took during the 1880s and 1890s support Hardy's insistence on his personal, home-grown pessimism, for they refer mainly to his youthful interests—Mill, Huxley, and Darwin. Moreover, Jerome Buckley points out that among late-Victorian intellectuals, "a revolt from liberal thought helped perhaps to create an audience for Schopenhauer's pessimistic philosophy" (202–3).

Critics have often noted that the mature Hardy breaks with his youthful religious faith but not that, like other late Victorian intellectuals, he rebels against liberal thought as well. While parents, friends, editors, and philosophers influence this rebellion, the growing success of sensationalist discourse accounts for it most fully. In particular, affected by the new murder mysteries and the national daily papers, Hardy displaces the ironic, omniscient totalities of Henry Fielding and George Eliot and prefigures the detached, alienating perspectives of James Joyce and William Faulkner. Hardy overturns the synthesizing moral ironies that in the older fiction bind the

---

reader into a community and moves toward the "neutral" description and sensationalist action that in modernist art alienates the reader, circumscribing a character's point of view and distancing the reader from it.

The ironic style of Fielding and Eliot assimilates the reader into the social totality; this style reveals to her the social contexts and norms that the characters violate, thereby elevating her to a superior position and showing her the rationality and justice of social action. By contrast, Hardy's pastoral fiction represents a social fragment, not the whole, and does not justify the social order in this ironic way. His characters come from rural settings, not from all corners of society. Corrupt aristocrats, self-serving lawyers, penny-pinching innkeepers, amorous maids, illiberal publishers, or decadent gentlemen find no place in his fiction except as the representatives of unhealthy urban life. His fiction concentrates on the rural point of view—furze cutters, shepherds, stonemasons, and other offspring of mythical Wessex. In Hardy's time, the success of social science, which studies "human nature" in a systematic way, diminishes the prestige acquired by the older "knowledge" of human nature. While Hume and the empiricists of Fielding's era analyze complex terms, John Stuart Mill, Herbert Spencer, and August Comte, esteemed by Hardy, produce a positive science of social organizations. In the nineteeth century, the laws of social science, not the recognition of our common human foibles, bring mankind together. The factual analysis of concrete contexts, not the ironic analysis of ethical terms or diverse perspectives, represents the late Victorian mode of empiricist thought. Popular murder mysteries, which become a distinct genre in the 1860s and 1870s, reflect this shift from ironic analysis to positive fact. The detective is factual and legal, not moral or liberal. Sherlock Holmes, whom Arthur Conan Doyle first presents to the public in 1891, does not criticize social convention or expose moral hypocrisy; he seeks violations of written law, evidence of illegal doings. The scientist and the detective share certain attitudes—an inductive approach, a causal analysis, a factual world.

Of course, Hardy does not write detective fiction or scientific treatises. However, in rejecting *The Poor Man and the Lady,* Hardy's first novel, George Meredith and other editors advised him to imitate the murder mysteries of the successful Wilkie Collins, and Hardy does so in *Desperate Remedies.* The selling of wives like Susan, the hanging of women like Tess, the murder and suicide of children such as Father Time—these are the kinds of events depicted by the sensationalist daily press, which did not gain a national readership until the 1890s. Moreover, these events are the kind that Hardy wrote into his fiction. The modernist pessimism distinguishing his later work is already implicit in the newspapers' depiction of arbitrary, accidental hangings, suicides, rapes, and murders.

The detective stories of Collins and the treatises of Huxley and Darwin, two of Hardy's favorite scientists, also encouraged him to adopt the neutral, distant tone that characterizes modernism. The scientific language of *The Mayor of Casterbridge* illustrates this uninvolved attitude. Henchard's fall from prosperity acquires "velocity" (215); Henchard's sale of Susan represents his "tampering with social law" (312); his flight from Casterbridge shows a "centrifugal tendency imparted by the weariness of the world" and "counteracted by the centripetal influence of his love for his stepdaughter" (323); his decline is a fall to a "lower stage of existence" (323); and curiosity is irrelevant in "concatenations of phenomena wherein each is known to have its accounting cause" (202). "Velocity," "social law," "centrifugal" and "centripetal tendency," "lower stage of existence," "concatenations of phenomena," and "accounting cause" are scientific terms suggesting that the narrator, who describes the causes of evil but does not judge it, examines it instead in a detached way. In *Jude the Obscure* also, the narrator describes Jude's fundamentalist religious beliefs in equally neutral tones: Jude "did not at that time see that medievalism was as dead as a fern-leaf in a lump of coal." Although the death of religion is a highly charged subject, the simile "fern-leaf in a lump of coal" treats this death as more a question of biological fact than of personal despair.

In his early fiction, when Hardy is trying to establish a reputation and readership, the lurid sensationalism and the scientific neutrality do not seriously disturb the optimism of liberal and theological discourses. Unbalanced by Bathsheba's valentine, the emotional Boldwood murders Sergeant Troy, but the murder has a providential outcome: the virtuous Gabriel Oak can marry the chastened Bathsheba. However, once Hardy acquires both reputation and readers, he can more easily afford to take risks: showing his disillusion with the dominant liberal and theological discourses, he gives sensationalism a philosophical voice that ultimately acquires Schopenhauerian tones. According to this philosophy, violence and brutality have little purpose; human life, minor importance; and moral values, insignificant power (see Hughes, 15–17, 166–91). In his terms, chance, "hap," the "immanent will," accident, and injustice not only undermine traditional religious and liberal beliefs but they articulate the "ache of modernism," a pointless, impulsive restlessness undermining the stoic fortitude espoused by traditional pastoral fiction.

Not only does the sensationalist discourse express modernist pessimism, it disrupts the ironic, totalizing style of conventional Victorian realism. The neutral, detached language of Hardy's fiction opposes the involved, judgmental language of Fielding and Eliot; Hardy describes, while they praise or condemn. Like them, Hardy criticizes vulgar interests and narrow designs. Unlike them, he does not affirm traditional values—charity, compassion, and community. He distances the reader, his severe neutrality alienating her. The neutral description elevates sensationalist discourse, whose melodrama kept it a minor genre, into the material of "honest" art; at the same time, such description disrupts the reader's faith in traditional social and theological values.

Thus, unlike the narrators of previous fiction, Hardy's narrators depict "immoral" characters, including Tess, who has a child out of wedlock and lives with but does not marry her debaucher Alec, and Sue and Jude, who live together and raise children but do not marry. The neutral tone of the narrators enables them to depict such characters without judging them, to seek a causal explanation of the sensational acts rather than an ethical analysis of the personalities. The narration means to explain why Tess murders her lover Alec and hangs or why Jude's son kills himself and his brothers and sisters but not to evaluate these actions. Like a detective story, the fiction only tries to account for such actions.

Unlike the detective story, though, the fiction never does explain them. The narrative may suggest causes for such actions, but a detective or narrator does not give us the definitive account of the crime. Instead, the fiction depicts what modern critics call a point of view, whose legitimacy or propriety is not itself in question. Hardy's narratives anticipate the modernist depiction of brutal, antisocial characters like Faulkner's Joe Christmas, whose life and outlook "account" for Anne Burden's sensational murder even though Faulkner does not identify motives, analyze clues, or explain crimes.

In this way, the detached, neutral narration is also involved and committed: instead of affirming traditional values in an ironic way, its modernist stance undermines conventional discourses by estranging them, by revealing their absurdity. As a "neutral" scientist, Hardy explains why his characters murder each other, why Tess hangs and Jude drinks. As an involved artist, however, he describes the sensational events and situations disrupting the reader's social and theological values, exploding her faith in rational activity and communal solidarity.

Conclusion

Hardy does ultimately acquire what critics attribute to him—Schopenhauer's existential pessimism. However, the modernist vision does not possess him in one sudden thunderclap. He develops it gradually, through the discourses that his fiction works and reworks. I have outlined this development in order to illustrate a poststructuralist approach that does not preclude interpretation. The language of Hardy's text may undermine established interpretations, yet situated within the opposed liberal, religious, sensational, and existential discourses informing Hardy's conditions of production, the language of the text acquires historical significance. My exploration of Hardy's development suggests that the text's overturning established readings of it does not render interpretation itself impossible. Hardy's narratives reveal the "facts"—vain illusion, social intolerance, unjust privilege, repressed desire, accidental violence, bloody death—which conventional, Victorian fiction failed to see but modernist narrative has made commonplace; still, this revelation does not put an end to our interpretive efforts. While reworked sensationalism, rather than ironic analysis, distances the reader from conventional, Victorian discourse and prefigures the art of the great modernists, the reader's alienated state does not stop interpretation. Rather, the interpretive strategies of the dominant methods remain viable. Our situating established interpretations of Hardy's fiction in its discursive context preserves the New Critical, humanist, reader-response, phenomenological, structuralist, and deconstructive accounts of the fiction even though the text, the author, the reader, and the language no longer represent autonomous, apolitical categories transcending history. This institutional approach reveals the ideological commitments and political ideals that New Critical, humanist, reader-response, structuralist, and deconstructive readings invoke but do not acknowledge. Indeed, this approach uncovers the "popular" discourses that these readings presuppose but do not recognize.

Although this eclectic approach may make institutional criticism seem more liberal than radical, the exposé and critique of the politics implicit in established approaches is a radical act. Such an approach acknowledges, as the liberal also does, that many methods can interpret a text, that interpretive communities, not transcendent entities, govern reading. Even Marxist criticism enters into complicity with these established communities. Nonetheless, this approach can effectively disrupt the conventional discourses that the literary institution perpetuates. As the Marxists have discovered, institutional discourses affirm the rituals and conventions of Western capitalism, thereby justifying and even glorifying unjust, degrading divisions between classes, races, and sexes. A critique of the institution's unacknowledged politics can undermine the literary reproduction of these divisions.

Abrams, M. H. "The Deconstructive Angel." *Critical Inquiry* 3 (Spring 1977): 425–38.

———. *The Mirror and the Lamp: Romantic Theory and the Critical Tradition.* New York: Oxford University Press, 1953.

Adams, Hazard. "The Dizziness of Freedom or, Why I Read William Blake." *College English* 48, no. 5 (September 1986): 431–43.

Adorno, Theodor W. *Against Epistemology: A Metacritique.* Translated by Willis Domingo. Cambridge, Mass.: MIT Press, 1985.

———. "Commitment." In *The Essential Frankfurt School Reader,* edited by Andrew Arato and others, and introduced by Paul Piccone, 300–318. New York: Continuum, 1985.

———. *The Jargon of Authenticity.* Translated by Knut Tarnowski and Frederic Will. Evanston, Ill.: Northwestern Univerity Press, 1973.

———. "On the Logic of the Social Sciences." In *The Positivist Dispute in German Sociology,* edited by Theodor Adorno and others. London: Gower, 1976.

———. "Subject and Object." In *The Essential Frankfurt School Reader,* edited by Andrew Arato and others, and introduced by Paul Piccone, 497–511. New York: Continuum, 1985.

Adorno, Theodor W., and Max Horkheimer. *Dialectic of Enlightenment.* Translated by John Cumming. New York: Continuum, 1972.

Alcorn, Marshall W., and Mark Bracher. "Literature, Psychoanalysis, and the Re-Formation of the Self: A New Direction for Reader-Response Theory." *PMLA* 100 (May 1985): 342–54.

Althusser, Louis. *Essays in Self-Criticism.* London: New Left Books, 1976.

————. *Lenin and Philosophy*. Translated by Ben Brewster. London: Monthly Review Press, 1971.

————. *Pour Marx*. 1965. Reprint. Paris: François Maspero, 1977.

Althusser, Louis, and Etienne Balibar. *Reading Capital*. Translated by Ben Brewster. London: New Left Books, 1970.

Altieri, Charles. "The Hermeneutics of Literary Indeterminacy: A Dissent from the New Orthodoxy." *NLH* 10, no. 1 (Autumn 1978): 71–100.

Anderson, Perry. "The Antinomies of Antonio Gramsci." *New Left Review* 100 (November 1976–January 1977): 5–78.

————. *Arguments Within English Marxism*. London: Verso Editions, 1980.

————. *Considerations on Western Marxism*. London: New Left Books, 1976.

————. *In the Tracks of Historical Materialism*. London: Verso Editions, 1983.

Ayer, A. J. *Language, Truth and Logic*. New York: Dover, 1936.

Baker, Houston A., Jr. *Blues, Ideology, and Afro-American Literature: A Vernacular Theory*. Chicago: University of Chicago Press, 1984.

Baldick, Chris. *The Social Mission of English Criticism 1848– 1932*. Oxford: Clarendon Press, 1983.

Balibar, Renée. *Les français fictifs: le rapport des styles littéraires au Français national*. Paris: Librarie Hachette, 1974.

Barthes, Roland. "Introduction to the Structural Analysis of Narrative." *Image-Music-Text*. Edited and translated by Stephen Heath, 79–124. New York: Hill and Wang, 1977.

————. *Mythologies*. Translated by Annette Lavers. New York: Hill and Wang, 1972.

————. *The Pleasure of the Text*. Translated by Richard Miller. New York: Hill and Wang, 1975.

————. "Science versus Literature." In *Introduction to Structuralism,* edited by Michael Lane, 410–16. New York: Basic Books, Inc., 1970.

————. *S/Z*. Translated by Richard Miller. New York: Hill and Wang, 1974.

————. *Writing Degree Zero*. Translated by Jonathan Cape. Boston: Beacon Press, 1967.

Batsleer, Janet, and others, eds. *Rewriting English: Cultural Politics of Gender and Class*. London: Methuen, 1985.

Belsey, Catherine. "Constructing the subject: deconstructing the Text." In *Feminist Criticism and Social Change,* edited by Judith Lowder Newton and Deborah Rosenfelt, 45–63. New York: Methuen, 1985.

————. *Critical Practice*. London: Methuen, 1980.

Bennett, Tony. *Formalism and Marxism*. London: Methuen, 1979.

————. "Marxism and Popular Fiction." *Literature and History* 7, no. 2 (Autumn 1981): 149–64.

————. "Texts in History: The Determinations of Readings and Their Texts." *Journal of the MMLA* 18, no. 1 (Fall 1985): 1–16.

————. "Texts, Readers, Reading Formations." *Bulletin of the Midwest Modern Language Association* 16, no. 1 (Spring 1983): 3–17.

Bennett, Tony, and Janet Woollacott. *Bond and Beyond: The Political Career of a Hero.* New York: Methuen, 1987.

Bernstein, J. M. *The Philosophy of the Novel: Lukács, Marxism, and the Dialectics of Form.* Minneapolis: University of Minnesota Press, 1984.

Berthoud, J. A. "Narrative and Ideology: A Critique of Fredric Jameson's *The Political Unconscious." In Narrative: From Malory to Motion Pictures,* edited by Jeremy Hawthorn. London: Edward Arnold Ltd., 1985.

Bledstein, Burton J. *The Culture of Professionalism: The Middle Class and the Development of Higher Education in America.* New York: W. W. Norton and Co., Inc., 1976.

Bleich, David. "Gender Interests in Reading and Language." In *Gender and Reading: Essays on Readers, Texts, and Contexts,* edited by Elizabeth A. Flynn and Patrocinio Schweickart. Baltimore: Johns Hopkins University Press, 1986.

————. "Intersubjective Reading." *NLH* 17, no. 3 (Spring 1986): 401–22.

————. *Subjective Criticism.* Baltimore: Johns Hopkins University Press, 1981.

Booth, Wayne. *The Rhetoric of Fiction.* Chicago: University of Chicago Press, 1961.

Bové, Paul. *Intellectuals in Power: A Genealogy of Critical Humanism.* New York: Columbia University Press, 1986.

Brenkman, John. "Theses on Cultural Marxism." *Social Text* 7 (1983): 19–33.

Brooks, Cleanth. *Modern Poetry and the Tradition.* 1939. Reprint. New York: Oxford University Press, 1965.

————. *The Well-Wrought Urn.* New York: Harcourt, Brace, & World, 1947.

Brooks, Cleanth, and William K. Wimsatt, Jr. *Literary Criticism: A Short History.* New York: Vintage 1957.

Brooks, Peter. *Thomas Hardy: The Poetic Structure.* Ithaca, N.Y.: Cornell University Press, 1971.

Buckley, Jerome. *The Victorian Temper.* New York: Random House, 1964.

Cain, William E. *The Crisis in Criticism: Theory, Literature, and Reform in English Studies.* Baltimore: Johns Hopkins University Press, 1984.

————. "English in America Reconsidered: Theory, Criticism, Marxism, and Social Change." In *Criticism in the University,* edited by Gerald Graff and Reginald Gibbons. Evanston: Northwestern University Press, 1985.

―――. "The Institutionalization of the New Criticism." *MLN* 97 (1983): 1100–1120.

Caute, David. *The Illusion: An Essay on Politics, Theatre and the Novel.* London: Andre Deutsch, 1971.

Christian, Barbara. "The Race for Theory." *Cultural Critique* 6 (Spring 1987): 51–64.

Cohen, Ralph. "History and Genre." *NLH* 17, no. 2 (Winter 1986): 203–18.

Cohen, Stephen F. *Rethinking the Soviet Experience: Politics and History since 1917.* New York: Oxford University Press, 1985.

Crane, R. S. *The Languages of Criticism and the Structure of Poetry.* Toronto: University of Toronto Press, 1953.

Culler, Jonathan. "Criticism and Institutions: The American University." In *Post-structuralism and the Question of History,* edited by Derek Attridge and others. Cambridge: Cambridge University Press, 1987.

―――. *On Deconstruction: Theory and Criticism after Structuralism.* Ithaca, N.Y.: Cornell University Press, 1982.

―――. *The Pursuit of Signs: Semiotics, Literature, Deconstruction.* Ithaca, N.Y.: Cornell University Press, 1981.

―――. *Roland Barthes.* New York: Oxford University Press, 1983.

―――. *Structuralist Poetics: Structuralism, Linguistics and the Study of Literature.* Ithaca, N.Y.: Cornell University Press, 1975.

Davis, Walter A. "The Fisher King: *Wille zur Macht* in Baltimore." *Critical Inquiry* 10 (June 1984): 668–94.

DeLaura, David J. "The Ache of Modernism in Hardy's Later Novels." *ELH* 34 (1967): 380–99.

de Man, Paul. *Allegories of Reading.* New Haven: Yale University Press, 1979.

―――. *Blindness and Insight: Essays in the Rhetoric of Contemporary Criticism.* New York: Oxford University Press, 1971.

―――. "Shelley Disfigured." In *Deconstruction and Criticism,* edited by Geoffrey Hartman, 39–74. New York: Seabury Press, 1979.

Demetz, Peter. *Marx, Engels, and the Poets.* Chicago: University of Chicago Press, 1967.

Derrida, Jacques. *Dissemination.* Translated and introduced by Barbara Johnson. Chicago: University of Chicago Press, 1981.

―――. *Of Grammatology.* Translated by Gayatri Chakravorty Spivak. Baltimore: Johns Hopkins University Press, 1976.

―――. *Marges de la philosophie.* Paris: Les Editions de Minuit, 1972.

―――. *Otobiographies: L'enseignement de Nietzsche et la politique du nom propre.* Paris: Éditions Galilèe, 1984.

―――. *Positions.* Translated by Alan Bass. Chicago: University of Chicago Press, 1981.

————. *Speech and Phenomena.* Evanston: Northwestern University Press, 1973.

————. *Writing and Difference.* Translated by Alan Bass. Chicago: University of Chicago Press, 1978.

Doyle, Brian. "The Hidden History of English Studies." In *Re-Reading English,* edited by Peter Widdowson. London: Methuen, 1982.

Eagleton, Terry. *Criticism & Ideology.* London: Verso Editions, 1978.

————. *Exiles and Emigres: Studies in Modern Literature.* New York: Schocken, 1970.

————. "Fredric Jameson: The Politics of Style." *Diacritics* 12, no. 3 (Fall 1982): 14–22.

————. *The Function of Criticism: From The Spectator to Post-Structuralism.* London: Verso Editions, 1984.

————. *Literary Theory: An Introduction.* Minneapolis: University of Minnesota Press, 1983.

————. *Marxism and Literary Criticism.* Berkeley: University of California Press, 1976.

————. *Myths of Power: A Marxist Study of the Brontës.* London: Macmillan, 1975.

————. *The Rape of Clarissa: Writing, Sexuality, and Class Struggle in Samuel Richardson.* Minneapolis: University of Minnesota Press, 1982.

————. "The Revolt of the Reader." *NLH* 13 (1982): 449–52.

————. *Shakespeare and Society: Critical Studies in Shakespearean Drama.* New York: Schocken, 1967.

————. *Walter Benjamin, or Towards a Revolutionary Criticism.* London: Verso Editions, 1981.

Ellenstein, Jean. *The Stalin Phenomenon.* Translated by R. Latham. London: Lawrence & Wishart, 1976.

Elliott, Susan M. "A New Critical Epistemology." *Hartford Studies in Literature* 7 (1975): 170–89.

Ellis, John M. "What Does Deconstruction Contribute to Theory of Criticism?" *NLH* 19, no. 2 (Winter 1988): 259–80.

Engels, Frederick. *Ludwig Feuerbach and the Outcome of Classical German Philosophy.* 1888. Reprint. New York: International Publishers, 1941.

Erlich, Bruce. "Amphibolies: On the Critical Self-Contradictions of 'Pluralism.'" *Critical Inquiry* 12 (Spring 1986): 521–49.

Feenberg, Andrew. *Lukács, Marx and the Sources of Critical Theory.* Totowa, N.J.: Rowman and Littlefield, 1981.

Fekete, John. *The Critical Twilight: Explorations in the Ideology of Anglo-American Literary Theory from Eliot to McLuhan.* London: Routledge & Kegan Paul, 1977.

————. "Modernity in the Literary Institution." In *The Structural Allegory: Reconstructive Encounters with the New French Thought,* edited and introduced by John Fekete. Minneapolis: University of Minnesota Press, 1984.

Feuer, Lewis S. *Ideology and the Ideologists.* New York: Harper & Row, 1975.

Fielding, Henry. *The History of the Adventures Of Joseph Andrews And Of His Friend Abraham Adams.* Introduction by Maynard Mack. 1742. Reprint. New York: Holt, Rinehart and Winston, 1960.

Fischer, Michael. *Does Deconstruction Make Any Difference? Poststructuralism and the Defense of Poetry in Modern Criticism.* Bloomington: Indiana University Press, 1985.

Fish, Stanley. "Anti-Professionalism." *NLH* 17, no.1 (Autumn 1985): 89–108.

————. "Consequences." *Critical Inquiry* 11, no. 5 (March 1985): 433–58.

————. *Is There a Text in this Class? The Authority of Interpretive Communities.* Cambridge, Mass.: Harvard University Press, 1980.

————. "Literature in the Reader: Affective Stylistics," In *From Formalism to Post-structuralism,* edited by Jane P. Tompkins, 70–100. Baltimore: John Hopkins University Press, 1980.

Flynn, Elizabeth A., and Patrocinio Schweickart, eds. *Gender and Reading: Essays on Readers, Texts, and Contexts.* Baltimore: Johns Hopkins University Press, 1986.

Forster, E. M. *Aspects of the Novel.* New York: Harcourt, Brace, & World, 1927.

Foster, Richard. *The New Romantics: A Reappraisal of the New Criticism.* Bloomington: Indiana University Press, 1962.

Foucault, Michel. *The Archaeology of Knowledge.* Translated by A. M. Sheridan Smith. New York: Harper & Row, 1976.

————. *Histoire de la folie à l'âge classique.* 1961. Reprint. Paris: Éditions Gallimard, 1972.

————. *Histoire de la sexualité: La volonté de savoir.* Paris: Éditions Gallimard, 1976.

————. *Les mots et les choses: une archéologie des sciences humaines.* Paris: Éditions Gallimard, 1966.

————. *Surveiller et punir: Naissance de la prison.* Paris: Éditions Gallimard, 1975.

Frank, Joseph. *The Widening Gyre: Crisis and Mastery in Modern Literature.* Bloomington: Indiana University Press, 1963.

Fromm, Eric. *Marx's Concept of Man.* New York: Frederick Unger, 1961.

Frow, John. *Marxism and Literary History.* Cambridge, Mass.: Harvard University Press, 1986.

Frye, Northrop. "The Four Forms of Fiction." In *The Theory of the Novel,* edited by Philip Stevick, 31–44. New York: The Free Press, 1967.

Gasché, Rodolphe. "Deconstruction as Criticism." *Glyph* 6 (1979): 177–216.

———. *The Tain of the Mirror: Derrida and the Philosophy of Reflection.* Cambridge, Mass.: Harvard University Press, 1986.

Gates, Henry Louis, Jr. "Authority, (White) Power and the (Black) Critic; Or, It's All Greek to Me." *Cultural Critique* 7 (Fall 1987): 19–46.

———. *Figures in Black: Words, Signs, and the "Racial" Self.* New York: Oxford University Press, 1987.

Gendron, Bernard. "Theodor Adorno Meets the Cadillacs." In *Studies in Entertainment: Critical Approaches to Mass Culture,* edited by Tania Modleski, 18–38. Bloomington: Indiana University Press, 1986.

Gilbert, Sandra M., and Susan Gubar. "'Forward into the Past': The Complex Female Affiliation Complex." In *Historical Studies and Literary Criticism,* edited by Jerome J. McGann. Madison: University of Wisconsin Press, 1985.

———. *The Madwoman in the Attic: The Woman Writer and the Nineteenth-Century Literary Imagination.* New Haven: Yale University Press, 1979.

———. "The Man on the Dump versus the United Dames of America; or, What Does Frank Lentricchia Want?" *Critical Inquiry* 14 (Winter 1988): 386–406.

———. "Sexual Linguistics: Gender, Language, Sexuality." *NLH* 16, no. 3 (Spring 1985): 515–44.

———. "Tradition and the Female Talent." In *The Poetics of Gender,* edited by Nancy K. Miller. New York: Columbia University Press, 1986.

Gittings, Robert. *The Older Thomas Hardy.* New York: Penguin, 1980.

———. *Young Thomas Hardy.* New York: Penguin Books, 1978.

Glucksmann, André. *Les Maîtres Penseurs.* Paris: Bernard Grasset, 1977.

Goldmann, Lucien. *Lukács and Heidegger: Towards a New Philosophy.* Translated by William Q. Boelbower. Boston: Routledge & Kegan Paul, 1977.

———. *Pour une sociologie du roman.* Paris: Éditions Gallimard, 1964.

———. "Structure: Reality and Concept." In *The Structuralist Controversy: The Languages of Criticism and the Sciences of Man,* edited by Richard Macksey and Eugenio Donato, 98–124. Baltimore: Johns Hopkins University Press, 1970.

Graff, Gerald. "Interpretation on Tlön: A Response to Stanley Fish." *NLH* 17, no. 1 (Autumn 1985): 109–18.

———. *Literature Against Itself: Literary Ideas in Modern Society.* Chicago: University of Chicago Press, 1979.

———. *Poetic Statement and Critical Dogma.* Chicago: University of Chicago Press, 1970.

————. *Professing Literature: An Institutional History*. Chicago: University of Chicago Press, 1987.

————. "The Pseudo-Politics of Interpretation." *Critical Inquiry* 9 (March 1983): 597–610.

Guerard, Albert. *Thomas Hardy: The Novels and the Stories*. Cambridge, Mass.: Harvard University Press, 1949.

Guillory, John. "Canonical and Non-Canonical: A Critique of the Current Debate." *ELH* 54, no. 3 (Fall 1987): 483–527.

Habermas, Jürgen. *Knowledge and Human Interests*. Translated by Jeremy J. Shapiro. Boston: Beacon Press, 1971.

————. *The Theory of Communicative Action*. Vol. 1. Translated by Thomas McCarthy. Boston: Beacon Press, 1981.

Hardy, Barbara. *The Appropriate Form: An Essay on the Novel*. London: University of London Press, 1964.

Hardy, Florence. *The Life of Thomas Hardy*. 1928. Reprint. London: Macmillan, 1962.

Hardy, Thomas. *Jude the Obscure*. Edited and introduced by Robert B. Heilman. 1895. Reprint. New York: Harper & Row, 1966.

————. *The Life and Death of the Mayor of Casterbridge*. 1886. Reprint. New York: New American Library, 1962.

————. *Tess of the D'Urbervilles*. Edited by William E. Buckler. 1891. Reprint. Boston: Houghton Mifflin, 1960.

Heidegger, Martin. "The Origin of the Work of Art." In *Poetry, Language, and Thought,* translated by Albert Hofstadter. New York: Harper & Row, 1975.

Hegel, G. W. F. *Phenomenology of Mind*. 2d ed. Translated and introduced by J. B. Baillie. New York: Macmillan, 1949.

Highet, Gilbert. *The Classical Tradition: Greek and Roman Influences on Western Literature*. New York: Oxford University Press, 1957.

Hirsch, E. D., Jr. *The Aims of Interpretation*. Chicago: University of Chicago Press, 1976.

————. *Validity in Interpretation*. New Haven: Yale University Press, 1967.

Hirst, Paul. *On Law and Ideology*. Atlantic Highlands, N.J.: Humanities Press, 1979.

————. *Marxism and Historical Writing*. London: Routledge & Kegan Paul, 1985.

Hohendahl, Peter Uwe. *The Institution of Criticism*. Ithaca, N.Y.: Cornell University Press, 1982.

Holland, Norman. *Five Readers Reading*. New Haven: Yale University Press, 1975.

————. *The "I"*. New Haven: Yale University Press, 1985.

————. "The New Paradigm: Subjective or Transactive?" *NLH* 7 (Winter 1976): 335–46.

————. "Unity Identity Text Self." Reprinted in *Reader Response Criticism,* edited by Jane Tompkins. Baltimore: Johns Hopkins University Press, 1980.

Holland, Norman N., and Leona F. Sherman. "Gothic Possibilities." In *Gender and Reading: Essays on Readers, Texts, and Contexts,* edited by Elizabeth A. Flynn and Patrocinio Schweickart. Baltimore: Johns Hopkins University Press, 1986.

Horkheimer, Max. "The Authoritarian State." In *The Essential Frankfurt School Reader,* edited by Andrew Arato and others, and introduced by Paul Piccone, 95–118. New York: Continuum, 1985.

Howe, Irving. *Thomas Hardy.* New York: Macmillan, 1967.

Hughes, Winifred. *The Maniac in the Cellar.* Princeton, N.J.: Princeton University Press, 1980.

Hume, David. *A Treatise of Human Nature.* Edited by L. A. Selby-Bigge. 1739. Reprint. London: Oxford Unversity Press, 1967.

Husserl, Edmund. *Ideas: General Introduction to Pure Phenomenology.* Translated by W. R. Boyce Gibson. 1931. Reprint. New York: Collier Books, 1962.

————. *Phenomenology and the Crisis of Philosophy.* Translated and introduced by Quentin Lauer. New York: Harper & Row, 1965.

Ingarden, Roman. *The Literary Work of Art.* Translated by George C. Grabowicz. Evanston: Northwestern University Press, 1973.

Iser, Wolfgang. *The Act of Reading: A Theory of Aesthetic Response.* Baltimore: John Hopkins University Press, 1972.

Jacoby, Russell. *The Last Intellectuals: American Culture in the Age of Academe.* New York: Basic Books, 1987.

Jameson, Fredric. "Criticism in History." In *Weapons of Criticism.* edited by Norman Rudich, 31–50. Palo Alto, Calif.: Ramparts Press, 1976.

————. *Fables of Aggression: Wyndham Lewis, the Modernist as Fascist.* Los Angeles: University of California Press, 1979.

————. "Introduction" to *The Historical Novel,* by Georg Lukács. Translated by Hannah Mitchell and Stanley Mitchell. 1962. Reprint. Lincoln: University of Nebraska Press, 1983.

————. *Marxism and Form: Twentieth-Century Dialectical Theories of Literature.* Princeton, N.J.: Princeton University Press, 1971.

————. "Periodizing the Sixties." In *The Sixties Without Apology,* edited by Sohnya Sayres and others. Minneapolis: University of Minnesota Press, 1984.

————. *The Political Unconscious: Narrative as a Socially Symbolic Act.* Ithaca, N.Y.: Cornell University Press, 1981.

―――. "The Politics of Theory." *New German Critique* 53 (Fall 1984): 53–65.

―――. "Postmodernism, or The Cultural Logic of Late Capitalism." *New Left Review* 146 (July–August 1984): 53–92.

―――. "Regarding Postmodernism—A Conversation with Fredric Jameson." *Social Text* 17: 29–54.

―――. *The Prison-House of Language.* Princeton, N.J.: Princeton University Press, 1972.

Jay, Martin. *Adorno.* Cambridge, Mass.: Harvard University Press, 1984.

Johnson, Barbara. *The Critical Difference: Essays in the Contemporary Rhetoric of Reading.* Baltimore: Johns Hopkins University Press, 1980.

―――. *A World of Difference.* Baltimore: Johns Hopkins University Press, 1987.

Koelb, Clayton. "Kafka's Rhetorical Moment." *PMLA* 98 (January 1983): 37–46.

Kramer, Dale. *Thomas Hardy: The Forms of Tragedy.* London: Macmillan Press, 1975.

Krieger, Murray. *The New Apologists for Poetry.* Minneapolis: University of Minnesota Press, 1956.

―――. *The Theory of Criticism.* Baltimore: Johns Hopkins University Press, 1976.

Krupnick, Mark. "The Two Worlds of Cultural Criticism." In *Criticism in the University,* edited by Gerald Graff and Reginald Gibbons. Evanston: Northwestern University Press, 1985.

Kuenzli, Rudolf E. "The Intersubjective Structure of the Reading Process: A Communication-Oriented Theory of Literature." *Diacritics* 10 (Summer 1980): 47–74.

Kuhn, Thomas. *The Structure of Scientific Revolutions.* Chicago: University of Chicago Press, 1972.

Le Court, Dominique. *Marxism and Epistemology.* Atlantic Highlands, N.J.: Humanities Press, 1969.

Lemert, Charles C., and Garth Gillan. *Michel Foucault: Social Theory and Transgression.* New York: Columbia University Press, 1982.

Lentricchia, Frank. *After the New Criticism.* Chicago: University of Chicago Press, 1980.

―――. "Patriarchy Against Itself—The Young Manhood of Wallace Stevens." *Critical Inquiry* 13 (Summer 1987): 742–86.

―――. "Reading Foucault (Punishment, Labor, Resistance)." *Raritan* 1, no. 4, and 2, no. 1.

Lerner, Lawrence. *Thomas Hardy's The Mayor of Casterbridge— Tragedy of Social History.* London: Sussex University Press, 1975.

Lodge, David. *Working with Structuralism: Essays and Reviews on Nine-*

teenth- and Twentieth-Century Literature. Boston: Routledge & Kegan Paul, 1981.

Löwith, Karl. *From Hegel to Nietzsche.* Translated by David Green. Garden City, N.Y.: Doubleday, 1967.

Löwy, Michael. *Georg Lukács—From Romanticism to Bolshevism.* Translated by Patrick Camiller. London: New Left Books, 1979.

Lukács, Georg. *History and Class Consciousness: Studies in Marxist Dialectics.* Translated by Rodney Livingstone. Cambridge, Mass.: MIT Press, 1971.

———. *Marxism and Human Liberation.* Edited by E. San Juan, Jr. New York: Dell, 1973.

———. *Realism in our Time: Literature and the Class Struggle.* New York: Harper & Row, 1971.

———. *Studies in European Realism.* London: Hillway, 1950.

McCallum, Pamela. *Literature and Method: Towards a Critique of I. A. Richards, T. S. Eliot, and F. R. Leavis.* Atlantic Highlands, N.J.: Humanities Press, 1983.

Macdonell, Diane. *Theories of Discourse: An Introduction.* New York: Basil Blackwell, 1986.

Macherey, Pierre. *Hegel ou Spinoza.* Paris: Maspero, 1979.

———. *A Theory of Literary Production.* Translated by Geoffrey Wall. London: Routledge & Kegan Paul, 1978.

Macherey, Pierre, and Etienne Balibar. "Literature as an Ideological Form: Some Marxist Propositions." *Praxis* 5 (1981): 43–58.

McLellan, David. *Ideology.* Minneapolis: University of Minnesota Press, 1986.

Mailloux, Stephen. *Interpretive Conventions: The Reader in the Study of American Fiction.* Ithaca, N.Y.: Cornell University Press, 1982.

Marcuse, Herbert. *One-Dimensional Man.* Boston: Beacon Press, 1964.

Margolis, Joseph. "Deconstruction; or the Mystery of the Mystery of the Text." In *Hermeneutics and Deconstruction,* edited by Hugh S. Silverman and Don Ihde. Albany: State University of New York Press, 1985.

Marx, Karl. *Capital.* 1887. Reprint. Moscow: Progress Publishers, 1965.

———. *A Contribution to the Critique of Political Economy.* 1859. Reprint. Translated N. I. Stone. Chicago: Charles H. Kerr, 1904.

Marx, Karl, and Frederick Engels. *The German Ideology.* Edited by R. Pascal. New York: International Publishers, Inc., 1947.

———. *Selected Correspondence.* Moscow: Progress Publishers, 1965.

Megill, Allan. *Prophets of Extremity: Nietzsche, Heidegger, Foucault, Derrida.* Berkeley: University of Califorinia Press, 1985.

Miller, J. Hillis. "The Critic as Host." In *Deconstruction and Criticism,* edited by Geoffrey Hartman, 217–55. New York: Seabury Press, 1979.

————. *Fiction and Repetition: Seven English Novels.* Oxford: Basil Blackwell, 1982.

————. *Thomas Hardy: Distance and Desire.* Cambridge, Mass.: Harvard University Press, 1970.

Mizener, Arthur. "*Jude the Obscure* as a Tragedy." *Southern Review* 6 (1940): 193–213.

Moharty, S. P. "History at the Edge of Discourse: Marxism, Culture, Interpretation." *Diacritics* 12 (Fall 1982): 33–46.

Moi, Toril. *Sexual/Textual Politics: Feminist Literary Theory.* London: Methuen, 1985.

Montag, Warren. "Marxism and Psychoanalysis: The Impossible Encounter." *The Minnesota Review* 23 (Fall 1984): 70–85.

Newton, Judith Lowder. *Women, Power & Subversion: Social Strategies in British Fiction, 1778-1860.* New York: Methuen, 1981.

Newton, Judith Lowder, and Deborah Rosenfelt. "Toward a Materialist-Feminist Criticism." In *Feminist Criticism and Social Change,* edited by Judith Lowder Newton and Deborah Rosenfelt, xv–xxxix. New York: Methuen, 1985.

Ohmann, Richard. *English in America: A Radical View of the Profession.* New York: Oxford University Press, 1976.

Ollman, Bertell. *Alienation: Marx's Conception of Man in Capitalist Society.* Cambridge: Cambridge University Press, 1971.

O'Neill, John. "Breaking the Signs: Roland Barthes and the Literary Body." In *The Structural Allegory: Reconstructive Encounters with the New French Thought,* edited by John Fekete, 183–200. Minneapolis: University of Minnesota Press, 1984.

Palmer, D. J. *The Rise of English Studies: An Account of the Study of English Language and Literature from its Origins to the Making of the Oxford English School.* New York: Oxford University Press, 1965.

Pinion, F. B. *A Hardy Companion.* London: St. Martin's Press, 1968.

Podhoretz, Norman. *The Bloody Crossroads: Where Literature and Politics Meet.* New York: Simon and Schuster, 1986.

Poirier, Richard. *The Renewal of Literature: Emersonian Reflections.* New York: Random House, 1987.

Polan, Dana. "Brief Encounters: Mass Culture and the Evacuation of Sense." In *Studies in Entertainment: Critical Approaches to Mass Culture,* edited by Tania Modleski, 167–87. Bloomington: Indiana University Press, 1986.

Poster, Mark. *Foucault, Marxism, and History: Mode of Production versus Mode of Information.* Cambridge: Polity Press, 1984.

Poulantzas, Nicos. *L'État, le Pouvoir, le Socialisme.* Paris: Presses Universitaires de France, 1978.

Poulet, Georges. "Criticism and the Experience of Interiority." In *Reader-Response Criticism: From Formalism to Post-structuralism,* edited by Jane Tompkins, 41–49. Baltimore: Johns Hopkins University Press, 1980.

Randall, John Herman, Jr. *The Career of Philosophy.* 2 vols. New York: Columbia University Press, 1970.

Ransom, John Crowe. *The World's Body.* New York: Charles Scribner's Sons, 1938.

Ray, William. *Literary Meaning: From Phenomenology to Deconstruction.* New York: Basil Blackwell, 1984.

Rendall, Stephen. "Fish vs Fish." *Diacritics* 12 (Winter 1982): 49–56.

Richards, I. A. *Practical Criticism: A Study of Literary Judgment.* New York: Harcourt, Brace & World, 1929.

Richards , I. A., and C. K. Ogden. *The Meaning of Meaning.* New York: Harcourt, Brace, & World, 1923.

Ringer, Fritz. K. *The Decline of the German Mandarins: The German Academic Community, 1880–1933.* Cambridge, Mass.: Harvard University Press, 1969.

Rooney, Ellen. "Who's Left Out? A Rose by Any Other Name Is Still Red; Or, The Politics of 'Pluralism.'" *Critical Inquiry* 12 (Spring 1986): 550–63.

Rorty, Richard. *Philosophy and the Mirror of Nature.* Princeton: Princeton University Press, 1979.

———. *Consequences of Pragmatism (Essays: 1972–1980).* Minneapolis: University of Minnesota Press, 1982.

Russo, John Paul. "I. A. Richards in Retrospect." *Critical Inquiry* 8 (Summer 1982): 743–60.

Ryan, Michael. *Marxism and Deconstruction: A Critical Articulation.* Baltimore: Johns Hopkins University Press, 1982.

Said, Edward. *Beginnings: Intention and Method.* Baltimore: Johns Hopkins University Press, 1978.

———. "The Problem of Textuality: Two Exemplary Positions." *Critical Inquiry* 4 (1978): 673–714.

———. *The World, the Text and the Critic.* Cambridge, Mass.: Harvard University Press, 1983.

Sayres, Sohnya, and others, eds. *The Sixties Without Apology.* Minneapolis: University of Minnesota Press, 1984.

Scholes, Robert. *Textual Power: Literary Theory and the Teaching of English.* New Haven: Yale University Press, 1985.

Scholes, Robert, and Robert Kellogg. *The Nature of Narrative.* London: Oxford University Press, 1966.

Schwartz, Delmore. "Poetry and Belief in Thomas Hardy." In *Hardy: A*

Collection of Critical Essays, edited by Albert Guerard. Englewood Cliffs, N.J.: Prentice-Hall, 1963.

Sheridan, Alan. *The Will to Truth.* New York: Methuen, 1980.

Showalter, Elaine. *A Literature of Their Own: British Women Novelists from Brontë to Lessing.* Princeton: Princeton University Press, 1977.

————. "Critical Cross-Dressing; Male Feminists and the Woman of the Year." In *Men in Feminism,* edited by Alice Jardine and Paul Smith, 116–32. New York: Methuen, 1987.

————. "Feminist Criticism in the Wilderness." In *The New Feminist Criticism: Essays on Women, Literature, and Theory,* edited by Elaine Showalter. New York: Pantheon, 1985.

————. "Piecing and Writing," In *The Poetics of Gender,* edited by Nancy K. Miller. New York: Columbia University Press, 1986.

Silverman, Kaja. *The Subject of Semiotics.* New York: Oxford University Press, 1983.

Solzhenitsyn, Aleksandr. *Cancer Ward.* Translated by N. Bethel and D. Burg. New York: Bantam, 1969.

Spivak, Gayatri Chakravorty. "Feminism and Critical Theory." In *For Alma Mater: Theory and Practice in Feminist Scholarship,* edited by Paula A. Treichler and others, 119–42. Urbana: University of Illinois Press, 1985.

————. "Marx after Derrida." *Philosophical Approaches to Literature: New Essays on Nineteenth- and Twentieth-Century Texts,* edited by William E. Cain. Lewisburg, Pa.: Bucknell University Press, 1984.

————. "Revolutions That As Yet Have No Model: Derrida's *Limited Inc.*" *Diacritics* 10, no. 4 (Winter 1980): 29–49.

Sprinker, Michael. *Imaginary Relations: Aesthetics and Ideology in the Theory of Historical Materialism.* New York: Verso Editions, 1987.

————. "Reinventing Historicism: An Introduction to the Work of Fredric Jameson." In *American Critics at Work: Examinations of Contemporary Literary Theories,* edited by Victor A. Kramer. Troy, N.Y.: Whitson Publishing Co., 1984.

————. "What is Living and What is Dead in Chicago Criticism." *Boundary 2,* 12 (Winter/Spring 1985): 189–212.

Swingewood, Alan. *The Novel and Revolution.* London: Macmillan, 1975.

Tanner, Tony. "Colour and Movement in Hardy's *Tess of the d'Urbervilles.*" *In The Victorian Novel: Modern Essays in Criticism,* edited by Ian Watt, 407–31. London: Oxford University Press, 1971.

Thompson, E. P. *The Poverty of Theory and other essays.* London; Merlin Press, 1978.

Todorov, Tzvetan. *Introduction to the Literature of Fantasy.* Translated by Richard Howard. Cleveland: Case Western Reserve Press, 1973.

Tompkins, Jane P. "Indians: Textualism, Morality, and the Problem of History." *Critical Inquiry* 13, no. 1 (1986): 101–19.

———. "Me and My Shadow," *NLH* 19, no. 1 (Autumn 1987): 169–78

———. "The Reader in History." In *Reader-Response Criticism: From Formalism to Post-structuralism,* edited by Jane P. Tompkins, 201–32. Baltimore: John Hopkins University Press, 1980.

———. *Sensational Designs: The Cultural Work of American Fiction 1790–1860.* New York: Oxford University Press, 1985.

Toulmin, Stephen. *Foresight and Understanding.* New York: Harper & Row, 1961.

Trilling, Lionel. *The Liberal Imagination: Essays on Literature and Society.* Garden City, N.Y.: Doubleday, 1953.

———. *The Opposing Self.* New York: Harcourt, Brace, Jovanovich, 1955.

———. *Sincerity and Authenticity.* Cambridge, Mass.: Harvard University Press, 1972.

Vernier, France. *L'écriture et les texts.* Paris: Éditions Sociales, 1971.

Walzer, Michael. *Interpretation and Social Criticism.* Cambridge, Mass.: Harvard University Press, 1987.

Watkins, Evan. *The Critical Act: Criticism and Community.* New Haven: Yale University Press, 1978.

Watt, Ian. *The Rise of the Novel: Studies in Defoe, Richardson and Fielding.* Berkeley: University of California Press, 1957.

Weber, Samuel. "Capitalizing History: Notes on *The Political Unconscious.*" *Diacritics* 13 (Summer 1983): 14–26.

———. "Caught in the Act of Reading." In *Demarcating the Disciplines: Philosophy, Literature, Art,* edited by Samuel Weber. Minneapolis: University of Minnesota Press, 1986.

Webster, Harvey Curtis. *On a Darkling Plain.* Chicago: University of Chicago Press, 1947.

Weeks, Jeffrey. *Sex, Politics and Society: The Regulation of Sexuality since 1800.* New York: Longman, 1981.

Weimann, Robert. *Structure and Society in Literary History: Studies in the History and Theory of Historical Criticism.* Charlottesville: University Press of Virginia, 1976.

Wellek, René. *Concepts of Criticism.* Edited by Stephen G. Nichols, Jr. New Haven: Yale University Press, 1963.

———. "The New Criticism: Pro and Contra," *Critical Inquiry* 4 (Summer 1978): 611–24.

Wellek, René, and Austin Warren. *Theory of Literature.* New York: Harcourt, Brace, & World, 1956.

Wernick, Andrew. "Structuralism and the Dislocation of the French Rationalist Project." In *The Structural Allegory: Reconstructive Encounters with the New French Thought,* edited and introduced by John Fekete. Minneapolis: University of Minnesota Press, 1984.

Widdowson, Peter, ed. *Re-Reading English.* London: Methuen, 1982.

Williams, Merryn. *A Preface to Hardy.* New York: Longman, 1976.

Williams, Raymond. *The Country and the City.* 1973. Reprint. New York: Oxford University Press, 1982.

———. *Culture and Society.* 1958. Reprint. New York: Columbia University Press, 1983.

———.*The English Novel from Dickens to Lawrence.* New York: Oxford University Press, 1970.

———. *Keywords: A Vocabulary of Culture and Society.* 2d ed. New York: Oxford University Press, 1983.

———. *Marxism and Literature.* New York: Oxford University Press, 1976.

———. *Problems in Materialism and Culture.* London: Verso Editions, 1980.

———. *Writing in Society.* London: Verso Editions, 1985.

Wimsatt, W. K., Jr. *The Verbal Icon: Studies in the Meaning of Poetry.* Lexington: University of Kentucky Press, 1954.

Wimsatt, W. K., Jr., and Monroe C. Beardsley "The Intentional Fallacy." In *The Verbal Icon: Studies in the Meaning of Poetry,* by W. K. Wimsatt, Jr. Lexington: University of Kentucky Press, 1954.

———. "The Affective Fallacy." In *The Verbal Icon: Studies in the Meaning of Poetry,* by W. K. Wimsatt, Jr. Lexington: University of Kentucky Press, 1954.

Zabel, Zabel. "Hardy in Defense of His Art; The Aesthetic of Incongruity." In *Hardy: A Collection of Critical Essays,* edited by Albert Guerard. Englewood Cliffs, N.J.: Prentice-Hall, Inc., 1963.

The Politics of Literary Theory

Bennett, William, 1
Bernstein, J. M., 12, 18
Berthoud, J. A.: on Jameson and Conrad's *Lord Jim*, 154
Bledstein, Burton J., 9, 69
Bleich, David: and Hobbes, 107, 108, 109; and ideology, 110; and language, 108–10; and objectivity, 107–8; on the reader's community, 108
Bloom, Allen, 1
Bové, Paul, 29, 36; and New Critical conservatism, 49–50; and Richards, 35; on Said, 195
Brooks, Cleanth: and the canon, 40–41; and hierarchy, 38–39; and *MacBeth*, 37–38; and paraphrase, 36–37; and Richards, 36
Brooks, Cleanth, and W. K. Wimsatt: *Literary Criticism: A Short History*, 32–33
Brooks, Peter: on Hardy's imagery and symbolism, 201–2
Buckley, Jerome: on the late-Victorian revolt against liberalism, 214

Cain, William, 5, 29, 41; on indeterminacy, 164; on New Criticism, 65
Caute, David, 10
Christian, Barbara, 3
Cohen, Stephen, 11
Culler, Jonathan: on American universities, 145; on Barthes, 138; and Cartesian, rationalism, 144–45; on interpretive conventions, 143–44; on literary language, 143–44; on mistakes, 145; *The Pursuit of Signs,* 144–45

DeLaura, David J.: on Hardy's pessimism, 200
de Man, Paul: on circular interpretation, 177; on literary language and interpretation, 177–78; and Platonic ignorance, 179; and skepticism, 176

Derrida, Jacques: "Differance," 165–66; on differance, 168; and Heidegger, 165–66; on historical determinism, 167, 173; *Otobiographies*, 165; "The Pharmacy of Plato," 167; on skepticism, 164–65. *See also* Ellis, John; Fischer, Michael; Gasché, Rodolphe; Lentricchia, Frank; Margolis, Joseph; Ryan, Michael; Said, Edward; Spivak, Gayatri
Dowling, William, 6
Doyle, Brian, 9, 68, 69

Eagleton, Terry: and Barthes, 140; *Criticism and Ideology*, 60; and education, 9; and eighteenth-century criticism, 68; *Exiles and Emigrés*, 59; and the failure of theory, 140–41; and Freudian dream theory, 148; on Jameson's speculative Marxism, 160; on liberal Derrideans, 184; *Literary Theory: An Introduction*, 64; and Macherey, 139; on a Marxist literary language, 185; and modes of production, 61; *Myths of Power*, 63; and New Critical formalism, 60–61; and postructuralist textuality, 62–63; *The Rape of Clarissa*, 63; on reader-oriented criticism, 101; on science/ideology, 60–62, 139–40; *Shakespeare and Society*, 59; *Walter Benjamin, or Towards a Revolutionary Criticism*, 63, 184–85. *See also* Frow, John
Ellenstein, Jean, 11
Ellis, John: on deconstruction, 163, 166
Engels, Friedrich: and culture, 8; and ideology, 7. *See also* Marx, Karl; Marxism
Erlich, Bruce, 67

Fekete, John, 29–30, 134; on Brooks, 38; and New Critical formalism, 47–49

Feuer, Lewis: on intellectuals and politics, 3–4

Fischer, Michael: on deconstruction, 163, 166

Fish, Stanley: "affective stylistics," 111; and Althusser and Foucault, 196–97; on "interpretive communities," 112; on indeterminacy, 196; on literary language, 111; on the limits of theory, 196; on ordinary language, 163; on political criticism, 113, 197

Forster, E. M.: on Hardy's artistic skill, 201

Foster, Richard, 29

Foucault, Michel, 68; Derridean critiques of, 173; and discourse, 169–71; and epistemological rupture, 169–70; on historical critique, 171–72; on ordinary language, 163; on the state, 172–73. *See also* Althusser, Louis; Fish, Stanley; Lentricchia, Frank; Said, Edward; Wellek, René

Frank, Joseph, 59

Frankfurt School: and Lukács, 17; and the working class, 20. *See also* Adorno, Theodor; Jameson, Fredric; Marcuse, Herbert

Frow, John: on Eagleton, 140

Frye, Northrop, 70

Gasché, Rodolphe: on Derrida's account of writing, 168; on differance, 167

Gates, Henry Louis, Jr.: on African-American figural language, 54–55; on the African-American tradition, 57–58; and New Criticism, 55–57; and political criticism, 58–59

Gilbert, Sandra, and Susan Gubar: and Lentricchia, 53, 54; *The Madwoman in the Attic*, 50–52; and New Criticism 51, 53; "Sexual Linguistics," 52; and Toril Moi, 53; and twentieth-century writers, 52

Glucksman, André, 5

Goldmann, Lucien: and *The Hidden God*, 78–79; and Hirsch, 77; and historicism, 78; on Lukács, 18, 21; and structure, 77–78; and the "transindividual other," 78; *For a Sociology of the Novel*, 79

Graff, Gerald, 10; on Brooks, 38; and the canon, 84; on deconstruction, 163; *Literature Against Itself*, 82–83; and neutrality, 82; on New Criticism, 29–30, 47, 72; and poetic decorum, 82; *Poetic Statement and Critical Dogma*, 82–82; *Professing Literature*, 83–84

Gramsci, Antonio: and Althusser, 25; and Marx, 7. *See also* Marxism

Guerard, Albert J.: on Hardy and extrinsic interpretation, 202–3; on Hardy's artistic skill, 261

Guillory, John: on Tompkins, 114

Habermas, Jürgen, 130; and Hegel, 22; and Lukács, 22; on Marx, 8

Hardy, Barbara: on Hardy's artistic skill, 201

Hardy, Thomas: and British realist fiction, 203; and G. Eliot, 206–7, 214–15; *Jude the Obscure*, 211–12, 216, 217; and liberalism, 211, 214; *The Mayor of Casterbridge*, 216; pessimism and artistic productivity, 205, 213; and sensationalist discourse, 214–16; and social science, 215; *Tess of the d'Urbervilles*, and traditional values, 217; and Victorian feminism, 211. *See also* Brooks, Peter; Guerard, Albert; Howe, Irving; Kramer, Dale; Lodge, David; Miller, J. Hillis; Tanner, Tony

Heidegger, Martin: and despotism, 125; on language, 124–25; "The Origin of the Work of Art," 122–25; on truth, 113. *See also* Adorno, Theodor; de Man,

Paul; Derrida, Jacques; Husserl, Edmund; Iser, Wolfgang

19; and historical method, 13–14; and Marxist humanism, 72; and reification, 18; and Stalinism, 12, 14; *The Theory of the Novel*, 12. *See also* Frankfurt School; Goldmann, Lucien; Jameson, Fredric; Williams, Raymond

McCallum, Pamela, 70; on Richards, 35
Macherey, Pierre: and Barthes, 139; and humanism, 80; and institutions, 81; *A Theory of Literary Production*, 138–39. *See also* Eagleton, Terry
Marcuse, Herbert, 20
Margolis, Joseph: on deconstruction, 167
Marx, Karl: and commodity fetishism, 18; on culture, 8; and Hegelian theory, 21–22; *The German Ideology*, 6–7. *See also* Althusser, Louis; Engels, Friedrich; Gramsci, Antonio; Lukács, Georg
Marxism: and culture, 8–11; death of, 5; and educational institutions, 9–10; and Solzhenitsyn, 10; and Stalinism, 10–11
Marxist feminism: and history, 143; and structuralist science, 141. *See also* Belsey, Catherine; Silverman, Kaja
Miller, J. Hillis: "The Critic as Host," 174–75; on the empirical text, 175; on Hardy and the reader's self-consciousness, 208; on Hardy's pessimism, 200; on repetition, 175; on *Tess of the d'Urbervilles*, 200, 213
Mizener, Arthur: on Hardy's artistic skill, 201
Moi, Toril, 53; on Showalter, 94, 96
Montag, Warren, 25

New Criticism: and empiricism, 31–2; and literary institutions, 30, 49; and politics, 29; and traditional Marxism, 48–49

Newton, Judith: on ideology, 97; on poststructuralism, 97; *Women, Power, & Subversion*, 96; on women's power, 96–97

Ohmann, Richard, 1, 30, 49
O'Neill, John: on Barthes, 141

Palmer, D. J., 68
Pinion, F. B.: on Hardy and Schopenhauer, 214
Podhoretz, Norman, 5
Poirier, Richard, 1–2
Poster, Mark: on Foucault and Hegel, 156
Poulantzas, Nicos, 9

Randall, J. H., 31
Ransom, John Crowe, 39
Richards, I. A.: on the civilized reader, 35; and ideology, 34–35; *The Meaning of Meaning*, 34
Rooney, Ellen, 67
Ryan, Michael: on Adorno and Derrida, 132; on Althusser, 186–87; on concepts, 186; on deconstruction and socialism, 186–87; on deconstruction and social theory, 186; *Marxism and Deconstruction*, 186–87; and Stalinism, 187

Said, Edward, 28; on culture and the state, 193–94; on deconstruction, 167; and de Man, 178–79; and Derrida, 168; on Foucault and resistance, 195–96; on the historical archive, 194; on indeterminacy, 164
Saussure, Ferdinand de: on linguistic conventions, 134
Schwartz, Delmore: on Hardy's pessimism, 200
Showalter, Elaine: on gynocritics, 95; *A Literature of Their Own*, 93–94; on science, 95; on women's artistic conditions, 94
Silverman, Kaja: on Lacan,